GUARDING THE PERIPHERY

THE AUSTRALIAN ARMY IN
PAPUA NEW GUINEA, 1951–75

Based around the Pacific Islands Regiment, the Australian Army's units in
Papua New Guinea had a dual identity: integral to Australia's defence, but
also part of its largest colony and viewed as a foreign people. With Papua
New Guineans comprising the largest minority within the Australian armed
forces, the Australian Army in PNG found itself commanding units of
astonishing diversity, encompassing hundreds of languages and cultures. It
did so to defend Australia from threats to its north and west, while also
managing the force's place within Australian colonial rule in PNG,
occasionally resulting in a tense relationship with the Australian colonial
government during a period of significant change.

In *Guarding the Periphery: The Australian Army in Papua New Guinea,
1951–75*, Tristan Moss explores the operational, social and racial aspects of
this unique force during the height of the colonial era in PNG and during the
progression to independence.

Combining the rich detail of both archival material and oral histories,
Guarding the Periphery recounts a part of Australian military history that is
often overlooked by studies of Australia's colonial and military past.

Tristan Moss is a researcher on the Official Histories of Australian
Operations in Iraq and Afghanistan and Australian Peacekeeping
Operations in East Timor at the Australian War Memorial. He is an
Adjunct Lecturer at the University of New South Wales, Canberra, and is
also the winner of the C.E.W. Bean Prize for Military History.

OTHER TITLES IN THE AUSTRALIAN ARMY HISTORY SERIES

Series Editor
Peter Stanley

GUARDING THE PERIPHERY

THE AUSTRALIAN ARMY IN PAPUA NEW GUINEA, 1951–75

TRISTAN MOSS

CAMBRIDGE
UNIVERSITY PRESS

University Printing House, Cambridge CB2 8BS, United Kingdom

One Liberty Plaza, 20th Floor, New York, NY 10006, USA

477 Williamstown Road, Port Melbourne, VIC 3207, Australia

4843/24, 2nd Floor, Ansari Road, Daryaganj, Delhi - 110002, India

79 Anson Road, #06-04/06, Singapore 079906

Cambridge University Press is part of the University of Cambridge.

It furthers the University's mission by disseminating knowledge in the pursuit of education, learning and research at the highest international levels of excellence.

www.cambridge.org
Information on this title: www.cambridge.org/9781107195967

© Tristan Moss 2017

First published 2017

Cover designed by Anne-Marie Reeves
Typeset by Aptara Corp.
Printed in China by C & C Offset Printing Co. Ltd, May 2017

A catalogue record for this publication is available from the British Library

A Cataloguing-in-Publication entry is available from the catalogue of the National Library of Australia at www.nla.gov.au

ISBN 978-1-107-19596-7 Hardback

To Meggie

CONTENTS

Maps and figures

PREFACE

The Australian Army has a long and admirable record in fostering serious research and publication about its history. For more than a century the Army has seen the value of history to its future. From its outset 'military history' was part of the formal education of officers at the Royal Military College, Duntroon, and for a time officers' promotion depended upon candidates being able to give a coherent analysis of 'Stonewall' Jackson's Shenandoah Valley campaigns in promotion exams. An understanding of the Army's history and traditions remains central to its *esprit de corps*, in its most literal meaning.

From the 1970s (as a consequence of educating officers at university level) the Army has produced several generations of educated soldiers, several of whom became historians of note, including Robert O'Neill, David Horner, Peter Pedersen, John Mordike, Bob Hall, Jean Bou, Bob Stevenson and Craig Stockings. The creation of an Army History Unit in the late 1990s demonstrated the Army's commitment to encouraging and facilitating serious history. Under Dr Roger Lee it had a profound influence on managing the Army's museums, in supporting research on army history and in publishing the Army's history.

One of the most impressive demonstrations of the Army's commitment to history has been its long association with several major publishers, and notably with Cambridge University Press. This has been a productive relationship, brokered by Roger Lee and the former long-serving general editor of the Army History Series, Professor David Horner.

The Cambridge Army History Series brings to an academic and popular readership historical work of importance across the range of the Army's interests and across the span of its history. The series, which I now have the honour to edit, seeks to publish research and writing of the highest quality relating to the Army's operational experience and to its existence as an organisation, as a part of its contribution to the national narrative.

The Army History Unit has created a community of writers and readers (including soldiers in both roles), the product of whose questions, research, debate and writing informs the Army's understanding of itself and its part in Australia's history. It is a history to be proud of in every sense.

Tristan Moss's *Guarding the Periphery: The Australian Army in Papua New Guinea, 1951–1975* reminds the Army, and indeed the Australian community, of Australia's long relationship with the people of Papua New Guinea. While the campaigns of 1942–45 represent the Army's most intensive encounter with Papua New Guinea, as Tristan shows, the Army played a vital part in the decades preceding independence. The Army's long and complex relationship with the territory demonstrates how it coped with the most ethnically diverse component it has ever included, and how it played a part in mentoring the defenders of Australia's closest neighbour. This is an unsung chapter of the Army's history that remains relevant to its continuing engagement with the defence forces of our region.

Professor Peter Stanley
General Editor, Australian Army History Series
UNSW Canberra

ACKNOWLEDGEMENTS

This book is the result of the support of many people in Australia and Papua New Guinea. Based as it is on my doctoral research, this book had its genesis almost seven years ago, and I owe thanks to so many who have helped or encouraged me along the way. Dr Garth Pratten never failed to encourage me to greater efforts, and always cast an insightful and incisive eye over my work. His straightforward approach to my writing kept me on track and enthused throughout my candidature. Dr Peter Londey guided me through the difficult first years of my studies, and I am grateful for his continued interest in and support of my research. I owe a debt of gratitude to Professor Joan Beaumont for her astute advice and for the countless opportunities she has given me to grow as an historian. She is always generous with her time, and has shown by example on our research trips to the wilds of Burma and Thailand that historians can be adventurers both in the jungle and on the page.

The staff at the Strategic and Defence Studies Centre at the Australian National University provided a wonderful environment in which to complete my research. Associate Professor Peter Dean, Professor John Blaxland, Professor David Horner, Professor Dan Marston, Dr Joanne Wallis, Dr Jean Bou, Dr Rhys Crawley and Mike Gisick all gave me invaluable advice and assistance, for which I am profoundly grateful. More broadly, Professor Timothy Parsons and Professor Ted Wolfers gave helpful guidance for turning my thesis into this book. My current colleagues on the Official Histories of Australian Operations in Iraq and Afghanistan, and Australian Peacekeeping Operations in East Timor provided me the encouragement necessary to finish the final stages of this book, while the historians at the Australian Defence Force Academy were always available for a chat about Australia's military past and were a wonderful source of inspiration. I am deeply saddened that Professor Jeffrey Grey will not see this book's production. Jeff was always generous in his support of my work, as he has been for so many young scholars, and his sudden death is a profound loss to the history community.

In researching this book I was ably and kindly assisted by many librarians and archivists in Australia and PNG. I would like to thank the staff at the National Archives of Australia, Canberra, Brisbane and Melbourne. I am grateful to the staff in the reading room at the Australian War Memorial, who were always friendly to an often-harried researcher. Dr Roger Lee, Bill Houston and the staff at the Australian Army History Unit allowed me to access their rich archival material, and supported my research through an Army History Unit Research Grant. At the Australian Army Psychology Corps, I would like to thank Nicole Steele and Geoff Gallas for allowing me access to the incredible series of research reports on Papua New Guineans produced by the Army. In PNG, the staff at the Papua New Guinea National Archives and the archives of the University of Papua New Guinea were extremely helpful. Finally, I am grateful to the United Services Institute of the Australian Capital Territory for awarding me a scholarship in support of my research.

Professor Peter Stanley deserves my thanks as editor of the Australian Army History Series for so enthusiastically accepting my book into this series. The team at Cambridge University Press have also been of great help along the way: in particular Vilija Stephens and Cathryn Game. The maps were produced by CartoGIS at the Australian National University, while the pictures that grace this book's pages have been generously provided by the Australian Army Infantry Museum, the Chalkies Association and Veronica Peek.

I would like to express my immense gratitude to those who agreed to be interviewed for this project. Although too numerous to list here, all invited me into their homes, shared their stories and encouraged me in my research. However, a handful of people deserve particular mention. In Australia: Frank Cordingley, Terry Edwinsmith, Major General Hori Howard, Greg Ivey, Major General Michael Jeffery, Ian Ogston, Lieutenant Colonel Maurie Pears and Kevin Smith. My two research trips to PNG were made possible by the assistance of a number of generous people: the staff at the National Research Institute, the officers of PNGDF Headquarters, Dr Karl Claxton and Lachlan McGovern at the Australian High Commission, John Gibson, Thomas Hukahu, Clarence Hukahu, Major Frank Moripi, Colonel Reg Renagi, Dr Jon Ritchie, Alan Robinson and Major General Jerry Singirok.

My friends and family made the process of research and writing this book possible. In Melbourne, my grandfather has always been a source of cheer, while my friends, in particular Sam, Amanda, Settle, Burnett, Liley and Laura, were a font of diversion during my research. My father has always provided patient encouragement during my academic endeavours, and I owe a great deal to his years of support.

Finally, it is no exaggeration to say that this book would never have been completed without Meggie. Her wonderful patience, vital assistance, kind ear, welcome distraction and gentle cajoling were the *sine qua non* of my research and writing, even as she worked on her own research. I will never cease to be grateful for her friendship, love and support, and this book is dedicated to her.

A NOTE ON TERMINOLOGY

The nation known today as Papua New Guinea (PNG) has been referred to by a number of formal and informal names over the course of its history, including Papua/New Guinea, Papua and New Guinea, the Territory of Papua New Guinea (TPNG), Nuigini or simply New Guinea (a term that also describes the whole island, including the now Indonesian province of Irian Jaya). In official documents during Australian rule there was little consistency. In the interests of simplicity, the term 'Papua New Guinea' and its acronym are used throughout the book to describe the area contained within the modern country's borders, while recognising that no such country existed for either Australians or indigenous people for most of the period discussed. Similarly, the book uses the term 'Papua New Guinean' to describe the indigenous people of this region, despite the great variety of languages, ethnicities and identifications of these millions of people, then as now.

The terms used for the armed forces in PNG are equally confusing. Many sources refer to the Pacific Islands Regiment when they mean both the regiment and the host of ancillary units and subunits in PNG at the time, even after all Australian Army units were placed under a single, cohesive formation, PNG Command. Where appropriate, the book refers to the highest formation with operational command in PNG. Before 1965 this was the PIR, as Area Command PNG was an administrative organisation only. After 1965 the Australian Army's Papua New Guinean units in PNG were part of first PNG Command, then Joint Force PNG and finally the PNG Defence Force. These terms are used interchangeably with 'the Australian Army in PNG' to refer to units that included Papua New Guineans, particularly in cases where the book discusses more than one of these organisations.

Glossary

1ATF	1st Australian Task Force, Vietnam
AACE	Australian Army Certificate of Education
AAHU	Australian Army History Unit
AAPSYCH	Australian Army Psychology Corps
AATTV	Australian Army Training Team, Vietnam
ABC	Australian Broadcasting Commission
ABS	Australian Bureau of Statistics
ADAG	Australian Defence Assistance Group
AGPS	Australian Government Publishing Service
AHQ	Army Headquarters
ARA	Australian Regular Army
AUSTEO	Australian Eyes Only
AWM	Australian War Memorial
BHQ	Battalion Headquarters
CGS	Chief of the General Staff
CMF	Citizen Military Forces
CO	Commanding Officer
CPC	Constitutional Planning Committee
CUP	Cambridge University Press
DCGS	Deputy Chief of the General Staff
DMO&P	Directorate of Military Operations and Plans
FCO	Foreign and Commonwealth Office
FESR	Far East Strategic Reserve
GOC	General Officer Commanding
HQ	Headquarters
JFHQ	Joint Force Headquarters
JPC	Joint Planning Committee
KAR	King's African Rifles
L/Cpl	Lance Corporal
MUP	Melbourne University Press

NAA	National Archives of Australia
NCO	Non-Commissioned Officer
NG	New Guinea
NGIB	New Guinea Infantry Battalion
NGVR	New Guinea Volunteer Rifles
NS	National Service
OC	Officer Commanding
OCS	Officer Cadet School
OUP	Oxford University Press
PI	Pacific Islander
PIB	Papuan Infantry Battalion
PIR	Pacific Islands Regiment
PNG	Papua New Guinea
PNGDCC	Papua New Guinea Defence Coordination Committee
PNGDF	Papua New Guinea Defence Force
PNGMD	Papua New Guinea Military District
PNGNA	Papua New Guinea National Archives
PNGVR	Papua New Guinea Volunteer Rifles
RAAEC	Royal Australian Army Education Corps
RAAF	Royal Australian Air Force
RAE	Royal Australian Engineers
RAEME	Royal Australian Electrical and Mechanical Engineers
RAN	Royal Australian Navy
RAR	Royal Australian Regiment
RMC	Royal Military College
RPNGC	Royal Papua New Guinea Constabulary
RSL	Returned and Services League
RSM	Regimental Sergeant Major
RSSAILA	Returned Sailors', Soldiers' and Airmen's Imperial League of Australia
SAS	Special Air Service
SMH	*Sydney Morning Herald*
SOFA	Status of Forces Agreement
TPNG	Territory of Papua New Guinea
UN	United Nations
UPNG	University of Papua New Guinea

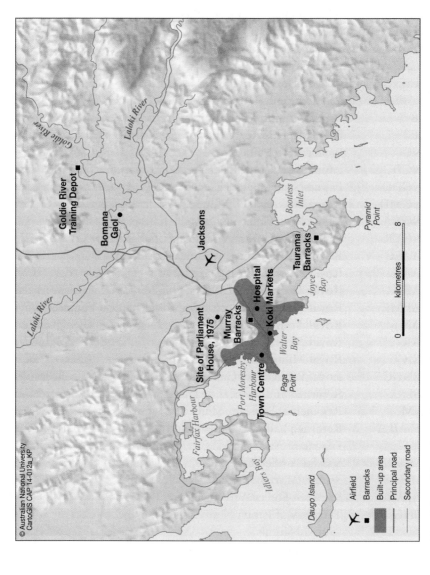

Map 1 Port Moresby and surrounds

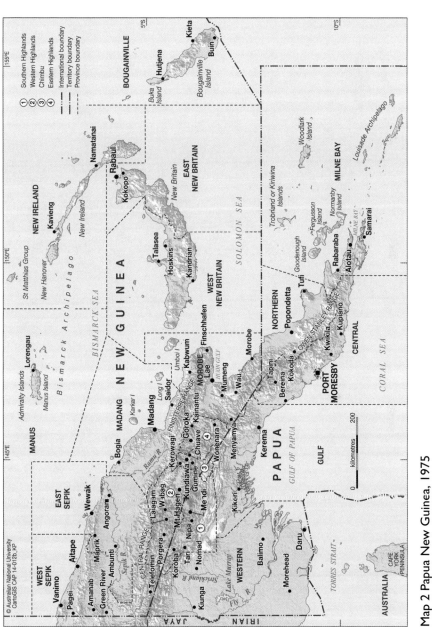

Map 2 Papua New Guinea, 1975

INTRODUCTION

On 16 September 1975, the flag of Papua New Guinea (PNG) was raised officially for the first time in Port Moresby, marking the end of almost a hundred years of Australian rule. The honour of this task was given to Warrant Officer George Aibo of the fledgling Papua New Guinea Defence Force (PNGDF), who not only represented the military at the ceremony but was also himself a product of the profound changes that had occurred in the twenty-four years since Australia raised the small peacetime Pacific Islands Regiment (PIR). Aibo had been the third Papua New Guinean to join the regiment and, in the years following, saw the single battalion of the PIR expand to a force five times its size, becoming the brigade-sized PNG Command in 1965 and, in 1973, the PNGDF.

Aibo's career exemplified the changing role of Papua New Guinean units within the Australian Army and the transformation of Papua New Guinean soldiers from subordinate 'colonial' troops in the eyes of Australians to well-educated, equipped and trained men who were represented at all ranks and in all positions, albeit solely in PNG rather than throughout the Australian Army. He had served throughout the PIR's problematic infancy, when it was considered of only secondary importance by the Australian Army, and had helped halt riots by Papua New Guinean troops in 1957 and 1961. Later, he patrolled the border with Indonesia at the height of Confrontation, at a time when PNG Command was charged with guarding this vital Australian region. During the late 1960s, as a solid and experienced non-commissioned officer (NCO),

Figure 0.1 The lowered Australian flag is removed, Independence Day, 16 September 1975. George Aibo is second from the left, at rear. (Dennis Williams and the *Post Courier*)

Aibo guided those new Papua New Guinean officers who would lead the PNGDF in an independent PNG.[1]

The history of the PIR, PNG Command and the PNGDF is at once a history of Australia and of Papua New Guinea. It is a history of men like Aibo, and of his Australian counterparts, of colonialism and decolonisation, and of peacetime and the threat of war. From the re-raising of the PIR in 1951, the Australian Army in PNG was, to varying degrees, both an important pillar of Australia's defence as well as a significant part of PNG's progression to independence. More broadly, Australian policies and attitudes towards Papua New Guinean units and the soldiers within them are one example of a multitude of colonial armies around the world at the time and before, albeit with a particular, and unique, Australian flavour. The experiences of the Australian Army's Papua New

Guinean units are therefore a window on race relations in PNG, and on the relationship between militaries and decolonisation.

This book takes as its focus the operational, social and racial aspects of the Australian Army in PNG. The PIR, and the other units later raised to command and support it, was first and foremost raised to defend Australia by guarding PNG, which was then the northernmost periphery of Australia's territory. As a result the role the Australian Army was intended to play in the defence of PNG, and how successful it was in preparing for it, are key to this history. At the same time, the Army did not act in a vacuum in PNG. Indeed, in some ways the Australian Army had to be more attuned to the local context than it was in Australia. As a result, the book considers the interaction between the Australian Army and its Papua New Guinean context, in particular the development of the Territory and the often-tense relationship with the Australian colonial government as the place of the military in the future nation was debated. Finally, as is often noted, armies are collections of people. In PNG, the Australian Army found itself commanding units of astonishing diversity, in which hundreds of languages and cultures were represented. This book explores the Australian Army in PNG as a point of cultural interaction, between the Army and its colonial charges, between Australian and Papua New Guinean soldiers, and between their families, all during a period of profound change in race relations in Australia and PNG.

It is a cliché when writing Australian military history to refer to the degree to which a particular battle, campaign, war or person has been neglected by historians. Often, this speaks as much to the particular narrative an author or group hopes to create about an event as to the number of people with knowledge of it, given the cachet associated with an 'untold' story. Undoubtedly, some historical periods are neglected for a variety of reasons, such as their complexity, lack of a clear narrative, paucity of sources and a dearth of drama or excitement. In particular, 'peacetime' or 'routine' military activities attract little attention, while battles and campaigns are studied time and time again. No conventional war was fought in PNG after 1945, although one with Indonesia was feared during the 1960s, and Papua New Guineans did not directly participate in Australia's Cold War conflicts. Consequently, the campaigns of the Second World War and the narrative of military deterioration, civil conflict and criminal violence after independence have overshadowed the experience of the military in PNG between 1951 and 1975. Moreover, as PNG is now an independent nation, the contribution of Papua New

Guineans to Australia's defence is seen as part of that country's past, and has been largely excised from Australian history.

Scholarly work on the Australian Army in PNG is scarce, and is limited to a handful of narrative regimental histories and theses, many written in the 1970s and therefore invariably suffering from a lack of access to the archival record, as well as a focus on the process of independence rather than the broader history of the PIR and later forces.[2] General histories of the Australian Army after 1945 have conceptualised its Papua New Guinean units as an interesting but remote corner of the institution. For instance, Jeffrey Grey's Australian Army, the most valuable of a handful of studies of the history of the institution, describes service in PNG 'as one of the defining features of service in the army in the 1950s and 1960s'. However, his allocation of only a small number of pages to the bookends of the PIR's existence – its raising and Papua New Guinean independence – is representative of other studies of the Australian Army's organisation and its post-Vietnam history, which recognise Papua New Guinean units as unique but do not, or cannot, study them in their own right.[3] In part, the absence of the Australian Army in PNG from this historical record is compounded by the broader academic neglect of the post-1945 period in Australia's military history, beyond studies of Korea, Malaya and Vietnam.[4] Although, as is often the case in Australian military history, while there might be only a little written about the Army in PNG, the Royal Australian Navy (RAN), which maintained a PNG Division of the RAN from 1949, and the Royal Australian Air Force (RAAF), which operated extensively in PNG during the Cold War, have received almost no historical attention.[5]

From the end of the nineteenth century, PNG was viewed by Australians both as a bulwark against attack and as a springboard to Asia, and as such figured significantly in Australia's defence planning and strategic thinking. However, only recently has PNG's place in Australia's strategic perceptions been examined. Historian Bruce Hunt argues that throughout most of the period of Australian administration of PNG, Australia 'made judgements about Papua New Guinea using external reference points as the focus of its assessments', namely Germany, Japan and Indonesia.[6] In the period immediately before independence, however, these reference points 'all but disappeared'. While internal stability and unity became an increasing security concern, the decline of PNG's strategic significance was of profound importance not only to the Army in PNG but also to Australia's willingness to grant independence to Papua New Guineans.[7] Others, such as T.B. Millar and Hank Nelson, have examined the role played by PNG in Australia's conceptions of its defence.[8] However, in each case, the implementation of strategy, and its implications for the units and the people within them, is absent from these discussions.

While the strategic and political context – as understood by Australians – dictated a great deal of the development of the force, this book moves beyond high-level decision-making, and is concerned primarily with the way government policies, civilian attitudes and the Army's own experiences combined to shape the development of a force of Papua New Guineans. Grey complains that the official historians of the First and Second World Wars do not 'devote much space to the essential building blocks of armies . . . doctrine, training, command, logistics, force structure'. As a result, in the official histories, 'Australian operations just "happen", with little real indication of the extraordinary preparations necessary'.[9] While the study of a force that trained for combat but did not engage in it presents particular challenges for an historian, this book addresses those essential building blocks of armies to which Grey referred by examining how the Army in PNG 'happened', adding to this list the issues of race, civil–military relations, and soldiers' family and social life.

PAPUA NEW GUINEANS: AUSTRALIA'S OTHER SOLDIERS

Papua New Guineans composed the largest minority to have served in the Australian Army in the post-war period. By 1972, the 2800 Papua New Guinean troops constituted almost one in ten regular soldiers in the Australian Army.[10] By way of contrast, an estimated five hundred Indigenous Australian soldiers served during the entire ten years of Australia's participation in the Vietnam War.[11] Yet, despite the fact that Papua New Guineans constituted the largest non-European group of soldiers in the Australian Army, their experience has been almost completely neglected by historians, even within the already 'overlooked and underrepresented' place of minorities in discussions of Australia's military past.[12] As interest grows in Indigenous Australians soldiers, sailors and airmen, an examination of Papua New Guineans in the context of their place as regular soldiers in Australian service reveals that the breadth of cultures within the Army extended far beyond mainland Australia, and substantially expands the understanding of race in the Australian Defence Forces and colonialism more generally.[13]

The Second World War has dominated the limited discussion of Papua New Guinean soldiers. Just as the physical legacy of the war can be seen throughout PNG, in airstrips, overgrown fortifications and the layout of towns and roads, so the war also pervades Australia's perception of PNG. As Hank Nelson has noted, 'three and [a] half years of World War II may have been more important and more enduring than nearly one hundred years of administrative history', given the effects of the war on the landscape and the people.[14] While PNG itself struggles to find a place for the war in its national memory, in Australia the war dominates perceptions of its former colony and closest northern neighbour.[15] Views of 'native' troops varied both during the conflict and in the post-war literature, but although portrayed in the official histories as performing well, they have often been presented in racial terms.[16]

As Liz Reed and others have shown, since the Second World War popular memory in Australia has focused on the archetype of the 'native' carrier, popularly known as the 'fuzzy wuzzy angel', as exemplified in George Silk's famous photograph of a Papuan man leading a wounded Australian soldier near Buna on Christmas Day, 1942.[17] Papua New Guineans are, through this image, accorded a place in Australia's perception of the war, yet it is a subordinate one. The common depiction of all carriers as willing and loyal participants simplifies their complex motivations and experiences, particularly given the widespread Australian practice of conscripting carriers and the fact that many Papua New Guineans laboured – willingly and unwillingly – for the Japanese.[18] Moreover, the focus on carriers and labourers in historical study and commemoration of the war denies the less subordinate (although equally valuable) role played by thousands of Papua New Guineans as soldiers during the war and is perhaps one factor in the lack of recognition of Papua New Guinean soldiers after 1945.

Simplistic images of Papua New Guineans as loyal carriers and 'fuzzy wuzzy angels' have continued in recent scholarship. It is still possible to find scholars referring to Papua New Guineans during the Second World War as 'innocent and ignorant', while the term 'native' still abounds in description of both soldiers and carriers.[19] At the same time, more scholarly work on the treatment of Papua New Guineans can depict Australians as universally callous and racist. Noah Riseman, for instance, argues that Australians were profligate with the lives of Papua New Guinean soldiers.[20] Papua New Guineans were undoubtedly treated as second-class soldiers, but the idea that Australian commanders wilfully threw away the lives of their soldiers is neither substantiated nor consistent with contemporary military practice. Ultimately, the description of Papua New Guineans as either innocent or cruelly exploited

Figure 0.2 Raphael Oimbari leads Private George Whittington, Buna, 25 December 1942 (AWM014028)

serves to simplify the complex place of Papua New Guineans within the military.

Certainly, the Australian Army, particularly during the 1940s and 1950s, viewed Papua New Guineans as subordinate, adopting a paternalistic attitude to their training and leadership. However, during the postwar period on which this book focuses the place of Papua New Guineans shifts from subordinate to all but equal. Within this transformation there existed a variety of Australian Army attitudes, ranging from racist to more progressive than the civilian world. Importantly, Papua New Guinean soldiers themselves were not naïve colonial soldiers, instead engaging with the Army in a range of ways, often proudly becoming part of an elite in PNG. Through these men – both Australian and Papua New Guinean – we have an unparalleled insight into the way in which the Australian Army adapted to shifts in race relations occurring around and within it. The omission of Papua New Guinean experiences from the history of race and Australia's defence is somewhat baffling.[21] In the small Australian armed force of the 1950s, Papua New Guinean units would have loomed large in Australian soldiers' conception of race within their ranks. Without an examination of the Army in PNG, any discussion of race and Australia's defence during the Cold War period is inadequate.

'THAT ARMY AGAIN': THE MILITARY AND COLONIAL PNG

The development of the PIR into the PNGDF can be understood only in the context of Australian rule in PNG and the process of decolonisation from the second half of the 1960s. However, the literature on this subject suffers from a lack of scholarly and public interest in Australia and PNG's shared history.[22] Academic study on PNG peaked immediately before and after independence as historians and political scientists examined the past and present in order to comment on the nascent country's future. As Stuart Doran points out, much of what has been written on Papua New Guinean independence has 'all too quickly moved to a narrative of what was or was not done' rather than examining the context of independence and the motivations of the various actors.[23] At the centre of critiques of Australian decolonisation are the interconnected questions of why Australia granted independence, and whether its approach took into account the needs and desires of Papua New Guineans. A common narrative is that Australia left too early, burdening PNG with national institutions ill-suited to its particular circumstances, of which the PNGDF is seen as a prime example.[24] Donald Denoon, in his analysis of the independence process, rightly argues that this narrow interpretation of decolonisation neglects the complex drivers of change in late 1960s PNG, denies the agency of Papua New Guineans, and assumes that 'continuing Australian rule would have resolved, rather than exacerbated, problems of governance'.[25]

There is little doubt that Australia acted in its own interests when determining the shape and timing of independence. However, as Doran and Denoon suggest, there is a distinct difference between self-interested leadership and deliberate neglect. Nelson most clearly argues that self-interest was always at the centre of Australia's decolonisation, but reminds us that given Australia's position as the dominant partner in the process, this should not be surprising. Concern over increasing tribal violence, protests in Bougainville and tensions along the Indonesian border were important but largely unarticulated reasons for the Australian withdrawal. Given these factors, Nelson speculates that 'in the event of violence the Australians would immediately become part of the problem' and that were Australia to remain, it would find itself in an unenviable situation: forced to act, but pilloried for doing so.[26] Australia's position on the international stage, as well as its own self-perception, also drove its withdrawal from the dwindling list of colonial powers.[27]

Despite the importance of the Army as an expensive and powerful force in PNG, the military figures little in discussions of Papua New Guinean decolonisation. Whether the PNGDF was suited to an independent PNG, the degree to which independence influenced the Army's policies and the way in which the Army engaged in nation-building all remain largely unexamined. To some extent, the experiences of several scholars in PNG during the independence period shaped their writing on these issues. Ian Downs, author of the most comprehensive study of the Australian Administration to date, addresses the Australian military only in the context of independence, overlooking the Army's presence in PNG in the two decades preceding 1975.[28] For him, and the Administration at the time (in which he served), the PIR and PNG Command were simply part of a separate government department, out of the Administration's control and therefore not part of the history of the Australian presence in PNG until the transfer of powers at independence. During the period of Australian rule this separation was sometimes reinforced by interdepartmental antagonisms and jealousies, stemming in part from the Administration's resentment at the Army's role in the Territory.

Adding to the tensions between the Army and Administration was a civilian fear of the military's potential to cause instability, through mutiny or an overthrow of the government. The example of African coups played a large part in fuelling this concern, and from the beginning of the 'wave of decolonisation' during the 1960s, Africa loomed large, if somewhat vaguely, in discussions and planning for PNG. Coups in the Congo, Nigeria and elsewhere suggested powerfully that the militaries of newly decolonised nations had the opportunity, organisation and inclination to impose their will on the shaky structures of a fledgling state.[29] As a result, and despite the vast differences between Africa and PNG in culture and history, the threat of a coup shadowed the military in the prelude to independence. Similarly, after 1975 the possibility of the PNGDF mounting or supporting a coup and its general deterioration in discipline and capability dominated scholarly discussion of the force.[30] Given that PNG's independence occurred more than a decade later than that of many other colonised nations, the development of the PIR into the PNGDF occurred against the backdrop of the troubled experiences of these new states, and in particular a multitude of military-led coups. Nevertheless, as several scholars have pointed out, there are limitations to the comparison of PNG with Africa, not least the nature of Australian colonialism, which was tightly controlled from the metropole, and the unique culture and diversity of Papua New Guineans.[31]

The possibility of a coup also shaped the construction of the PNGDF before independence. The Australian Army engaged in these debates, largely but not entirely within government channels, and devoted considerable resources to addressing concerns about instability in the ranks. However, recent studies have failed to interrogate why the coup narrative had such force, particularly around independence. In this way, Marcus Mietzner and Nicholas Farrelly ask why no coup occurred despite a 'number of observers' predicting in the 1970s that PNG would likely become dominated by the military.[32] Privileging such predictions, this view neglects the widespread civilian fear of 'arming the natives' during Australian rule, the poor relationship between PNG Command and the Administration and the broader context of anti–Vietnam War feeling at the time of independence. Ultimately, much of the scholarship on the Army's place within Australian rule in PNG and the country's independence relies too heavily on contemporary studies, which either neglect the military or reflect the tensions of the time.

THE AFRICAN EXAMPLE

Although a comparison between the Australian Army in PNG and other colonial armies is beyond the scope of this book, the wealth of literature on the subject helps illuminate the PNG case. In particular the work of scholars on such issues as 'martial race' theory, loyalty of indigenous people to the colonial power, exploitation of military minorities and cross-cultural relationships by scholars of colonial militaries informs my study. As Timothy Stapleton points out, although colonial soldiers have often been presented as 'naïve fools mesmerized by Europeans or optimistic mercenaries', the complex nature of indigenous soldiers' engagement with the colonial state has been acknowledged by a number of historians.[33]

David Killingray has led the field, and more recently Timothy Parsons has explored the breadth of African soldiers' experiences both serving and negotiating with the colonial state.[34] A growing body of historians follow Parsons and Killingray, moving on from the simplistic regimental narratives that previously typified the field to disentangle the web of loyalty, exploitation and indigenous agency within colonial armed forces. While Parsons has been criticised for privileging resistance and dissent over negotiation and agency, some more recent studies have acknowledged the multilayered nature of indigenous engagement with the colonial military. Examining Malawian soldiers in the King's African Rifles (KAR), Timothy Lovering writes that these men were 'successfully co-opted into the Army' but also 'were able to adapt military culture themselves'.[35] Kaushik Roy similarly examines the multifaceted nature of service among Indian soldiers, showing that 'loyalty' was produced by a combination of pride at being soldiers, personal bonds and economic factors, describing the Indian Army as 'a quasi-mercenary professional colonial army'.[36] Mutinies, riots and disaffection among colonial troops have also offered a rich area of investigation for historians, who have shown that far from being a rejection of colonial rule, as was often suggested at the time, mutinies were sometimes the result of a breach of contract – supposed or real – by the colonial government, most usually in regard to pay and conditions.[37]

Race, culture, ethnicity and the idea of the 'martial race' are central to almost all discussions of colonial militaries, in particular the way in which Europeans have perceived, treated and categorised colonial troops. PNG is no exception. As Gavin Schaffer has pointed out, 'for hundreds of years, soldiers have repeatedly been selected and remembered racially, according to criteria whereby notions of type prefigured the realities of service and sacrifice'.[38] Writing about Māori soldiers in New Zealand, for instance, Francesca Walker argues that historians have 'accepted the martial distinctiveness [of Māori soldiers] as historical truth', while Māori soldiers themselves at times made use of this myth to further their own interests.[39] The perception of difference within colonial forces has also been important to their existence. David Omissi contends that ethnicity and security were closely tied, as 'no imperial power could hope to maintain its rule . . . if it treated its subject population as a single, undifferentiated and potentially hostile mass'.[40] Similarly, Cynthia Enloe has argued that 'ethnically designed militaries are frequently used by governments as vehicles through which to exert and maintain their authority'. At the same time, the exploitation of ethnicity within militaries has had important effects on the relationship between certain groups and between subjects and the colonial government.[41] While race and ethnicity are important in explaining the development of the Australian Army's Papua New Guinean forces, as this book explores, Australian perceptions of Papua New Guinean soldiers was different from that of other parts of the colonial world. Partly, this was the result of the different place afforded these units within the colonial structure, given that they were never used as a direct instrument of colonial control, and were funded and controlled directly from the metropole. It was also the consequence of a particularly Australian view of Papua New Guinean soldiers, at least until the early 1960s, as primitive and not suited to 'modern' soldiering.

Hence I take issue with those scholars who have argued that the idea of 'martial race' was important in the military in PNG. Robert Hall, for instance, criticises the Australian Army for not acknowledging a long-standing 'Papua New Guinean military culture', implying that there was indeed a military culture to silence, despite the vast range of cultural forms in PNG and the absence of any Papua New Guinean national identity before European colonisation.[42] Comparing PNG with other colonial militaries, Riseman has argued that Papua New Guineans were seen as a martial race during the Second World War and that this was central to their treatment by Australia.[43] This idea is problematic. There is no doubt that Papua New Guineans were framed according to Australian ideas of race, but whether this translated into a perception that Papua New Guineans were inherently 'martial' is far from certain. In regard to the Indian Army, Gavin Rand and Kim Wagner have argued that 'the *concept* of the "martial race" has been ascribed too central a role in analyses of colonial recruiting', as it ignores the more prosaic economic and political influences at play.[44] In the limited history of the military in PNG, the idea of 'martial race', so prevalent in studies of other colonial forces, has also been too quickly used to explain the place of Papua New Guineans. As will be seen, the strength of the 'fuzzy wuzzy angel' myth, while evidence of a continued subordination of Papua New Guineans to Australian historical ownership of the war, as Riseman and Reed suggest, is nonetheless also indicative of an Australian perception of a lack of martiality among Papua New Guinean soldiers.

In its scope and periodisation, this book focuses on the Australian Army's Papua New Guinean–manned units from the peacetime re-raising of PIR in 1951 to the end of Australian rule in 1975. The wartime history of the PIR has been broadly studied, although further detailed archival work is needed, and is better examined in the context of the Second

World War. The period after independence, while also deserving of further historical scholarship, encompasses a different set of influences, not least an independent PNG government, and would rely far more heavily on limited Papua New Guinean archives. This book also takes as its subject those regular Australian Army units that included Papua New Guineans, rather than encompassing all military units that served in PNG during this period, such as engineers and survey troops.[45] Similarly, the smaller but important contribution of the RAN and the RAAF to the defence of PNG is not examined here.

The first chapter explores the formation of the PIR during the early 1950s, placing it within the context of Australia's colonial rule in the Territory of PNG, and examines the racial origins of the Australian Army's perception of its new unit and the soldiers within it as simple, inexpensive and auxiliary to the rest of the Army. Chapter 2 considers the problems that arose from these assumptions, which culminated in two 'disturbances' among Papua New Guinean troops in 1957 and in 1961, which had long-lasting effects. The third chapter examines the effect of the changing strategic circumstances facing Australia between 1962 and 1966 on the PIR, in particular the advent of Confrontation with Indonesia and that country's control over Dutch New Guinea, as well as the process of transforming the PIR into the much larger PNG Command. Alongside the PIR's expansion were profound shifts in the treatment and conception of Papua New Guinean soldiers. These are considered in chapter 4, which explores the influence of the dismantling of discriminatory laws and practices on the Army throughout the 1960s. The chapter also investigates the composition, character and motivations of the Papua New Guinean cohort of the Australian Army in detail, and the limits placed on their integration into the military. Chapter 5 examines the way in which the end of Confrontation in 1966 created room for discussion of the purpose of the Australian Army's forces in PNG, and the way in which the Australian Army began to focus its expansion and training efforts on PNG's independence. Chapter 6 moves beyond 'traditional' military history, and integrates the professional, personal and social experiences of Australian servicemen and their families into the history of the Army in PNG. The final chapter examines the Australian Army during the last five years of Australian rule in PNG, during which PNG Command and later the PNGDF were almost wholly focused on independence as the immediate and most pressing goal.

For twenty-four years, Papua New Guinean units made up a substantial portion of the Australian Army and were an important – sometimes a vital – part of the defence of PNG, to which Australia attached a significant degree of strategic importance. Equally, the development of the Army in PNG serves as a reminder that the Australian Army during the Cold War was not simply composed of Australians and based in Australia, but was a force of varied tasks and composition. Indeed, if Papua New Guinean soldiers are taken into account, the Australian Army was perhaps one of the most culturally and linguistically diverse forces on earth. Essentially, the Australian Army in PNG was a force with a dual identity. It was part of the Australian Army while also being perceived as a foreign and distinct force that was the potential precursor to a national Papua New Guinean military. This book provides an examination of these two identities, how they coexisted and the manner in which the PNGDF was finally separated from the Australian Army.

CHAPTER 1

AN 'EXPERIMENTAL ESTABLISHMENT'

THE RE-RAISING OF THE PACIFIC ISLANDS REGIMENT, 1951–57

Units of the Australian Army manned by Papua New Guineans were first raised during the Second World War in response to the Japanese threat to Australia and its possessions. The single Papuan Infantry Battalion (PIB) and the four New Guinea Infantry Battalions (NGIB) created during the war were combined by Army authorities to form the PIR in 1944, and the units ultimately performed a small but significant role as a reconnaissance and raiding force over three years of fighting in PNG. Despite its service, the PIR was viewed by Australians only as a wartime necessity, and was disbanded in 1946 in part owing to fears of Papua New Guinean soldiers, trained and armed, upsetting the colonial status quo. Just five years later, in November 1951, growing Australian concerns about the security of PNG led to the regiment being re-raised as a means by which to defend Australia's northern approaches. This about-face reflected the parallel influences on Australia's defence in PNG of the Army and the colonial administration. While the PIR would later form the basis for an independent PNGDF, its early years were shaped by the various demands on the stretched Australian Army during the early Cold War period as well as colonial ideas about race. In light of Australian experience during the war, and the broader colonial view of Papua New Guineans, soldiers of the PIR were perceived as men who were unsuited to modern warfare and who required close guidance from Australians. The result was a force that was reflective of the colonial state during the 1950s: hierarchical, based on racial ideas of Papua New Guinean inferiority, and constructed largely in Australia's interests.

AUSTRALIA'S COLONIAL OUTPOST

PNG's geography – that is, its terrain and place in the world – has influenced much of the country's history. It has shaped the composition and identity of the people collectively known today as Papua New Guineans and dictated the pace and extent of European colonisation. Most of the spine of New Guinea consists of mountainous country, cut by rivers and covered in jungle, while the coastal regions include plains, mangroves and archipelagos. Separated from each other by a difficult topography, the isolated regions of PNG form pockets of culture, language and ethnicity that rival the far-flung islands of the Pacific; indeed PNG arguably has more languages than any other nation.[1] Ethnic groups are a primary source of identity in PNG and remain so today, while the ubiquitous *wantok* system (literally 'one talk') creates a social structure of obligation and responsibility among families and members of the same ethnic group that influences Papua New Guinean life at every level, while coexisting with identification with broader regional categories.[2]

Although Europeans first came into contact with PNG in the 1600s, significant interaction between explorers, traders and missionaries began in earnest during the early 1800s. European imperialism followed, with Germany annexing the north-eastern section of the island of New Guinea in 1884, an event that helped spark an equation of PNG with defence in the minds of Australians that would last almost another hundred years. With the movement of imperial rivalries closer to Australia's borders, concerns were raised about security in the pre-Federation collection of colonies, particularly Queensland. In 1883 the Queensland Premier 'annexed' Papua, in an attempt to force a reluctant British Government to act to secure the northern approaches to the Australian continent.[3] The following year the British Government relented, declaring a protectorate over Papua and formally incorporating the region into the empire four years later.[4] Shortly after the outbreak of the First World War, an Australian expeditionary force easily captured German New Guinea, and in 1919 the Territory became a League of Nations Class C Mandate under Australian administration as part of the division of Germany's empire, a status that meant it operated under a different administrator and laws from its neighbour, Papua.[5]

PNG experienced minimal development in the first half of the twentieth century. The Australian and British Governments were largely apathetic towards a region that they considered backward and economically unimportant and which contained few European expatriates.[6] What little economic activity there was centred on plantations (mainly copra) and resources such as gold. The role of the two Australian administrations, largely limited to towns and surrounding countryside, was to curb violence among the population with which it had contact, and to manage European business in the territories.[7] The only other European influence in PNG came from those attempting to spread Western religion and, as a result, missions and missionaries were prominent in those areas in contact with Europeans.[8] However, despite the two administrations and the reach of the churches, large swathes of PNG had little or no direct contact with Europeans during the first half of the twentieth century, despite being nominally under their control.

While Australian governments had always conceptualised the possession of PNG in terms of Australia's security, the Japanese entry into the Second World War thrust the region into sharper focus and forced a conception of PNG not just as a geographical barrier but as a potential battlefield as well. It is impossible to overstate the importance of the war to PNG. It brought hundreds of thousands of European soldiers and civilians into contact with Papua New Guineans, who were themselves subject to the upheaval of recruitment or conscription as labourers and carriers or who experienced the war as it was fought over their land. A smaller number joined the PIB and the NGIB as soldiers.[9] The environment over which the war was fought was also shaped by the war. Towns were razed, crops destroyed, roads and airfields built and the landscape littered with the detritus of war. These changes, in turn, influenced the urban structures of the post-war period, with towns being built on and with wartime matériel.

After the military governance of the Australian New Guinea Administrative Unit, peacetime administration was reinstated in 1949.[10] For the first time since Australia had received the Mandate for New Guinea, the two halves of PNG were united under one Administration, based in Port Moresby.[11] While a bipartisan agreement not to politicise PNG had been a feature of Australia's governance of PNG, the Australian Government displayed a greater interest in the development of the Territory after 1945 than previously, and the appointment in 1951 of Paul Hasluck as Minister for Territories marked the first time that a minister took on this portfolio as his only responsibility. As a former official from the department with an interest in 'native affairs', Hasluck came to the portfolio determined to reinvigorate the governance of PNG.[12] On assuming his position, Hasluck set about making the new single Administration a more efficient organisation capable of managing a gradual and measured development of PNG and its people. This so-called Hasluck period was characterised by an Australian paternalism that focused on guided development. Under Hasluck's guidance, PNG's budget rose from £7 to £37 million during the 1950s, new systems of recruitment were introduced for the Territory's public service and the quality of personnel was improved.[13] Services for Papua New Guineans were also expanded. For instance, pupils in primary schools tripled between 1953 and 1959, in addition to children already in mission schools.[14] Changes in laws restricting Papua New Guineans, such as those concerning dress and access to public facilities, were incrementally relaxed over the course of the 1950s, although it was only during the following decade that legal, if not social, discrimination was fully eliminated. At the same time, the reach of the Administration was slowly and carefully expanded by patrols into unexplored 'restricted areas' not yet under government control, particularly in the Highlands region.[15]

The 450 people who made up the Administration during the 1950s were largely based in the centres of Port Moresby, Rabaul and Lae. In the rural areas of PNG, colonial rule was enforced by a system of district commissioners, district officers and patrol officers, colloquially termed 'kiaps', from the German word for captain. Either based in a population centre or patrolling their area of responsibility, these men had extensive powers to convene courts, pass sentences and ensure that they were carried out, all with little or no direct oversight. Kiaps could, for instance, use imprisonment as a way to manage local conflicts, gaoling people on spurious pretences in order to limit trouble.[16] During the 1950s, acts of 'petty intimidation' were still widely used to maintain government control.[17] Kiaps also had the power to instruct villages on matters such as hygiene, organisation and what crops to plant, acting through appointed local leaders, 'luluai' in Papua and village constables in New Guinea. Only in 1959 were Australian kiaps replaced in their role by the Native Local Government Councils, although the representatives of the Administration retained their extensive powers.[18] For most Papua New Guineans living away from the major centres, kiaps were literally the Administration, being the embodiment of colonial power.[19]

Although it was structured as a government, managing its own departments, budget and police force, the Administration was not an independent or self-contained entity. Instead, it was closely overseen by the Department of Territories in Canberra. In PNG, the Administration operated alongside other Australian government departments and organisations, such as the Army, with whom they had only informal coordination, not control. This was at times an awkward relationship that, although suitable for the small size of the two pre-war territories, became difficult as the post-1945 Administration attempted to steer PNG towards greater development.[20]

There were four Administrators between 1945 and 1973: J.K. Murray, D. Cleland, D.O. Hay and L.W. Johnson – after which the position became that of High Commissioner (with some residual responsibilities of Administrator), held by Johnson and T.K. Critchley. As the Administration was part of the Department of External Territories, the Administrator's role was one of a senior government official rather than a representative of the Crown. Nevertheless he was often seen within the Territory as the figurehead of a colonial government, and at times performed duties of a vice-regal nature.[21] The first post-war Administrator, Murray, was dismissed in 1952 as the result of difficulties in his relationship with the Department of Territories, particularly his belief that his position should be accorded greater respect, responsibility and independence.[22] Indeed, on his first trip to PNG as Minister, Hasluck was surprised and revolted to find 'colonialism of a comic kind' operating under Murray:

> [Murray] acted like a colonial governor and was accorded the deference due to a vice-regal rank which in fact he did not have . . . In and around civilian circles in Port Moresby close to the senior administrative staff, there were some of the oddities of an officers' mess full of temporary gentlemen in white ducks giving a repertory club performance of a pukka sahib who had just come in from a damned awful day of taking up the white man's burden.[23]

Hasluck complained that the eleven thousand Australians in Papua New Guinea at the time were a 'stuffily rank-conscious' community in which the indigenous people were never dealt with on an equal footing.[24] Major General Thomas Daly, who visited Port Moresby in 1957, described Port Moresby as 'a small country town, virtually isolated and extremely parochial. Parish politics are paramount and local opinion is narrow and noisy.'[25] Murray was replaced in 1951 by Donald Cleland, a former brigadier with service in the military administration in PNG during the war. Cleland served in PNG until 1966, outlasting Hasluck as Minister for Territories by three years. As a result, for more than ten years the same minister, Administrator and departmental secretary ran the Territory, all sharing a similar belief in a methodical and gradual process of development in PNG.

Governed by the Administration were PNG's 1.4 million indigenous inhabitants and around thirteen thousand expatriates.[26] Despite some new policy initiatives after the Second World War, in most ways life in the Territory for Papua New Guineans during the early 1950s reflected the *status quo antebellum*.[27] Papua New Guineans were second-class citizens in PNG, having little say in their treatment or governance.[28] They were restricted in what they could wear, which films they could watch, where they could travel, in their wages and in their relationship with Europeans. Words such as 'boi' and 'masta' were used in everyday language, and decisions were taken on behalf of the 'native', who was considered ill-prepared for the modern world.

'ARMING THE NATIVES': PNG IN THE SECOND WORLD WAR

Papua New Guinean soldiers were recruited by Australia only as an emergency measure. Before the Second World War, PNG was considered vital to Australia's defence as a jungle-clad and mountainous barrier that would keep any potential invader at arm's length until suitable forces could be arrayed against them. Lengthy mobilisation times, PNG's remote and torturous geography and the absence of important economic or population centres all made permanent forces in PNG seem largely unnecessary. The nature of Australian governance in PNG played a role as well. The terms of Australia's League of Nations Mandate prohibited the creation of an indigenous force or the construction of defences in former German New Guinea. Even the raising of a whites-only reserve force the New Guinea Volunteer Rifles (NGVR) in 1939 was legally questionable.[29] In Papua, fears of 'arming the natives' and the potential of trained, paid and educated men to upset the balance of colonial power were seen as powerful arguments against suggestions that local men be recruited to serve as soldiers before the war.[30] Moreover, in contrast to British colonies in Africa, Australia did not use the military to maintain control in PNG, and the Royal Papuan Constabulary and the New Guinea Police Force were the only officially armed instruments of colonial power supporting the officers of the Administration. Indeed, the need to free the police from guard duties contributed to the creation of the first unit in PNG, the PIB, in 1940.[31]

Papua New Guineans made a significant contribution to Australia's campaigns in relation to their numbers. In early 1942 the PIB was deployed to the north coast of Papua, and went into action for the first time on 23 July near Awala when a party of Japanese soldiers was ambushed.[32] The PIB went on to serve in the Papuan campaign (with the

Figure 1.1 March past of signals troops, PIR, Nadzab 1945 (AWM093308)

exception of Milne Bay) and in the New Guinea campaigns in 1943. Such was the usefulness of the battalion that two additional 'native' battalions, the 1st and 2nd NGIB, were formed in New Guinea during 1944, with two further battalions in training or being formed by the end of the war. By November 1944 these battalions were grouped together into the PIR, and saw service in the final campaigns of New Britain, Bougainville and Aitape–Wewak. For the Papua New Guineans who served in the PIR during the war, numbering around 3500, the experience of being a soldier was an educative one, with not a small degree of excitement and pride. As Nelson points out, 'The black man who carried an Owen gun had a power and prestige among foreigners undreamt of by those who had known the company and plantation labour lines of the 1930s.'[33]

Although the combat record of the PIR was excellent, the conduct of Papua New Guinean soldiers during the war was not without controversy. Operationally under the control of Australian forces in PNG, Papua New Guinean troops were often used in a line infantry role, for which they were not trained or equipped, or allocated as 'penny packets' away from their unit, sometimes simply to protect Australian soldiers at night. These roles negated many of the strengths of the PIR in reconnaissance and raiding.[34] Despite the fact that such situations were beyond the training and organisation of the PIR, some Australians were critical of the ability of 'the natives' to stand up to concentrated fire and engage in conventional combat.[35]

Discipline was a problem within the PIR throughout the war, and Papua New Guinean soldiers gained a reputation for being unruly and dangerous away from the front line. Papua New Guineans were accused of raiding villages, stealing crops and livestock, and numerous cases of rape. Many cases were investigated, but Australian officers reacted to some serious incidents, such as rape, with a 'restraint that bordered on indifference', imposing only fines and short gaol terms on offenders. These incidents contributed to calls for the PIB to be disbanded in late 1942, but military necessity trumped these concerns and the unit was retained.[36] Although less common, instances of mass disobedience among Papua New Guinean soldiers were taken far more seriously by military authorities. In February 1945 a platoon of Papua New Guinean soldiers freed a fellow soldier from police custody in Annaberg, New Guinea, after the man was arrested for raping a policeman's wife. In the ensuing scuffle soldiers fired on police. Elsewhere, Papua New Guinean soldiers rioted over pay and conditions, not least the policy of providing 'traditional' uniforms rather than those issued to white soldiers.[37]

Incidents such as these bolstered long-standing opposition among Australians in PNG towards a force of Papua New Guineans.[38] In a letter to the Minister for External Territories in 1946, for instance, the Pacific Territories Association warned that if the PIR was not disbanded 'there will be serious trouble and possible loss of life, and general disaffection of the native population'.[39] Ultimately, the threat of disaffection among native troops, and the wholesale demobilisation of the Army down to just three battalions of infantry, saw the disbandment of the PIR in 1946.

THE COLD WAR COMES TO PNG

At the end of the 1940s, the strategic situation looked far less certain than it had in 1945, precluding a return to the pre-war peacetime footing and leading to the formation of the PIR. The threat of Russia, China and international communism caused mounting concern within the Australian Government throughout the late 1940s, and shaped Australia's defence spending and policies.[40] However, during this period Australia's strategic outlook was closely tied to that of Britain and the United States, and as a result strategic planners believed that Europe was the region in which a conflict would most likely be decided. As during the Second World War, Australia expected to contribute by providing troops to the Middle East and Malaya.[41] After the outbreak of the Malayan Emergency in 1948, South-East Asia gradually overtook any commitments further west as the primary focus of Australian strategic thinking.[42] Closer to home, the new nation of Indonesia became a specific point of concern for Australia, and would remain so for the next decade and a half.[43]

However, despite creating a permanent Australian Regular Army (ARA) in 1947, consisting of three battalions of infantry, an armoured regiment and assorted support units, the Australian Government struggled to find troops for its various commitments and plans.[44] In October 1949, for instance, the government of Prime Minister Robert Menzies was forced to admit to a worried public that there were only a thousand trained regular infantrymen in the entire Army at the time, and that many of these were in Japan.[45] The outbreak of the Korean War in 1950 transformed Australia's defence policy, as Menzies embarked on a higher level of peacetime military spending than hitherto seen and reintroduced national service, believing that a world war was likely in the next three years.[46] Nevertheless, combined with a competitive labour market, the continual deployments of battalions overseas and the need to provide instructors for the national service scheme, the Army at the start of 1950s was short of manpower and would have trouble providing forces to meet any unexpected crises.[47]

PNG had only recently been Australia's front line against a foreign threat, and so figured prominently in the thinking of Australia's defence planners during this period. The island was, in their eyes, both a bastion from which to defend Australia's lines of communication (and therefore its ability to project force) and a final strategic barrier. However, with the demobilisation of the wartime armed forces, no combat forces remained in PNG after 1946, although the RAN maintained a supply base on the strategically placed Manus Island in the Bismarck Sea. It was here that the first Papua New Guinean peacetime military unit, the RAN PNG Division, was created. This unit, consisting of around sixty local men, was approved in 1948 as an inexpensive way to provide manpower for the supply and refuelling of visiting Australian and allied ships, but it was not a combat force.[48]

The absence of locally based frontline forces, the shared border with the Dutch West New Guinea, to which newly independent Indonesia laid claim, and the 'present world situation' captured the attention of the press on the mainland. The *Courier-Mail* decried 'Defence lack in N. Guinea', while the *Advertiser* detailed 'measures to stop reds in NG'.[49] Expatriate Australian residents were also vocal in their concern over PNG's defence. In 1949 Australians in PNG called for the raising of a unit of the Citizen Military Force (CMF), the Army's reserve force, on the lines of the wartime NGVR.[50] Reports of foreign submarines in the area added to the sense of PNG's vulnerability considering that, as Administrator Murray pointed out, 'there is, at the moment, no Naval, Air or Army unit in any part of the Territory, other than [the small naval base in] the Manus District'.[51] He considered it 'highly desirable' that he should be given power to raise 'emergency but properly attested units as an immediate provision for the defence of the Territory'.[52] In a similar vein, members of the Returned Soldiers, Sailors and Airmen's Imperial League of Australia (RSSAILA) called for the formation of rifle clubs to 'provide a nucleus for military training'. The proposal also reflected a long-standing fear of the local population; the whites-only rifle clubs were also seen as a way 'to provide protection in the event of subversive organisations fomenting uprisings among the natives'.[53] Similar suggestions were made to arm 'white planters' against 'subversive communist guerrillas' (particularly the Chinese population in PNG, which numbered around two thousand) in an effort to stave off a 'second Malaya', a suggestion that combined the fears of the Asian north, communism and the traditional uneasiness felt by colonial societies about their safety.[54]

No doubt External Territories reacted with some alarm that Administrator Murray, who would shortly be removed by Hasluck in part because of his vice-regal pretensions, wished to hold the power to raise an armed force under Administration control, and the idea went no further. Equally, neither the Administration nor Major General V.C. Seacombe, the General Officer Commanding (GOC) Northern Command, under whose military jurisdiction PNG fell, were enthusiastic about 'private armies' being raised.[55] Instead, a CMF unit under the control of the Australian Army, but cheaper than a regular, Australian battalion, was approved by Josiah Francis, Minister for the Army, in January 1950.[56] The new unit was to be termed the Papua New Guinea Volunteer Rifles (PNGVR), linking it to the NGVR, but serving the newly combined entities of Papua and New Guinea.[57] Its role would be to provide security for key points during wartime, to gather military intelligence and to act as a cadre for the expansion of Papua New Guinean units, and as such would have small depots scattered around PNG.[58]

The Regular Army cadre for the PNGVR arrived in Port Moresby in September 1950, although men for the PNGVR were not recruited immediately. The Army's approach was unhurried, and five months after the arrival of the first soldiers, a *South Pacific Post* editor complained that 'it is to be hoped that the record of the PNGVR is not symptomatic of Australia's attitude toward defence'.[59] Equally concerning was the low number of recruits the PNGVR attracted, despite initial optimism.[60] While the PNGVR did have a far higher rate of participation among eligible Australian men than was the case with CMF units in Australia, the Army admitted it had been 'rather deluded by the burst of enthusiasm to serve, and the promise to join up'.[61] As a result of this, and of veiled suggestions of some debauchery involving the drunken theft of an air raid siren, the commanding officer (CO), Lieutenant Colonel N.R. McLeod, was returned to Australia in January 1951. Lieutenant Colonel N.P. Maddern, an officer who had been captured with Sparrow Force on Timor during the Second World War and had been interned in Singapore, replaced him in March. Recruiting for the PNGVR began in Port Moresby shortly after his arrival, and around PNG in the following months.[62]

The 'experimental establishment'

The limitations of the PNGVR were recognised almost immediately by Army authorities, who saw the re-raising of a regular 'native unit' as a more solid foundation for PNG's defence shortly after approving the CMF unit.[63] Papua New Guinean troops represented a cheap and expeditious means by which to defend PNG, particularly as financial and manpower restrictions and the Korean War made it unlikely that a regular battalion would be posted there permanently. Nonetheless, in taking the decision to raise the PIR, the Australian Government was at pains to ensure that the decision did not attract negative attention at the United Nations. Although the terms of Australia's trusteeship over New Guinea allowed for the development of a local force for the defence of the Territory, it nonetheless sought precedent in other similar forces around the world.[64] Whatever the window dressing, the decision to raise a local unit was one taken to ensure the defence of Australia rather than of PNG, and the force was always under Army, rather than Administration, control.

In contrast to the slow raising of the PNGVR, the first recruiting for the PIR began shortly after the arrival of the temporary CO, Major W.R.J. Shields, in February 1951.[65] The first draft of eighty-one Papua New Guineans enlisted by Shields came from Port Moresby and contained a number of men with wartime experience, such as the first recruit, Boino Warko, who had served with the police during the war. The criteria for enlistment were relatively simple. Papua New Guineans were to enlist for a three-year term, with each man required to be physically fit without any serious medical conditions and to provide a certificate of character from his local Administration officer. Given the lack of documentation for most potential recruits, there was no age limit.[66] Literacy was not a requirement, nor were recruits expected to understand English; this was not surprising given the dearth of educational opportunities throughout the Territory. However, despite even these low standards the Army was initially disappointed with the quality of recruits, particularly their health and suitability for service, for which the Army blamed the practice of using the Administration, a competitor for labour, as a recruiter.[67] By August 1951 only a single company had been raised, consisting of 192 men, with another fifteen having been discharged.[68]

The first CO of the PIR, Lieutenant Colonel H.L. Sabin, arrived on 2 October 1951, and immediately abandoned the policy of using the Administration as a recruiting agency. Sabin, like Maddern a former prisoner of the Japanese, instead used teams of PIR officers to recruit around the Territory. Despite continuing complaints about the quality of some recruits, Australian officers had no trouble finding enough troops to form a full battalion once they took over recruiting, and the PIR achieved its full establishment of around six hundred Papua New Guineans in November 1952. Indeed, the surfeit of potential recruits meant the PIR could recruit new men 'virtually on an as required basis'.[69]

The expansion of the battalion necessitated the construction of new facilities, many of which were built on the site of wartime camps. Initially based at Murray Barracks with the Area HQ and PNGVR, the PIR moved to a site around eight kilometres along a dirt road to the east of the town, known during the war as Eggy's Corner and renamed Taurama Barracks.[70] The site was chosen because the drainage, roads and concrete foundations of the wartime 2/1st and 2/5th Australian General Hospitals remained, which assisted the construction of new facilities.[71] Moreover, being situated on a peninsula, the site enjoys sea breezes and ready access to a beach, both extremely desirable in the hot and dusty environment of Port Moresby. The distance of the camp from the attractions of the town, such as they were during the 1950s, was probably also a recommendation, although later events would show that troops were not averse to walking the eight kilometres to town. Work on the new barracks was slow, forcing the Army to replace the Administration contractors with its own

Figure 1.2 PIR troops practise bayonet training during the 1950s (Australian Army Infantry Museum)

engineers. Despite their efforts, two companies were still accommodated in tents in 1952.[72]

Beyond being a demonstration of Australia's commitment to defend PNG, the role the PIR was to undertake in the event of war was modelled on its Second World War experience. During wartime the battalion would initially fight to delay the enemy and later act as a reconnaissance force for Australian units deployed from the mainland. It was also to be capable of conducting long-duration fighting patrols in difficult terrain.[73] While the PIR was structured in order to operate as a complete battalion, this cannot have been a realistic expectation given its planned deployment in company groups around PNG to defend key points and its role as a reconnaissance force. Reflecting its role, the PIR was an 'experimental establishment', structured as a pared-back infantry battalion, lacking heavier weapons such as mortars and machine-guns, and without the medical, quartermaster and signals platoons that supported a regular battalion.[74] The PIR could never defend PNG alone, but this was not its purpose. Instead, the PIR was the Australian Army's northern trip wire, as well as a symbol of Australia's defence of its territories, in keeping with the emphasis of successive Strategic Basis Papers on securing sea and air communications from Australia to Asia and beyond. The PIR was intended to identify a threat, provide the first line of defence and lead the more powerful and conventionally structured units of the Australian Army into the fight. Initially, senior officers suggested that the PIR also have an internal security role during peacetime. Seacombe for instance believed that there was a threat to PNG from so-called European dissidents – communists – and their potential 'to bring about the subversion of the native peoples by propaganda and incitement against the established government'. However, the idea of PIR involvement in internal security was abandoned, most likely as an unnecessary and unwelcome encroachment on the role of the Administration-controlled police.[75]

SETTLING IN

The regiment spent its first years establishing itself in PNG under the operational control of Northern Command, based in Brisbane. The most crucial aspect of the regiment's role as the first line of detection and defence against foreign aggression was the foundation of a series of outstations at key points from which patrols could be mounted. Initially, Northern Command intended to have three companies divided between outstations at Vanimo on the north coast of New Guinea near the Dutch border, at Rabaul and on Manus Island. These outstations, according to the Army Minister, were constructed explicitly to keep a 'watch on Indonesia', which was agitating for control of Dutch New Guinea.[76] The first outstation, at Vanimo, was built quickly by 24 Construction Squadron, and was first occupied in January 1953.[77] However, the establishment of an outstation at Rabaul was prevented by the refusal of local and Australian landowners to sell land at a price considered reasonable by the Army.[78] Instead, a second outstation was established at Nutt Point on Manus Island, close to the RAN's strategically important forward base at HMAS *Tarangau*, using the wartime US base there, and was occupied in December 1954.[79]

These outstations, particularly that at Vanimo, formed a central part of the PIR's activities for decades, while domestically the presence of a company at Manus presented an image of the Army addressing the issue of the defence of PNG; the Director of the Directorate of Military Operations and Plans (DMO&P) for instance believed that 'politically, even a company at Manus does something to offset the cry of "our defenceless north"'.[80] Both Vanimo and Manus were almost the archetype of tropical beach locations, with clear water, palm trees and abundant fish.

Vanimo outstation came replete with an open 'haus win' (i.e. house wind) overlooking the beach where officers could take advantage of a cool breeze to relax with a drink at the end of the day. Militarily, both outstations afforded 'somewhere a bit different to conduct training', being more remote than Port Moresby.[81] However, although those stationed at Nutt Point could socialise with the sailors at the RAN base and visiting warships, both outstations were possibly the most remote postings for a member of the Australian Army. All supplies came by ship, and during the 1950s aeroplane visits were few and far between. Such was the isolation that at least one local representative of the Administration committed suicide at Vanimo.[82]

Patrols were conducted from the outstations and by other groups of soldiers transported throughout the Territory. The lack of infrastructure in PNG meant that, before helicopters and plentiful air support became available during the 1960s, patrols were managed much as they had been during the Second World War.[83] They lasted for a maximum of two weeks, and any patrol longer than eight days required the hiring of carriers, who were paid in 'trade goods' and coins, as paper money had little worth in isolated villages.[84] However, as with so many aspects of the Army's role in PNG, Army policy was only belatedly adapted to the requirements of the Pacific Islands Regiment (PIR): it was not until 1958 that Treasury stopped insisting that PIR patrols procure receipts from villagers for food purchased while on patrol, despite repeatedly being told of the difficulties of weather, distance and almost universal illiteracy![85] Although in most cases Papua New Guineans were friendly, the PIR had to be prepared for a hostile reaction by groups who felt uncomfortable with foreigners on their land. In some instances, consideration was given to issuing a greater quantity of ammunition to patrols against the possibility of attack from locals, as had occurred in 1953 to two Administration officials at Telefomin, near the Dutch border.[86]

The remoteness of the PIR from Northern Command meant that the regiment lacked access to the Army's infrastructure in Australia. In the words of the regiment's third CO, Lieutenant Colonel Bert Wansley, 'we were neglected up there . . . we could do what we bloody well liked'. Although this was a 'jolly good experience', few allowances were made for the extra tasks required of the regiment, which, in addition to its usual training and routine tasks, was expected to recruit men and train them itself as well as carry out administrative tasks that were usually the responsibility of a higher headquarters.[87] In response to these difficulties, an Area Command PNG was created shortly after the PIR's re-raising, and the structure of the PIR gradually changed to include more officers and NCOs to cope with the workload. The new headquarters came under the command of the CO PNGVR, Lieutenant Colonel Maddern, and coordinated Army logistics and administrative matters in PNG, although the PIR still answered directly to Northern Command on operational matters.[88] This relieved some of the pressure, but the PIR still had to perform many of the tasks that in Australia were undertaken by specialised units, a fact exacerbated by the general shortage of officers across the Army.[89]

Compared with British colonies in Africa and elsewhere, PNG was anomalous in that the local government did not have control over military forces raised in the Territory. Although the Administration did engage with the Army on issues that fell into its purview, such as patrolling, recruiting tours and labour, during the 1950s the PIR was for the most part treated as if it did not exist.[90] In part, this lack of coordination was the product of a degree of antipathy from the Administration towards the Army, which it saw as an outsider that threatened the established hierarchy in PNG. In a letter to Northern Command, Major Don Barrett, a member of the PNGVR and a Rabaul businessman with a long association with both the Army and the Territory, attributed this hostility to equal parts interdepartmental rivalry and traditional fear of 'the native', telling Northern Command that it 'is the climate of fear that prompts some; it is the green eye of jealousy that prompts others', a sentiment echoed by Maddern.[91] In some cases Papua New Guinean soldiers bore some of this antagonism. In 1955 Barrett publicly claimed that PIR soldiers were 'treated like pigs' by Administration officials while on leave.[92] Although the claims could not be substantiated at the time, all district officers were reminded of their duties towards soldiers in their areas.[93] Such incidents did little to foster goodwill between the Army and the Administration.

SIMPLE SOLDIERS

The Australian Government turned to Papua New Guineans to provide the military manpower for the defence of PNG, but financial concerns, rather than any suggestion of Papua New Guineans being martial material, were the primary driver behind the establishment of the PIR. Indeed, the perception of Papua New Guineans as particularly unmartial was a powerful influence on the development of the regiment. In August 1950, for instance, a *Courier-Mail* headline heralded the 'Dusky guardians of Australia's back door: Thanks to the Fuzzy-Wuzzies we can sleep easier'.[94]

The conflation of Papua New Guinean soldiers with wartime carriers demonstrates the hold that the 'fuzzy wuzzy angel' myth already had on Australia's war memory, and the broader connotations of non-combatant and loyal service rather than aggressive and skilled soldiering that it represented.[95] The Army saw Papua New Guineans as biddable, loyal and adapted to the jungle, yet they were not seen as natural soldiers capable of fighting alongside Australians. Instead, they were seen as simple men who worked for rather than with Australian soldiers, as they could not undertake the same tasks, and the PIR was structured accordingly.

The belief that Papua New Guineans had adapted to the jungle with 'ease and alacrity' during the Second World War reflected the Australian perception that their utility in war came from their familiarity with PNG's geography, rather than any martial skills.[96] Australian officers described Papua New Guineans as 'unsophisticated', having 'little better than a primitive culture and background', but as 'intensely loyal' and displaying a 'childish enthusiasm'.[97] These perceptions led to their employment in situations where intimate knowledge of the environment could be expected to tell on the battlefield, such as during low-intensity, hit-and-run raids and patrolling, rather than in conventional warfare, which required 'modern' approaches to fighting.[98] The belief that Papua New Guineans lacked discipline similarly supported Australian perceptions of them as simple soldiers. Even displays of aggressiveness during rioting in 1957, described in chapter 2, were seen as evidence that Papua New Guineans had 'no warrior tradition whatsoever' and that 'the extent of their fighting lay in the treacherous sneak attack, or in some simulated battle'.[99] If, as Cynthia Enloe argues, the perfect characteristics of a 'martial race' were warlike, useful aggression and loyalty, the limited role imagined for Papua New Guinean soldiers in wartime and the Australian belief that they were prone to indiscipline suggests that they were not seen in this manner.[100]

The circumstances of PNG's colonisation, in particular its lack of development and isolation, played a role in the conceptualisation of Papua New Guineans as unmartial. The perceived lack of organised resistance among Papua New Guineans to Australian annexation of PNG contributed to their perception as non-warlike, in contrast to such groups as the Maori and Sikhs, who actively fought British encroachment and were therefore hailed as particularly martial.[101] Small punitive expeditions by armed police and white civilians before the Second World War proved sufficient to maintain Australian rule in those areas in which it had an interest.[102] As a result, there was no need to search for a group of loyal soldiers among Papua New Guineans for use in internal security duties,

in contrast to the extensive use of troops for internal security throughout the British Empire.[103] Moreover, as Parsons has shown, whatever
the beliefs of the colonial authorities, the construction of 'martial races'
was often largely driven by economic factors, social status and politics,
rather than any particular historical experience with conflict.[104] PNG's
economically and educationally undeveloped state before the 1960s most
likely precluded the formation of social groups that laid claim to 'martial
race' status.

Indeed, the sheer diversity of Papua New Guinean groups, of which the
Army was acutely aware, precluded the nomination of one as 'martial',
particularly as most were too small to provide enough men by themselves.
Moreover, the sheer scope of linguistic and cultural groups in PNG, and
their potential animosity to each other, undermined a sense of Papua
New Guineans as good soldiers. Sabin, for instance, believed that the
problem of ethnic tension had to be 'carefully watched in view of the
lessons learned in World War 2'.[105] Similarly, the Administrator advised
Seacombe in 1951 that poorly managed 'mixing of various tribes' might
cause problems within the regiment.[106] Consequently, from the start the
PIR was to be 'composed of a complete mixture of tribal types', achieved
by recruiting equally from the accessible areas of the three main regions
of the Territory: Papua, New Guinea and the islands (principally New
Britain, New Ireland, Manus and Bougainville).[107] Once recruited to the
PIR, these groups were spread throughout the unit to prevent factionalism, an idea that had precedent in the policy of plantation managers
of recruiting from different language groups in order to prevent a cabal
emerging among workers.[108]

A lack of Western education and unfamiliarity with Western standards of living meant that military training of new recruits and their
more general education had to occur simultaneously.[109] Many Papua
New Guineans did not know basic Western hygiene practices, and all
recruits were tested in elementary tasks such as 'use of a latrine', 'washing
eating utensils' and 'sweeping a floor'. Sabin argued that only after these
basic skills had been learned could more complex military tasks be taught.
During his tenure as CO, Sabin constructed the training of Papua New
Guineans around his reading of Papua New Guinean primitiveness, bas-
ing his perceptions in race rather than culture. He believed that working
with 'the Papua New Guinean' represented a 'peculiar problem' as 'He
is a slow thinker' with a poor memory who 'requires considerable reca-
pitulation before the subject matter of technique is retained'. Moreover,
Sabin believed, Papua New Guineans found it 'difficult to apply his basic

Figure 1.3 PIR troops on patrol during the 1950s (Australian Army Infantry Museum)

knowledge in moments of mild stress'.[110] These views appear to have been common, and many Australian officers were sceptical of Papua New Guineans' ability to work alongside Australians in the Army. A Northern Command officer in 1956 argued that it was 'doubtful if the native soldier can yet be trained efficiently in MMG [Medium Machine Guns] and mortars in the time of his engagement'. Papua New Guineans also 'proved incapable of carrying out the detailed clerical work required in a company'.[111]

In light of these views, managing the PIR was seen by the Australian Army as a matter of instruction rather than leadership. Indeed, the idea that Australian soldiers could simply impart and impose normal Army practices, rather than adapt them to the PNG context, was part of the appeal of the PIR as uncomplicated. The view was most clearly reflected in the appointment of warrant officers with experience as instructors to command platoons in place of lieutenants.[112] Here, the Army hoped it could kill two birds with one stone, adding to its order of battle without the need to draw on its small pool of junior officers. This wishful thinking was judged 'a failure' by 1957, as will be explored later, and Australian lieutenants were given command of infantry platoons in the PIR.[113]

Nonetheless, non-military education was recognised as important early on in the regiment's history, although the Army addressed the issue only slowly.[114] The Army initially turned to the Administration for teachers, and was again sorely disappointed, having to dismiss two men within months of one another.[115] Only in 1954 did the PIR receive an education instructor, Warrant Officer N. Clark.[116] Although three additional education officers later joined Clark, they could not hope to reach all members of the PIR.[117] Clark could not speak Tok Pisin, so that only a quarter of each hour was spent on verbal instruction and 'the rest of the time is taken up with gestures'.[118] By 1957 most Papua New Guineans in the Army remained unable to read or write.[119]

MANAGING PAPUA NEW GUINEAN SOLDIERS

Papua New Guineans were subordinate to Australians within the Army, as they were in wider society. Their unequal place was cemented in a December 1951 amendment to the Australian Defence Act, the legislation that regulated the armed forces. Here, the Australian Government ensured that it could 'make provisions for, and in relation to, the control, regulation and discipline of a native force'.[120] Although this section of the Act technically extended to Indigenous Australians, as no specifically Aboriginal force existed at the time (these men instead served singly throughout the armed forces), only Papua New Guineans were affected. While potentially allowing for different codes of discipline (something for which the Army later unsuccessfully pushed), ultimately this section ensured that only Papua New Guineans were permitted to enlist in the PIR and RAN PNG Division and that there were different scales of pay and conditions for Papua New Guineans, which were substantially lower than those for Australian soldiers but commensurate with those for the Royal Papua New Guinea Constabulary (RPNGC).[121]

Less officially, the Administration was quick to try to ensure that Australian officers arriving in PNG understood the desirability of maintaining 'proper relations' with Papua New Guineans.[122] The Administration 'repeatedly stressed' the need for strong Australian leadership in PNG, arguing that 'natives who were not under constant influence of white men became very confused as to where their loyalties lay'.[123] The RSSAILA went as far as to argue that 'experienced Territorians' be appointed as officers in the PIR. This suggested that its members believed that leading Papua New Guineans was more about 'understanding the native' and his place rather than any military or technical skill. In response to a threat to withdraw public support for the PIR if these demands were not met, the

Army challenged the League to supply men willing to train as officers for the requisite number of years in Australia. None accepted.[124]

Whether owing to the urging of the Administration or the Army's own views, efforts were made to ensure that the 'prestige' of Australians was maintained in the PIR. Following wartime practice, it was Army policy that all Australian soldiers sent to PNG, bar certain specialists, would hold the rank of sergeant or above so as not to create a situation where Australians were commanded by Papua New Guineans.[125] Similarly, in 1956 Northern Command instructed that all officers be given a Papua New Guinean batman, as it was 'undesirable in the interests of prestige and the established standards in the Territory for an officer or warrant officer to perform such tasks as washing and ironing clothes...or any other kind of domestic duty'.[126]

The selection process for Australian officers to serve in the PIR suggested that the Army did not see it as a posting that required particular skills. Most of those Australians sent to the PIR were neither specifically chosen for any particular experience in PNG, nor did most receive any special training. Even six years after the creation of the PIR, the head of the Australian Army Psychological Corps, for instance, stated that 'as far as is known, no specific training in the background of native culture, leadership of native soldiers and the problems of communication is given to Europeans posted to PIR'.[127] Although 'unfortunate incidents' during the war had convinced the Army that 'all NCOs should be natives' so that tighter and closer control could be exerted over Papua New Guinean soldiers, the idea that all those in command should understand their charges does not seem to have been internalised.[128] Just four of the sixteen officers serving with the PIR in 1953 had prior experience with Papua New Guineans: three with the NGIB and one with the PIB depot battalion, in some cases only for a handful of months. An additional officer had experience as the Officer Commanding (OC) the Nauru Defence Force for three months, but whether this provided a useful and transferable experience is uncertain.[129] Most tellingly, more than a quarter of the officers posted to the PIR in its first three years returned to Australia before the end of their three-year posting.[130] In the face of this, Sabin went as far to complain: 'Several Australian members [of the PIR] were quite unsuitable for the task and were returned to the mainland. Others were not trained or sufficiently experienced for their posting and made the burden heavier for those who were conversant with their duties.'[131] Maddern, in his role as OC Area Command PNG, similarly believed that Australian personnel sent to PNG were a poor representation of what the Army had to offer.[132]

Nor did these men attempt to learn the language of their soldiers: in 1957 only one man of eighteen could speak Tok Pisin. As few Papua New Guineans were literate, the result was not only poor communication and misunderstanding but also the exclusion of Papua New Guineans from basic clerical roles that would normally have been undertaken by junior NCOs.[133]

In an attempt to address the difficulties of language, the Army instituted a policy to teach English to Papua New Guineans in 1954. By learning English, the Army hoped, soldiers could eventually be trained to occupy more technical positions such as signallers or mortar men, and could be sent to mainland Army technical schools.[134] However, some Australian soldiers believed that the teaching of English ruined the 'tranquillity' of the PIR and introduced an overly fast pace of change for Papua New Guineans.[135] Regardless of these views, by the end of 1959 the Area Command Education Officer and his assistant were teaching English to more than two hundred pupils a month.[136] Nevertheless, at no point did English completely overtake Tok Pisin, and a situation existed whereby the local language was spoken in the ranks and English with officers where possible.

The inferior status of Papua New Guineans was evident in their uniform, which drew on colonial visions of what was suitable for 'the native'. Soldiers received a 'Number One' ceremonial uniform of shorts and shirts, while everyday wear during the 1950s consisted of a green 'laplap' and shirt. New recruits received even less, and were issued shirts only when they had completed their training.[137] This clothing policy had its origins in the pre-war requirement that Papua New Guinean civilians wear only a 'laplap' or the female version, the 'lava lava'. Any civilian found wearing a shirt or a hat was liable to be thrown in gaol. Only during the 1940s was the ban on Western clothes lifted, but wearing dirty or unsanitary clothing remained a punishable offence.[138] Much of this was out of the Army's hands, however, as conformity with the Administration on issues of pay, rationing and accommodation was thought necessary so as not to destabilise the Territory's economy by creating a group of Papua New Guineans with far more money and material goods than the remainder of the population.

The policy of not issuing footwear to Papua New Guinean soldiers was another sign of their inferior status. Sandals were provided, but these were only for ceremonies; soldiers were expected to go barefoot on operations.[139] Some Australian soldiers believed that Papua New Guineans' feet were conditioned to marching barefoot, given that they had usually spent most of their pre-Army lives without shoes, and that some of the usefulness of Papua New Guinean troops came from an innate ability to walk through the jungle stealthily, which would be limited by the issue of boots. PIR officers also argued that the issuing of boots would result in a 'softening of the feet [which] would detract from the value of the native when he must infiltrate enemy lines as he would be readily identifiable with footwear and soft feet'.[140] Why a barefoot Papua New Guinean armed with a rifle and kit would be less identifiable than one with shoes was not explained.

Rations were also different for Australians and Papua New Guineans, consisting of only seven items for the latter. Papua New Guineans were allocate tinned or fresh meat, wheatmeal biscuits, rice, margarine, salt, sugar and tea. Breakfast was rice, meat and vegetables, while at lunch, according to an Australian sergeant, 'they got two wheatmeal biscuits and black tea, and the evening meal was the same as breakfast. It didn't vary much.'[141] The simplicity of the ration was the product of the limited avail-ability of food in PNG, but was far less varied than that given Australian soldiers. Although bland, food was on a scale that meant many Papua New Guineans actually gained weight during initial training, despite the intense physical activity, and was 'sufficient to create a very fit-looking soldier'.[142]

Nonetheless, the monotony of the rations caused both Australian and Papua New Guinean soldiers to supplement their diets when they could. Such was the food situation at Vanimo in 1953 that Major Robert Dick and the soldiers under his command augmented their meagre rations by fishing with explosives. In some cases, mortar practice doubled as a fishing expedition, with the rounds being directed out to sea. The issue of poor food came to light when a Papua New Guinean was injured in one such fishing adventure, resulting in Dick's court martial. However, Dick was charged with 'fishing with explosives without a permit' rather than any more serious offence.[143] This was far from an isolated incident. The same year, an Australian sergeant was charged with issuing rifle ammunition to his platoon in order to hunt wallabies and birds, and in 1954 a platoon of Papua New Guineans under Australian sergeant Jack Dihm killed six cattle worth £600, or around thirty times the yearly wage of a new recruit. Dihm attempted to explain this action by claiming that the soldiers had 'mistaken' the cattle for wild pigs, although the owner understandably saw this as a 'pretty tame excuse'.[144] PIR officers sided with Dihm, who was quickly acquitted in a five-minute court martial and sent back to Australia.[145]

Despite the poor conditions relative to Australians, the excess of willing recruits demonstrates that the Army was a desirable career for many Papua New Guineans. The pay was still generous in Territory terms, with privates receiving between £18 and £72 per annum depending on the length of service, and sergeants up to £180, compared with an average wage of £18 for an unskilled worker in Port Moresby in 1950.[146] As during the war, the PIR also carried a prestige unmatched in the Territory, save for perhaps the police, with whom there was an intense rivalry.

DISCIPLINE

Discipline was a constant concern for the Army in PNG, given the supposed 'primitive' character of the soldiers and a history of wartime disobedience. A 'disturbance', or riot, during the PIR's first year revealed some of the challenges of raising a unit in PNG, and presaged problems to come. On the evening of 1 December 1952, Sarea Harofere, a soldier under detention for a minor offence, twice refused an order by regimental military policeman Kado Belto to cut grass as his punishment. That Belto was from Morobe province and Harofere from the Kerema region contributed to the tension between the two. Harofere attempted to hit the policeman and was placed in the detention compound as a result. Reflecting the power of *wantok* ties, other Keremas in the regiment saw this as mistreatment of one of their own and, armed with sticks, went in search of Belto. Australian personnel broke up the resulting fifteen-minute affray, and no one was injured; one suggestion was that the bugler sounded the call to dinner, which helped end the fight.[147]

This, however, was not the end of the matter. The concentration of Papua New Guineans in the mess hall most likely contributed to the tension, as soldiers were able to discuss the day's events. As a result, despite being spoken to by their CO, at 6.30pm a far larger group of Keremas once again confronted Belto and his colleagues in the regimental police, thereby widening the conflict to involve men from yet more regions.[148] This time the soldiers armed themselves with weapons that had been previously secreted away, including sharpened sticks, barbed wire flails and iron bars. This second round of fighting was again brought under control by Australian staff, with help from Papua New Guinean NCOs. Although far larger, the second incident involved only minor injuries.[149]

Sabin reported to Seacombe at Northern Command that among Australian officers the '"official attitude"... was one of disgust and annoyance'; in effect, this was a deplorable act of ill-discipline, but not an unexpected or catastrophic one.[150] Seacombe and others believed that given the 'experience of the history of PIR and NGIB [in] 1943/46', this incident was a predictable result of a battalion finding its feet and 'such incidents are to be expected until military discipline and loyalty to his white officers overcomes the tribal affiliations of the native'.[151] The fact that the regiment had not had an opportunity to train recently was also taken into account; Seacombe believed the regiment to be 'similar to a horse which has had too much oats' and that exercises and outstation duties would 'overcome brooding over imaginary injustices'.[152] Ron Lange, a young second lieutenant in 1952, similarly felt that some officers 'made a mountain out of a mole hill' in their reactions to the disturbance.[153]

The disturbance was a reflection of the complexity of Papua New Guinean engagement with military life, in which traditional social structures and animosities were overlaid by an Army hierarchy and culture.[154] Yet, although there was a strong reaction among Australian officers, Papua New Guineans did not see these two systems as incompatible. Rather, they believed they had identified the boundaries between the two. In this way, although Papua New Guinean soldiers had access to their rifles and bayonets, they did not choose to use them during the fighting, relying instead on more traditional, and largely blunt, weapons. Moreover, the quarrel was accepted as being between the two groups of Papua New Guineans, and not with Australian personnel, who during both fights were allowed to walk through the melée disarming participants. This was not lost on Australian officers, and Sabin reported the stockpiling of weapons to be normal Papua New Guinean practice.[155]

Nevertheless, such lapses of discipline could not be tolerated by the Army, and twenty soldiers were dismissed from the PIR.[156] Given the desirability of a career in the Army and the number of men willing to join, discipline was reinforced by the threat of discharge and, as after the 1952 disturbance, Australian officers had no qualms about dismissing men who caused trouble. More broadly, discipline in the PIR was seen as separate from that meted out to Australian troops. Immediately before the disturbance, harsher punishments were recommended by Army Headquarters (AHQ) for the PIR. These were to be 'awarded promptly and be of a semi-physical nature' and should have 'a further effect of making the individual concerned feel thoroughly ashamed of himself and repentant'.[157] Courts martial were considered 'wholly foreign to the native's nature and upbringing, and repugnant to his idea of justice' and were to be reserved for serious offences only.[158]

Although not as serious as the 1952 disturbance in Australian eyes, other discipline problems arose from this tension between Papua New Guinean culture and the Army's expectations of its soldiers. In Australia the Army was, broadly speaking, a reflection of the society from which it drew its soldiers; this was far from the case in PNG. The problems associated with leave in the first years of the PIR are illustrative. In 1953 the first batch of soldiers from the PIR were granted their one month's leave and at least one, Private Lekira Ajima, went absent without permission for an additional month to care for his sick father. The defence of Ajima, who was described as 'average . . . but definitely not bright' in the subsequent court martial, rested on the lack of explanation given to PIR soldiers about the conditions of leave, which 'were not generally known by all troops'. Nevertheless, Ajima was sentenced to twenty-eight days confinement.[159] Ajima's case was not unique. In 1954 Private Lawani Mati went absent without leave for fifty-seven days, and similarly argued that his father's death had led him to forget the date his leave finished.[160] For Ajima, Mati and countless other Papua New Guineans, ties with their home and family were a fundamental part of their lives; travelling home to care for a sick relative was common and accepted. The idea that the time spent with a dying father should be limited by the Army, not least when illiteracy and distance precluded other communication, must have been incomprehensible. The absence of Ajima and Mati also speaks to a more fluid engagement with employment and service than was the case in Australia. In Australia, which drew on centuries of military service, the Army was a calling as well as work. No such tradition existed in PNG; for many the Army was no different from plantation work or labouring.

Ajima and Mati's unauthorised absences were indicative of the fact that both Papua New Guineans and Australians were on unfamiliar ground in the PIR. During its first years, the Australian Army treated PNG as a remote outpost, secondary to the Army's other commitments. To a significant degree, this attitude was conditioned by Australian perceptions of Papua New Guineans as simple soldiers, useful only as auxiliaries to regular Australian troops, and to be instructed and led, rather than understood and worked with. In its treatment of Papua New Guineans, the Australian Army followed the hierarchical structure of PNG at the time. The PIR of the 1950s was, essentially, a product of Australia's requirements and the colonial nature of Australia's rule in PNG.

CHAPTER | 2

A 'FOOL'S PARADISE'

THE DISTURBANCES, 1957–61

The perception of the PIR as a straightforward addition to Australia's defence was challenged on the weekend of 14–15 December 1957, when simmering tensions between Papua New Guinean soldiers and local civilians erupted into a series of violent clashes in Port Moresby. The *South Pacific Post* headline 'Native soldiers riot! Army officers lose control', speaks to the shock of the event.[1] More alarming still to the *Post* was the attack by soldiers on the civilian court established to try them the following Monday, and the rejection of Australian authority that it seemed to represent. Three years later more than a hundred Papua New Guinean soldiers rioted again, this time protesting against inadequate pay, assaulting their officers as they marched to free comrades arrested for encouraging a strike.

These two events were the result of immediate and local grievances, but were exacerbated by the Army's belief that as 'native' soldiers, Papua New Guineans were unworthy of close attention, strong leadership and resources. Military and civilian authorities labelled both events 'disturbances'. Although a euphemism, this term accurately described their small nature and specific, immediate and identifiable origins, not least the Australian Army's *laissez-faire* attitude to the management of the PIR during the 1950s. By late 1957 the PIR was considered an established and stable unit of the Australian Army, having been on the order of battle for six years. After a rapid expansion to its official strength of around six hundred Papua New Guineans and fifty Australian officers and men, the regiment settled into its program of training, outstation duty and patrolling

Figure 2.1 Soldiers on parade at the opening of the Legislative Assembly, Port Moresby, 1957 (Australian Army Infantry Museum)

and was increasingly a feature of Army life.[2] In 1954 it provided a pipe band for the Queen's visit to Australia and became allied with the British Army's 7th Duke of Edinburgh's Own Ghurkha Rifles. Most significantly for the identity of the regiment, the PIR was presented its own Queen's and Regimental Colours by Australia's Governor-General, Field Marshal Sir William Slim, on 4 July 1956.[3]

Despite being granted the official trappings of an Australian unit, the PIR was nonetheless considered a secondary part of the Australian Army. As a result of severe manpower shortages, the PIR was undermanned, particularly as the battalions sent to Malaya from 1955 were accorded priority in Australian personnel. Such a shortage was problematic for any unit, but particularly so for the PIR given its additional responsibilities and intensive patrolling schedule. Before the creation of a depot company for training recruits in 1957, just before the first disturbance, few additional personnel were added to the regiment's establishment to manage these tasks. Moreover, illness, leave, and gaps between departing officers and their replacements, often of months, took their toll on the quantity of officers in the unit. However, despite AHQ's acknowledgement of the problem, only minor changes were made.[4] Compounding the issue of the PIR's management was a high turnover of COs. With the arrival of Lieutenant Colonel L. McGuinn in 1957, the unit received its fourth

CO in six years, while four officers also passed through the most senior position in Area Command PNG, giving little stability and little chance for the senior officers to become familiar with the PIR and Papua New Guineans or, importantly, their concerns.[5]

The first disturbance was sparked by an altercation between a PIR soldier and a civilian at Port Moresby's bustling Koki market, on Saturday 7 December 1957. Near the waterfront to the east of the town centre, Koki market and the adjoining village were a central part of life in the capital and attracted a relatively cosmopolitan mix of Papua New Guineans from around the Territory. Soldiers were transported to the markets at weekends by Army trucks, by hitching a ride in civilian vehicles, or by walking down Taurama Road. All troops were required to obtain leave passes to travel to town, but this was a common practice at weekends and soldiers were a familiar sight at the market. They were also instantly recognisable in their uniform, which they were required to wear while on leave. Their distinctiveness marked them out as an elite, but also made them targets for those Papua New Guinean civilians who envied their status. As a result, small confrontations were relatively common. When Private Jarute, accompanied by Privates Omai and Eboa, entered into an argument with two women from the Kerema region, at the markets on the Saturday evening, he was therefore a recognisable representative of the PIR and was aware of the tension between civilians and soldiers.

What transpired between Jarute and the Kerema women on 7 December remains contested, and different accounts circulated in Port Moresby after the event.[6] Civilian participants alleged that Jarute, who was drunk, manhandled one woman (unnamed in all accounts), prompting the second woman, Elizabeth Kiki, to come to her aid. Australian and Papua New Guinean soldiers later claimed that the two women had sparked the argument by insulting the PIR, prompting the soldiers to respond to defend the regiment's honour. The most likely scenario comes from the Superintendent of Police, who reported that two women walked between the soldiers, who were talking on the footpath. Incensed at this implied disrespect, one of the soldiers 'grasped one of the native women by the arm and asked her whether she had insufficient manners . . . to excuse herself when walking past a person'.[7] At this point all accounts agree that Elizabeth's husband, Albert Maori Kiki, came to her aid and, outnumbered, was severely beaten by Jarute and the two other privates. After the fracas the three soldiers were arrested by police and were taken before a civil court the following Thursday (12 December) where Jarute – the other two soldiers presumably having been only marginally involved – was fined £1.[8] Such incidents were considered relatively unremarkable by local authorities, being a product of young men out on the town, and the Army took no further action to discipline Jarute.

However, Kerema people believed that Jarute's fine was not commensurate with Kiki's beating and that it, in Kiki's words, 'could not atone for the shedding of blood'. Kiki and his fellow Keremas – his *wantoks* – felt bound to defend themselves against further depredations. Equally, they held the PIR collectively responsible, suggesting that some saw the Army as its own *wantok* in such situations. Keremas called for retribution for the attack on Kiki, and Keremas met at Koki market the following Saturday to fight any PIR soldier who appeared.[9] Shortly before 4pm two soldiers, 'going about their legitimate business' and unsuspecting of Kerema plans, were set upon. Police arrived and all involved in the clash – civilian and soldier – were arrested.[10] In accordance with normal procedure, the PIR was informed that two of its soldiers were in custody and the PIR's Australian Regimental Sergeant Major (RSM), Warrant Officer Smith, with the duty NCO of Area Command, Corporal Patterson, were dispatched to collect them. While passing Koki, Smith and Patterson witnessed yet another soldier under attack by civilians and, in attempting to come to his rescue, were themselves beaten by the mob. Having managed to make it back to their jeep, the arrested soldiers presumably forgotten, the pair sped back to Taurama. Their flight was interpreted by Keremas as conveying a 'challenge to the PIR', while the arrival of a bloodied RSM back at barracks infuriated the troops there.[11]

It was at this point that the disparity between the PIR's tasks and its structure and manning began to tell, and Australian officers, still enjoying their weekend, remained largely unaware of the growing anger among their troops. As it was the weekend, most Australian officers had travelled back to their quarters at Murray Barracks (there were no married quarters at Taurama at the time), leaving only a handful of duty personnel at Taurama on the Saturday night, limiting the ability of Australians to assess the situation brewing in the barracks.[12] More importantly, none of the Australians anywhere in Port Moresby spoke Tok Pisin, as the only officer fluent in the language was on a recruiting tour in Bougainville.[13]

On the Saturday evening, Papua New Guinean troops decided to take the fight to the Keremas, and duly marched on Koki markets early the following morning. At 7.30am on Sunday 15 December, police headquarters in Port Moresby received an excited telephone call from the duty officer at Taurama Barracks, Lieutenant Musgrave, warning them that around two hundred angry Papua New Guinean soldiers were marching towards the town. Having advised the police and his fellow officers at Murray Barracks, Musgrave followed the departing troops, catching up with them at the Port Moresby Hospital, where he and Papua New Guinean NCOs prevented the troops from running amok. However, the troops continued on the road towards Koki and Keremas, meeting a roadblock manned by police, Australian soldiers and Papua New Guinean NCOs from Murray Barracks who had been alerted by Musgrave. Here, the situation was almost fatally escalated when a police officer and an Australian civilian drew pistols, but Australian officers, 'at considerable personal risk to themselves', disarmed these individuals.[14] The potential consequences of a shooting can only be imagined. Such action went strongly against the Australian Army policy of never, in any but the most extreme circumstances, resorting to arms in the face of disobedience.[15] The incident was perhaps a sign of the hasty nature of the roadblock, and authorities were able to round up only half of the riotous troops around Badili, adjacent to Koki markets, shortly after 9am.

The remaining soldiers carried on to Koki village where they proceeded to attack all Kerema people they found.[16] Once at Koki, according to one Australian witness, 'our Army natives rushed into simply built native houses, pulled out their occupants and kept hitting them with the metal buckles of their belts'.[17] While the *South Pacific Post* described the soldiers as engaging in 'a brutal, crazed vendetta against Kerema natives', according to Port Moresby Hospital only nineteen civilians received injuries, all of them minor.[18] Tellingly, the Commissioner of Police later complained that a 'great body of native people watched the rioting without fear of attack, in fact, some hundreds followed and occasionally hampered police', which belied the savagery described by the press.[19] Nor was there any direct threat to Europeans; the Superintendent of Police reported that many 'camera enthusiasts' (who, given the cost of cameras, could only have been Europeans) similarly disrupted the efforts of police and Army officers.[20] Brawling continued around Koki until 9.45am, when the troops, fatigued and having lost cohesion as a result of the first roadblock, were rounded up by PIR officers, police and the fire brigade.[21] By 10.30am all troops had returned to Taurama Barracks, although violence also broke out between civilians around Koki and continued throughout the day.[22] In an effort to calm them, troops were given a cup of tea on return to the barracks, but reports that Keremas were marching on Taurama kept the soldiers 'up practically all night . . . ready to repel an attack'. In the end no attack eventuated, but the soldiers remained on edge.[23]

Violence in the courtroom

For the Army and the Administration, the shock of the weekend's riots was compounded by the invasion by Papua New Guinean soldiers of the court set up to try them on 16 December. Having been welcomed back to barracks with tea the day before, the troops were angered by the decision to try them, having assumed that their actions would go largely unpunished.[24] The Army and the Administration agreed that a civilian court should be held at Taurama, given that the soldiers' crimes were civilian in nature and the base offered the only suitably sized venue, yet for men who had only the day before been defending the honour of their regiment against civilian insults, the imposition of an outside authority was intolerable. The situation was exacerbated by the decision to hold the court in the education hut, which was considered a place of advancement by the troops, and the fact that the two companies concerned, A and D, were left parading in the sun while the court was established.[25]

Such was the tension in the ranks of soldiers standing in the sun that the sentencing of the first soldier, Corporal Make Soia, to one month's imprisonment with hard labour was considered *tumas* ('too much'): around sixty soldiers stormed the courtroom to confront the magistrate, F.J. Winkle, and his staff.[26] Australian officers attempted to restore order while the magistrate was escorted out of the building, but managed to calm the troops only when the court had been evacuated.[27] Remarkably, many of the twenty men of the first batch of accused also helped defend the court from the invading troops. Magistrate Winkle was taken to safety elsewhere in the barracks, where he waited until the Police Commissioner arrived with around 120 policemen. Their presence cemented Australian Army officers' control of the situation and persuaded the soldiers to accept the courts. The situation became sufficiently calm for most police to remain in their trucks. Indeed, in a sign that little hard feeling existed and that the court invasion was a spontaneous outburst of anger, the soldiers happily conversed with the police and brought them drinks throughout the night, while at the same time facing the court.[28]

The reconstituted court began anew at 5.30pm and continued for the next three hours. McGuinn and other PIR officers felt that the process of the court was a 'farce', given that troops were tried in batches and in English, a language many of them barely understood. Possibly not understanding the nature of their crimes, or out of solidarity with one another, the charged soldiers unanimously admitted to fighting. Consequently, 'without any defence or attempt to discriminate who were the main offenders', almost a hundred soldiers were fined £2.[29] As the wage for a private was between £18 and £72 per annum, this was a significant sum. In light of the role played by Soia and his fellow NCOs in defending the court, all sentences of men considered ringleaders were downgraded from imprisonment with hard labour to a fine. In the end, the only soldier sentenced to imprisonment (of two months) was the hapless Jarute, who not only sparked the whole affair on 7 December but had also taken part in the rioting of both Saturday and Sunday.[30]

In January 1958 the second round of trials held to try those who had invaded the courtroom on 16 December began, and were testament to the Administration's desire to punish those who it saw as threats to its authority, regardless of its role in causing them. Astoundingly, the trials were again chaired by Winkle, who told a journalist before the trial that in prosecuting these soldiers, he 'wanted to avoid a loss of prestige of the Court'.[31] Not surprisingly, the Army was suspicious of these trials. McGuinn expressed his belief that the Army should 'protect the rights of the troops', and the Army sent a legal representative, Major J.P. Shanahan, who found the evidence against the accused 'shadowy and lack[ing] substance'.[32] In the end, the court found fifteen Papua New Guinean soldiers guilty and, despite the Army's reservations about the trial, McGuinn had these men discharged.[33]

RECRIMINATIONS

The 1957 disturbance thrust the PIR into the minds of senior officials in the Australian Army and the Department of Territories. Such was the gravity with which the Army viewed the incident that Major-General Thomas Daly, GOC Northern Command, arrived in Port Moresby to assess the situation on 17 December, a day after the courtroom riot. Similarly, Hasluck, as Minister for External Territories, was concerned about the effects of the disturbance on the 'stability' of PNG, and followed events closely.[34] Among the press and the wider public in PNG, the disturbance was met with widespread unease, verging on outrage in some quarters, about the stability of the PIR. The riots themselves were seen by hundreds of people, Papua New Guinean and Australian, while the presence of two journalists at the court on the Monday ensured that the attack on the magistrate and his court was fully reported. The Port Moresby

Advisory Town Council, an Australian-run organisation whose monthly meeting coincidentally occurred immediately after the riots, demanded that the Army 'remove the PIR Establishment from the vicinity of Port Moresby, in order to ensure the safety of its inhabitants'. That 1957 was the hundredth anniversary of the Indian Mutiny was not lost on some counsellors, and some called for the deployment of at least a company of Australian troops in PNG, 'based on the British experience in India'. However, cooler heads prevailed, and this motion was not passed.[35] Press attention in Australia did little to explain the nuance of the disturbance, which was presented in some papers as typical of the unsophisticated nature of Papua New Guineans. The *Canberra Times* described the entire affair as 'said to be over a woman'.[36] The *Sydney Morning Herald* was more alarmist; their correspondent wrote that the 'seriousness of the raid on the courtroom cannot be overstressed' as 'it was an attack on the Government'.[37]

The aftermath of the disturbance was coloured and exacerbated by the poor relationship between the Administration and the Army. Never a friend of the Army like former brigadier Administrator Cleland, who was on leave at the time of the riot, Acting Administrator John Gunther was the source of particularly harsh and public criticism of the PIR. He reported to Hasluck that Papua New Guinean soldiers had 'gone berserk' and that he 'would personally describe their behaviour as mutiny'. For Gunther, blame for the disturbance lay firmly in the Army's staffing policies, which had resulted in too few Australian personnel who knew the men they were to command or spoke their language. This, as the Army would later also conclude, was a key cause of the riots, but by focusing on this alone Gunther overlooked the role played by the Keremas and, in the courtroom drama that followed, the effect of Winkle's insistence on making an example of unruly soldiers. Gunther did little to foster discussion between the Army and the Administration in his public statements after the disturbance, particularly as he presented the police – who were part of the Administration – as having saved the day. Gunther also misrepresented the Army's attitude as unrepentant, writing to Hasluck that 'no attempt has been made by the Army to condemn what was disgraceful behaviour', despite the immediate courts martial and the discharge of those involved.[38] Adding to this was the accusation, condemned by officers and members of the Administration alike, that the Army had 'turned tail' during the riots, leaving the police alone.[39] Privately, Daly accused the Administration of having 'dodged the issue of the Keremas for a long time', referring to previous clashes between this group and soldiers, and argued that the police had 'faded from sight' during the riots.[40] This mutual suspicion was eased only when Administrator Cleland returned from leave in March and issued a statement informing the Legislative Assembly that the matter was resolved satisfactorily.[41]

Although defensive in the face of criticisms from the Administration and civilians, the Army understood that the disturbance had revealed substantial problems in its management of the PIR, but many did not agree on their causes. Some officers believed that the clashes were a continuation of tribal tensions, suggesting that those soldiers who marched on Koki on the Sunday were mainly from the Morobe region.[42] However, as no data was collected on the origins of the soldiers, it is impossible verify whether tribal allegiances played a significant role. Nonetheless, no reference was made to the tribal allegiances of the troops by the press, in the trials or in the Army and civilian accounts of the incident. Moreover, Keremas attacked all soldiers indiscriminately.[43] That one of the soldiers involved in the initial clash between Jarute and Kiki was from Kerema further undermines the claim that the violence had any origin in ethnicity.[44]

McGuinn, as CO of PIR, reported to his superiors on 16 December, but his short analysis was noticeably silent on the matter of the failure by himself or other Australian soldiers to anticipate the rioting. Instead, he blamed events on the excitability of Papua New Guinean soldiers: 'When these native troops become worked up they are absolutely oblivious to everything except the matter in hand. They do not recognise authority, nor orders, nor force but are completely obsessed with a lust for blood.'[45] However much officers of the PIR wished to lay the blame for the disturbance elsewhere, the events of December 1957 can largely be attributed to their shortcomings. This was fully grasped by Daly, who visited the troubled unit shortly after the disturbance. A no-nonsense officer, Daly believed that the riot was 'due principally to the officers not knowing their men sufficiently well and in consequence being unable to command their complete confidence and unquestioning obedience in an emergency'.[46] In particular, he singled out junior officers as not being close enough to Papua New Guineans, arguing that their 'calibre...leaves much to be desired'. Officers had not learnt Tok Pisin and had little understanding of PNG and its people. More broadly, the PIR was hobbled by the Army's inability and unwillingness to ensure that it received its full complement of officers and NCOs.[47] Moreover, the full term for an Australian soldier in PNG was only two years, often less in practice, and few had time to become familiar with their task in the PIR and, importantly, to earn the

Figure 2.2 Departure of Lieutenant Colonel W. (Bert) Wansley, accompanied by his successor, Lieutenant Colonel L. McGuinn, 1957 (Sinclair, *To Find a Path*)

trust of the men.[48] Daly admitted that this ignorance existed in Northern Command as well, particularly as few staff officers bothered to visit PNG.[49] As a result, a complete change in thinking regarding the PIR was needed, and Daly believed he could not 'emphasise too strongly' that the regiment was an 'extremely delicate and intricate unit' in which more, not fewer, officers were required than an Australian unit, and that these should be 'of a definite type'. Fundamentally, Daly believed, 'the PIR officer must not only be a good officer, he must, in addition, be capable of understanding the native mentality and in order to do this he must have some affinity towards him'.[50]

Nonetheless, the motivations of the Papua New Guinean soldiers involved in the disturbance remained largely unexamined by Australians, and Papua New Guinean voices were almost entirely absent from the investigations. The actions of Papua New Guinean soldiers to defend the PIR suggested that they had developed a strong affinity with their regiment during the six years of its existence, and saw the PIR as outside or more important than civilian structures. This loyalty to the regiment explains some of the clash with civilians and the disregard for police during the riot: a correspondent from the *Sydney Morning Herald* was half right when he wrote that there was no excuse for the soldiers' actions in the courtroom because they had been 'taught for the last half-century' that 'the government is law'.[51] For most Papua New Guineans, 'the law' and 'the government' were personified in a 'big man' who had control over their lives, whether a tribal leader or a kiap. In the PIR, however, the principal authority was their CO, while civilian officers, such as Magistrate Winkle, represented outside power with no standing in the barracks.[52] A Papua New Guinean's loyalty therefore was not necessarily vested in the state but in the Army.

Moreover, their involvement in the disturbances suggests that Papua New Guinean soldiers had a different conception about the limits of their service. For them, the violence at Koki market was outside their role as soldiers, given that it was a weekend and they were permitted to leave the barracks. In the aftermath of the disturbances there was no discussion of the occupation of Keremas involved in the violence; it is possible that Papua New Guinean soldiers, with little understanding of the particular cachet of military service, believed that their own occupation was similarly irrelevant. After all, there were no similarly outraged press reports when civilians rioted in Port Moresby, as they often did. The fact that Papua New Guinean soldiers did not take their Army-provided weapons, such as bayonets, but relied instead on arms available to civilians, further suggests that Papua New Guineans differentiated between military and civilian spheres. Most significantly, as the courtroom violence shows, Papua New Guinean soldiers' loyalties were multifaceted and situational.[53] Soldiers such as Soia who had been happy to defend their comrades from the depredations of Keremas in Port Moresby also defended the court against these same soldiers when they attacked the judge and his staff. For these men, both actions were in support of the Army: the riot in the market was in defence of the PIR's status whereas the protection of the court was in defence of its discipline.

'OUR WORRY': THE 1961 DISTURBANCE

In the years following the 1957 disturbance, the PIR remained a small part of the Army's order of battle. In 1959 McGuinn was replaced by Lieutenant Colonel J. Norrie, who presided over the closure of the outstation on Manus Island and the construction of a new base at Moem, near Wewak on the north coast.[54] The Australian Army made minor changes to the way it managed the PIR and concentrated on improving the quality of its leadership, as Daly suggested. The experiment of

having Australian warrant officers as platoon commanders, already identified as a problem before the disturbances, was well and truly ended,
with five additional lieutenants being posted from Australia to the PIR
in 1958 to replace them.[55] Chaplains fluent in the language and familiar with Papua New Guineans were also appointed to act as a source
of informal advice to Australian officers. The first of these men, Roman
Catholic Chaplain Father Ray Quirk, formerly the civilian priest at Vanimo, joined the Army in 1959 and was to become a towering figure in
the PIR, providing advice to the PIR and PNG Command until 1976.
In 1960 the Army established the 35th Cadet Battalion, while closer cooperation with the Administration was also sought in identifying potential sources of tension between soldiers and civilians.[56] However, this
continued to be only on a personal basis, and although Cleland was made
Honorary Colonel of the PIR, there was little formal coordination or
cooperation in Port Moresby or Canberra between the Departments of
External Territories and the Army.[57] Most importantly, the CO's capacity to create a cohort of officers well suited to working with Papua New
Guineans was strengthened by the granting of power to return those who
proved incapable of 'handling native troops'.[58] To encourage a closer
relationship between Australians and Papua New Guineans, the length of
a posting to PNG was extended from two to three years in 1960, and a
greater emphasis was also placed on officers learning Tok Pisin.[59] However, the Army's focus on the quality of its personnel in PNG remained
more of an aspiration than a reality, and the PIR remained of secondary
importance to the Australian Army, as a result of the restrictions placed
on the Army during the 1950s by limited finance and a small pool of
officers.

The inferior place accorded the PIR was most clearly evident in the
issue of pay for Papua New Guinean soldiers during the late 1950s and
led directly to a second disturbance. The Army and Treasury displayed
extreme tardiness in adjusting pay scales for Papua New Guinean soldiers, in the face of rising costs for the soldiers, greater movement in
the Papua New Guinean labour force and, most importantly, pay rises
for other comparable groups in the Territory. In July 1959 the RPNGC
received a 30 per cent pay increase, arousing anger among members of
the PIR who saw themselves as equal to, if not better than, the police.[60]
At the formation of the PIR, the regiment's pay scales were based on
those of the RPNGC, and pay and conditions were kept roughly equal
between the two institutions throughout the decade.[61] The pay rate for the
police was decided by the Department of Territories on the advice of the

Administration, whereas Army pay was decided in the Department of the Army and in Treasury.[62]

In the eighteen months after the RPNGC pay rise, the AHQ pay committee repeatedly stressed to Treasury the importance of adjusting the PIR's pay, or instituting an interim rise, to no avail.[63] Australian officers, in a move that would later haunt them, assured the troops that a pay rise would be forthcoming, no doubt assuming, as Papua New Guineans did, that the pay discrepancy between the PIR and the police was unfair and would therefore soon be addressed. Anger mounted among the troops as their pay rise failed to materialise, despite explanations about the different administrative structures that the Army was forced to navigate. Adding to the soldiers' resentment, in December 1960 urban workers in Papua New Guinea also received a significant increase to their basic wage. For Papua New Guinean soldiers, the provision of a pay rise to urban labourers, a group of people they considered far less skilled, was a 'bombshell'.[64]

It was this festering tension that led to the second disturbance. In December 1960, only around half the battalion was in Port Moresby: two companies were at the outstations at Manus and Vanimo, and a company was exercising near Goldie River, leaving only Administration and A Company in Port Moresby.[65] By Friday 30 December tension in the ranks about pay had reached the point where a small group of Papua New Guinean soldiers were attempting to galvanise their peers in the mess, representing the pay problems in the PIR as a collective concern, referring to it as 'our worry'.[66] Discussions and meetings among soldiers continued over the weekend and, according to Lieutenant Peter Stokes of A Company, the first days of 1961 'were heavy with expected rain and foreboding' as the late wet season added to the tense atmosphere in the barracks.[67] In contrast to the 1957 disturbance, Australian personnel were well aware of the feeling among the soldiers, and Chaplain Quirk, in his new role as adviser to the CO, reported to Norrie that there was a 'lot of talk' in the lines. In response, Norrie ordered all officers to visit the two companies in the evenings, in an effort to calm the troops and explain the situation and maintain control.[68]

The soldiers themselves made little secret of their anger. On Monday 2 January around a hundred Papua New Guinean soldiers paraded themselves before Norrie to ask when they would receive pay increases.[69] Norrie reiterated what the other officers had told them: despite being the apparent supreme power in the PIR, capable of recruiting and discharging soldiers, the CO did not have the authority to change pay scales, but instead deferred to the Australian Government in Canberra. The soldiers, many of them with only a few years service, found it difficult to grasp this idea.[70] Given their training, position in PNG as an elite, the real hardship of patrolling and the potential dangers of combat, these men felt justified in demanding a better response to complaints they had been voicing for eighteen months. The disgust was evident in the constant discussion of the pay issue, both among themselves and with officers. Around the time of the parade before Norrie, for instance, Lance Corporal Kabeho Kaubabi complained to Captain Ian Campbell that 'The Army is doing a big work' compared with civilians, yet 'the Army only receives a small payment but civilians get a large payment'. Kaubabi believed the 'government' should visit from Australia and solve the matter: 'If the Government does not come', he told Campbell, 'then this Army can finish.'[71] The suggestion that Papua New Guinean soldiers might quit ('finish') was a sign of how serious the matter had become.

In contrast to McGuinn's inaction during the lead-up to the 1957 disturbance, Norrie's response to rising tension in the ranks was proactive. All available officers were called to Taurama Barracks, while the relevant civilian authorities were warned of the potential for trouble the following day. Late into the evening, Norrie discussed the plan of action for the following day with his officers, covering all possibilities, including 'sit-downs' and 'walk-outs'.[72] Believing, like many colonial officers faced with similar disobedience, that the majority of soldiers were being led astray by a few agitators, Norrie sought to arrest the leaders of the unrest, and to do so publically.[73] On 3 January Norrie paraded the regiment and read them a prepared speech in an effort to re-emphasise that the issue of pay was out of his hands, and admonish them to be patient. Not only was this probably received by the assembled troops as a repetition of the same excuses but also Norrie's speech was undermined by a poor command of Tok Pisin, such that he emphasised the wrong words.[74]

Unaware of the intensity of the soldiers' anger, Norrie proceeded with his plan to address the pay issue through the arrest of ringleaders, which would, in a show of force, stamp out the cause of the trouble. The sight of those junior NCOs who had led the fight for better wages being loaded into a police van and taken to Bomana Gaol proved to be the tipping point for soldiers already riled by the parade and the preceding week's inaction. According to Stokes, 'over a hundred revolutionary soldiers spewed out of the barracks and gave chase . . . hotly pursued by a motley crew of perplexed European Officers, Warrant Officers and native senior NCOs. It was the stuff of great theatre. They had no hope of catching the disappearing vehicles and we had no hope of stopping them.'[75] Unable to keep up with the van, some soldiers made for the barracks transport lines, hoping to steal a vehicle. During scuffles in the motor pool three Australian officers (Captains Campbell and Hamlyn, and Lieutenant Adamson) and Sergeant Osi, a Papua New Guinean, were hit by Papua New Guinean soldiers. According to one witness, having made the tactically unsound decision to enter the back of the truck among the angry soldiers, Adamson 'was launched, parallel to the ground for some distance, out of the back of the truck'. Despite the seriousness of the incident, this was 'one of the best comic events of the whole situation'.[76] Adamson's injuries notwithstanding, the Australians disabled the trucks and the men dispersed.[77] Denied transport, around a hundred men left the camp in pursuit of the ringleaders.[78] Judging from their later testimony, these men left the barracks and defied their officers as a result of a mix of anger and momentary excitement rather than as part of any premeditated plan. Private Kahpou Pahun, for instance, later told his court martial that contrary to Norrie's reading of the situation, the concerns of the ringleaders were indeed held by many of the other troops: 'It was the worry and the trouble of the whole battalion. We wanted to go with them.'[79]

Some no doubt felt the same, and others were simply caught up in the heat of the moment. Private Bonyu Titi, for instance, later recalled that 'when the seven men went up to BHQ and were taken to Bomana I started to get angry. When I was at BHQ I saw the troops running towards the road and I got up and ran after them to go with them.'[80] Stokes reported that also among those arrested was 'my poor bewildered batman who had run down from his ironing table at the Mess to see what was going on'. Other men, realising the futility of the march to Bomana and the probable consequences, quietly broke away from the group and stole back to barracks, thereby avoiding punishment later.[81] Importantly, in addition to those on outstation duty or training at Goldie River, most of the soldiers at Taurama Barracks did not become involved in the disturbance, either because they declined to join those leaving, or because they were unaware of the event.

Unable to stop the troops leaving Taurama Barracks, Norrie contacted the Commissioner of Police, who agreed to send police to meet the Australian personnel and Papua New Guinean NCOs already on the road. Following in Land Rovers, the officers and NCOs periodically attempted to stop the soldiers, with little success. At this point, the angry men were swinging their leather belts as they marched and more officers, including Stokes, were hit.[82] Being uncoordinated and spontaneous, the

Figure 2.3 Taurama Barracks front gate during the 1950s. Taurama Road is behind the camera (Australian Army Infantry Museum)

disturbance petered out along the road to Port Moresby. At 1.15pm, the combination of police with Australian soldiers from the Regular Army cadre of the PNGVR, as well as whoever could be found at Murray and Taurama Barracks, stopped the protesting soldiers near the hospital, about six kilometres from Taurama and a third of the way to Bomana Gaol.[83] The men were eventually persuaded to board trucks by their officers and NCOs, with fatigue probably also playing a role. Ironically, the seventy-seven soldiers arrested were then taken to the gaol, their original destination.[84] The day following the disturbance, 4 January, a large proportion of the PIR was sent on field exercises in order to 'cool down', a practice that later became a standard response to trouble in the regiment.[85]

COURTS MARTIAL

In contrast to the earlier disturbance, the two principal offences with which soldiers were charged were leaving barracks without permission and assaulting a superior, so the troops were tried and punished under military law. The CO dealt with fifty-four cases summarily, most of who were fined £5 and confined to barracks for seven days.[86] A further sixteen men, those considered the ringleaders or charged with more serious offences, were tried by court martial, and all but one man was found guilty.[87] Compared with the civilian trials, the Army's approach was relatively fair, as it was identical in composition and procedure to courts martial of Australian soldiers. The courts martial were made up of a president, usually a major, two officers of lower rank, a prosecutor and an officer for the defence. These men were chosen from officers not involved in the disturbance, and came from the PIR, the Territory's cadet battalion, the PNGVR and Area Command PNG. Their presence could be, and was, disputed by an accused soldier.[88] A judge advocate, Major B. Virtue from Northern Command, advised the court on matters of jurisprudence, and transcripts were recorded in shorthand by civilian stenographers from Brisbane and PNG. After the finding, the trial transcripts and evidence were sent for a two-stage review process, first to Northern Command and then to the Judge Advocate General and Adjutant General. The Judge Advocate General could quash a court martial's finding, and did so with a handful of trials from the 1961 disturbance, mainly for legal technicalities.[89] There were, however, problems of explaining the complex processes of the court to those accused. Many required translators, which in the case of Kaubabi led to difficulty given that the charge of being a ringleader before the disturbance was based on the nuance of what he had said to Campbell.[90]

A distinguishing feature of the courts martial was the fact that most of the officers knew those accused of striking them reasonably well.[91] This led to a degree of bitterness among the accused men, who felt they had been unfairly singled out while others escaped punishment. One of those who attacked Lieutenant Adamson was his batman. Similarly the bandmaster, Warrant Officer J.G. Whitecross, was struck by a member of the band, and Captain I.S. Fisher was struck by a mess steward with whom he was familiar.[92] In most cases, officers seem to have approached those soldiers known to them first, perhaps hoping to capitalise on their familiarity with these men. During the court martial of Private Takoni Pulei, for instance, Adamson told the court that 'knowing him fairly well I thought if I could get [him] out of the truck others would follow him'.[93] One result of this was that much of the evidence presented against the rioters consisted of the word of the officer who was struck against the accused, a fact that was noted by the Deputy Judge Advocate General.[94]

Statements given by the accused men during their courts martial suggest a divergence between Australian and Papua New Guinean understanding of the seriousness of the riots. In trials where a Papua New Guinean was charged with 'striking a superior officer', the pleas were uniformly 'not guilty'. While soldiers freely acknowledged that Australians had been hit, they invariably denied their own involvement, and declined to name others, even in the face of overwhelming evidence. A common excuse for those accused of striking officers was that they were only 'pretending' or that they had struck an officer by accident, suggesting that Australians were hurt only when they put themselves in the path of Papua New Guinean anger.[95] This is true to an extent, as there were no cases in which a Papua New Guinean explicitly sought out an Australian to offer violence. Nevertheless, Papua New Guineans did not refrain from hitting their superiors when they were confronted.

On the other hand, Daly suggested that the confusing responses given by Papua New Guinean troops during the courts martial might have reflected their unfamiliarity with the process, given that the CO usually dispensed justice. Faced with a complicated court martial, composed of unknown officers, all inferior to the CO, Daly argued, Papua New Guinean soldiers were 'confused, suspected traps, gave much conflicting evidence . . . and in the end were surly and resentful'.[96] Lieutenant L. Quinlivan, a defending officer in a number of courts martial, complained to the court during the trial of Private Utera Kipa, for instance, that 'it was difficult to get across to the native the weight a statement made on oath would carry later on'.[97] Whatever the reasons, as with the 1957 disturbance, Papua New Guinean voices are largely absent from Australian examinations of the disturbance, with the exception of the courts martial transcripts. As a result, the reasons behind soldiers' actions during the 1961 disturbance remain opaque.

The punishment for Papua New Guinean soldiers reflected both a desire on the Australian Army's part to mete out justice and to deter other soldiers from acting similarly. Some men were found not guilty on some charges, but most were convicted of at least leaving the barracks without permission, and received sentences of between twenty-nine and eighty-nine days imprisonment. Deterrence was provided by the discharge of all but eight of the seventy men involved in the riot at the completion of their sentences.[98]

TAKING STOCK OF MILITARY POLICY IN PNG

Having compounded the shock of the 1957 disturbance, the events of January 1961 sparked a wider-ranging examination of the Australian Army in PNG that addressed the conceptual failures of not just the Army but the Australian Government's policies on the PIR as well. Initially, however, reflection on the causes of the disturbance resembled the 'blame game' as commentators reacted to yet another breakdown of discipline.[99] The disturbance received wide press coverage in Australia, although with its origins in pay disputes, it was far easier to understand than the 1957 disturbance, somewhat lessening the shock of the violence. Indeed, a number of newspaper reports referred to 'demonstrations' rather than riots or disturbances.[100] Some Australians even expressed solidarity with the soldiers: a handful of Australian unions wrote to the government protesting against the treatment of Papua New Guineans in the PIR.[101]

In PNG, the riot was criticised as yet further evidence of the ill-discipline of Papua New Guinean soldiers, but this condemnation was not accompanied by calls for the PIR's disbandment, as had been the case in 1957.[102] The Kokopo Town Advisory Council in New Britain denounced the rioters, calling them a 'rabble', while the Rabaul Returned and Services League (RSL), probably composed of many of the same men, also called for improvements in discipline.[103] Assistant Administrator Gunther took the extreme view that the PIR was 'completely undisciplined'. He argued that 'physical violence should have been met with physical violence and that the Police would have been perfectly justified in using their batons', despite having praised the restraint of police and the Army after the previous disturbance.[104] Reflecting the view that 'native affairs' was the purview of the Administration, Gunther also called for a larger civilian role in the PIR, arguing that an experienced Administration officer should be placed in command. Administrator Cleland, who expressed satisfaction with the handling of the matter at each stage of the disturbance, did not share these views.[105] Both organisations had worked together well in 1961. Compared with the 1957 disturbance, the coordination between the Army and Administration had been smooth, the riot had been contained with a minimum of force, and no civilians were involved.[106]

Despite Cleland's satisfaction, the Administration and Department of Territories continued to harbour concerns that the rioters represented a potential threat to the stability of Australian rule in PNG. The disturbance came at a time of Australian anxiety about dissidents radicalising Papua New Guineans against the Australian Government, and the events of

January 1961 helped to fuel these fears. For instance, immediately before the disturbance, the Australian radical Brian Leonard Cooper had been arrested in PNG on sedition charges.[107] He was held in Bomana Gaol, was present when the soldiers were interned after the disturbance and was reported to have shouted at their officers that they should 'remember South Africa', referring to racial tension there.[108] The linking of the disturbances to potential political action by Australians had much in common with those of other colonial militaries. Historian Kaushik Roy, for instance, has shown that while indiscipline among Indian troops was mostly apolitical, some British officials 'looked for political undertones' in assessing the causes of certain incidents.[109] Similarly, for almost a year, Cleland reported to the Secretary of the Department of Territories on these men, although none conducted themselves in a way that threatened the Territory.[110]

Although the catalyst for the riot was the parade and the arrest of the seven ringleaders, few observers were in any doubt that Papua New Guinean concerns over their pay was its cause. As a result, in the short term the disturbance forced the Army and Treasury into action on pay issues. The day after the riot, the Minister for the Army announced that a pay rise for Papua New Guinean soldiers would be finalised within the week.[111] By 10 January, the pay increases were accepted by Cabinet, and were made retrospective to June the previous year.[112] The decision to grant a pay rise probably had more effect on the short-term stability of the PIR than the courts martial and discharge of those involved, but also raised the question as to why this haste had not been evident before the riot.

Although some in the Army tried to find the causes of the 1961 disturbance in tribal allegiances, it was Australian officers' inability to engage with and understand Papua New Guinean soldiers that contributed to the escalation of grievances and to the riot. While Tolais, from New Britain and particularly Rabaul, did make up thirty-six out of the seventy men later watched by the Administration, few were from the same village or area. More importantly, of the five convicted ringleaders only one was Tolai while the remainder hailed from around the Territory, making the ringleaders a diverse group.[113] Among the remaining men involved in the riots, there was no pattern along tribal or language lines.[114] Tolais did, however, make up a larger proportion of the Administration Company, as their relatively higher level of education made them more likely to be placed in technical positions. As there was only one other company in Taurama Barracks at the time, they therefore made up a larger proportion of the troops who were caught up in the disturbance. Moreover, being more skilled, the men of the Administration Company were probably more likely to feel aggrieved at receiving poor pay given their higher status in the regiment.[115]

More important was the age of those involved in rioting. The majority of the offenders were between 18 and 21 years old, and had only been in the PIR from between one to three years.[116] The Army clearly had not been successful in its indoctrination of its new soldiers. Lieutenant Quinlivan told the court martial of Private Kipa, for instance, that the actions of the accused soldiers were part of the cultural background of Papua New Guinean soldiers, for whom 'the normal thing is not to discuss things over long periods'. Instead, Quinlivan argued, 'if something goes wrong, if someone steals something from his garden, he goes over with his friends and beats the people up'.[117] Administration liaison officer Max Orken was scathing of the inability of Australians to understand the different mindset of Papua New Guinean troops, accusing them of living in a 'fools paradise by thinking that the troops of PIR have been fully and completely indoctrinated'.[118]

In this way, although tensions between civilians and soldiers and pay were the triggers for the two disturbances, an underlying lack of Australian experience with Papua New Guineans contributed to the scale of these events. In the three years after the 1957 disturbance, the suggestions to improve the cohort of Australians in PNG had had neither enough time to take effect, nor been pursued particularly rigorously. Daly recognised this, arguing again that in 1961 officers were 'inexperienced in handling natives'. No pool of officers experienced in working in PNG yet existed, and Daly argued that men in company commander positions were largely of the 'elderly major type', who were unlikely to advance sufficiently to return to the PIR as experienced senior officers.

It took the 1961 disturbance to force a wholesale reconceptualisation of the Australian Government's policy towards the PIR and its place within Australian defence planning. Daly's assessment that the disturbances were the result of the Australian Army and government's neglect of the PIR formed the basis for a new approach towards the PIR by the Australian Government, championed at the Cabinet level by the Army Minister, Joseph Cramer, who emphasised to his fellow ministers that 'we must regard the unit not simply as a small element of the Australian Regular Army with a particular role of reconnaissance and initial protection in New Guinea, but rather as a vital element in Australia's efforts to guide the peoples of New Guinea safely along the road to democratic self-government'.[119] Cabinet endorsed the view in September, deciding 'that the standard and standing of the Pacific Islands Regiment are of significance to Papua and New Guinea well beyond its purely military significance'.[120] This statement, while somewhat poorly worded, marked a significant turning point in Australia's management of the PIR. Cabinet encapsulated and cemented the dual nature of the Australian Army's units in PNG both as part of Australia's defence and of a unique cultural, economic and political environment that might one day become an independent nation. Australia's own defence needs were still to predominate, but the PIR and its later iterations were also recognised as a separate entity requiring a different approach to the remainder of the Army, despite their small size. However, although this decision came at a time when decolonisation around the world was gathering steam, there was little indication that Daly, Cramer or Cabinet were influenced by international events. Certainly, there was a general acceptance that PNG would be self-governing or independent at some point in the future, but the need to avoid a repetition of the disturbances seems to have been the driver of this shift in government policy.

Alongside the policy shifts engendered by the disturbances, these two events also shaped discussion of the Army until independence in 1975. Among Australian soldiers, attitudes towards the disturbances varied between professional interest and unease. Yet, although the disturbances were undoubtedly uncomfortable for the Australian Army, given its multiple failures in recognising and controlling them, throughout the 1960s and 1970s the Administration and members of the Territory's expatriate population retained a strong sense of anxiety regarding the PIR, given what they saw as its long history of instability. The Director of Military Operations and Plans at AHQ, for instance, complained in 1968 that 'much is made of past disturbances in PIR', and later documents refer to 'the disturbances' or 'recent unrest', rather than recognising the two events as discrete and localised.[121] The view that the PIR was unstable informed later debates about the role of the Army in an independent PNG and, in the lead-up to independence, was conflated with the possibility of the PNGDF leading a coup against a democratically elected government.[122]

CHAPTER 3

'REAL DUTY'

CONFRONTATION AND THE CREATION OF PNG COMMAND, 1962–66

By early 1966 the Australian Army was actively engaged on operations throughout the Asia–Pacific. In Vietnam, the 5th and 6th Battalions of the Royal Australian Regiment (5RAR and 6RAR) formed the core of the newly created 1st Australian Task Force (1ATF), while in Borneo 4RAR supported British efforts to defeat Indonesian incursions across the border. Other units were stationed around South-East Asia, were prepared in Australia for their own deployments, or were in the process of forming as part of the unprecedented peacetime expansion of the Australian armed forces. The activities of the Australian soldiers in PNG were no less focused on Australia's defence. The PIR, which by 1966 consisted of two battalions under the newly created PNG Command, patrolled the PNG–Indonesia border to detect possible Indonesian infiltration similar to those encountered in Borneo and trained to defeat it.

Although no conflict broke out, the Australian Government considered it a real possibility throughout the early 1960s. Consequently, PNG Command's preparations represented a third focus point of Australia's defence after Vietnam and Malaysia, providing protection for a strategically significant region. Indeed, while Australia's largest 'peacetime' deployment of troops overseas was to Vietnam in 1965, during the first years of the decade Australia was preoccupied by Indonesia. In 1962 Indonesia assumed control of West Papua from the Dutch, a move that provoked strong reactions in Australia.[1] The Defence Committee, responsible for advising the government on strategic matters, saw this development in no uncertain terms, as 'for the first time, Australia will . . . share a common land frontier with a country whose long term friendship cannot be assumed'.[2] Indonesia had already 'declared her antipathy' to the inclusion of the Borneo states into the Malaysian Federation during the early 1960s by declaring a policy of Confrontation, which was emphasised with a series of raids against the Malaysian Peninsula and in Borneo. The Defence Committee worried that Indonesia might expand these efforts and 'turn its attention at some time in the future towards Eastern New Guinea'. Were this to eventuate, the committee believed the Australian armed forces in 1963 were too small to 'make an effective and sustained contribution to South-East Asia and at the same time deter Indonesia from possible activities inimical to our strategic interest'.[3]

Certainly, during the early 1960s, the Australian Army had only a limited ability to meet its operational requirements. By 1963, one of the Army's three regular Australian-manned infantry battalions (2RAR) was based in Malaysia with the Far East Strategic Reserve, leaving only two battalions (1RAR and 3RAR) as the basis for the Army's two battle groups. The upshot was that the Army had little flexibility to conduct more than one small deployment at a time, given training requirements and the need to maintain a ready reserve for emergencies.[4] In addition, the Army provided personnel to the Australian Army Training Team Vietnam (AATTV) from 1962, placing an added strain on its pool of experienced officers and NCOs. In response to this and the possibility of Australian deployments elsewhere in the region, the Menzies Government announced an increase in defence spending in May 1963, including the purchase of additional Mirage fighters and transport aircraft for the RAAF, ships and an extension of the fixed wing capability for the RAN, and an increase of the regular Army to 28 000 soldiers.[5]

Papua New Guinean–manned units were expanded alongside the rest of the Australian Army.[6] Specifically, four initial decisions were made regarding defence in PNG: adequate forewarning of threats was to be provided by the establishment of an Australian intelligence capacity within the Territory, coastal security was to be boosted through the formation of a Papua New Guinean patrol boat squadron, Boram airfield outside Wewak was to be upgraded to take fighter aircraft and, most significantly, Cabinet called for the PIR to be expanded from its current, peacetime, 'lower establishment' to a full battalion, while a larger training depot and a composite company with pioneers, signals and supply troops were also to be created. This was in keeping with many of the changes advocated by the PIR's senior officers and Northern Command since the 1950s; in effect this initial expansion addressed many of the PIR's shortcomings, and fashioned it into a more rounded and capable battalion. The Defence Committee saw this step as the first of three phases. The second phase included the raising of another battalion and additional support units, while in the third and final phase, a third battalion would be formed and existing support units expanded. To support these three battalions, the Army would create an expanded headquarters formation and institute a building program to house new personnel and their dependants.[7]

Events during 1964 only reinforced the need to prepare the Australian military for conflict around the region. In response to Indonesian attacks in Borneo, the Menzies Government authorised the deployment of 3RAR to counter-terrorist operations on the Malay–Thai border, releasing British forces for deployment in Borneo.[8] In August, the battalion helped capture Indonesian raiding parties landed on the Malaysian Peninsula, heralding the start of Australian involvement in low-level conflict with Indonesia and bringing closer the possibility of a conventional war in which Australia would undoubtedly be involved. The conflict in Vietnam also became a pressing issue for Australia by the middle of 1964, as the United States increased its involvement. For Australia, the Cold War was fast becoming less of an abstraction.

Australian concern about the changing strategic situation is illustrated in the Strategic Basis Papers of the early 1960s. These documents, the precursor to Defence White Papers, laid out the threats facing the country and the means by which these might be avoided or confronted. Whereas during the 1950s there had been a Strategic Basis Paper outlining Australia's defence posture on average every three years, three of these foundational documents were produced in as many years up to 1964.[9] In the February 1963 document, defence planners stated their expectation that if Indonesia became hostile towards Australia, it might 'turn its attention... to eastern New Guinea'.[10] The following year, planners believed that 'Australia could become involved in war if Indonesia under-estimated Commonwealth reaction to her confrontation activities'. In this eventuality, conflict was likely in New Guinea, although it was expected to be of a similar intensity to the Borneo fighting, which consisted of small-scale and covert clashes. Conventional war, although possible if the situation deteriorated, was considered less likely.[11] It was in this context that the government authorised the PIR to expand to the full three battalions envisaged by the Defence Committee (approximately 3500 troops), with the expansion to be completed by 1968.[12] In addition to its contribution to the defence of a likely area of conflict, the PIR remained a cheap addition to the Australian Army, with more potential recruits than it could accept at any given time.[13] For instance, the Joint Planning Committee (JPC), which formulated plans for the Defence Committee, reported in 1968 that the 650 Australian personnel then in PNG cost $4.1 million, while the 2350 Papua New Guinean soldiers cost just $5.6 million. A Papua New Guinean soldier therefore required about a third of the financial outlay of his Australian counterpart to pay, feed and house.

The PIR was expanded in the interests of Australian security first and foremost, but the possibility of Papua New Guinean self-governance or independence in the future was a secondary influence on Army planning. When assessing the role of the PIR in June 1961, five months after the disturbance, the GOC Northern Command, Major General R. Wade, noted that the 'speed of [the] emergence of New Guinea to a status of self-government' meant that the 'Army in New Guinea must take note of this new, dramatic and fast moving background'.[14] Permeating planning for the expansion was Cabinet's 1961 decision that policy regarding the PIR should take into account the regiment's effects on the Territory. By 1963 the Defence Committee accepted that it had to take into account 'the requirements of the Territory for indigenous military forces at the time of self-determination'. An armed force raised from Papua New Guineans would provide a 'stabilising influence' leading up to self-determination, the committee believed, while 'the presence of an adequate, efficient and loyal armed force will provide valuable backing for the civil authorities'.[15] Following the Defence Committee's recommendation, Major General M. Brogan, GOC Northern Command, framed his plan for the expansion of the PIR in terms of 'the transition of a country from a dependent to an independent status', which could only be 'non-violent and administratively harmonious' if the structures of state, such as the military, were already established.[16]

Nonetheless, the conception of the expanded PIR as the forerunner to an independent defence force remained secondary to the government's plans. During the early 1960s the Australian Government believed that Australia's security in the context of the Cold War should be the principal driver of policy in the Pacific. In addition, ministers felt that as a result of the underdeveloped state of the Pacific territories, gradualism was the best approach and that the timetable of independence in PNG should not be influenced by decolonisation in other parts of the world or international pressure.[17] Politics played a role: Cabinet believed that the decision to expand the PIR provided the people of Papua New Guinea and Australia 'with visible evidence of capacity and intention to act in the defence of the

Territory'.[18] The Defence Committee also considered it 'desirable both for reasons within New Guinea and for external political reasons' that any Indonesian action be dealt with as far as possible by local forces, without the need for forces from mainland Australia.[19] However, it is worth noting that there was no direct requirement for the Army to include PNG's possible independence in its planning; that it did so illustrates the degree to which, even at this early stage, the Army engaged with the PNG context in which it operated.

IMPLEMENTING THE EXPANSION

The change wrought by the decision to expand the PIR was all the more significant considering that the regiment had experienced few significant adjustments in its role and structure during its first decade.[20] Before the expansion had been implemented Cramer, as Minister for the Army, complained that the PIR was seen as 'just another Army unit, maintaining its tactical role as allotted ten years ago – namely that of reconnaissance and initial protection of vital areas'.[21] The new role envisaged for the expanded PIR was far broader. The PIR continued its earlier function as a reconnaissance, first reaction and delaying force, but with an increased focus on the border region and counter-insurgency operations over the defence of key points.[22] Rather than being an auxiliary force, PNG Command was to be equipped and trained to assume the burden of fighting the opening stages of a war in PNG. The expanded force was still expected to operate in individual subunits – companies or platoons – in the event of Confrontation-style operations along the border, following British and Australian practice countering Indonesian incursions in Borneo. Like any infantry unit, it was to be supported by more powerful forces as needed.

To be best placed to deter, detect, train for and defend against Indonesian incursions, the three battalions were to be based around PNG during peacetime. Responsibility for patrolling and border surveillance in PNG would be split between two battalions based in Wewak and Port Moresby, which would, respectively, send companies to outstations at Vanimo in New Guinea and temporarily established bases in Papua. The third battalion, based in Lae near a proposed airbase at Nadzab, would be responsible for internal security and defence of key installations, as well as patrolling in the islands and eastern areas of the PNG mainland. Each battalion would have responsibility for its own outstations, and would remain at its own barracks rather than rotate to a new area, given the cost of moving thousands of men and dependants. However, to ensure that all units were familiar with areas outside their responsibility, each would train and patrol throughout PNG as a matter of course.[23]

The structure of the three PIR battalions was based on the Army's lighter 'tropical' establishment, which consisted of four rifle companies, headquarters and supporting elements, but without heavy weaponry and equipment such as anti-tank weapons and trucks, which were of less use in the jungle than in open terrain and difficult to transport. Troops were, however, armed with light machine-guns, and 81mm mortars were issued in 1964.[24] The PIR was therefore unique among Australian post-war battalions in that it did not adopt the new and short-lived pentropic structure, unlike the RAR. Introduced in 1960 and abandoned in 1964, the pentropic concept was intended to enable the Army to fight in a nuclear battlefield in South-East Asia, but the divisional structure of five infantry battalions, each composed of five companies, proved unwieldy. The Army never considered changing the structure of the PIR, given the 'diverse' and independent role of the regiment, which was not expected to operate as a single unit, let alone as part of the battle groups envisaged in the pentropic division.[25]

The expansion proceeded 'at full effective speed' after Menzies's approval of the second phase in 1964.[26] By the end of that year, the PIR had grown from 660 to 810 Papua New Guineans and the Australian component rose to more than a hundred. By 1965 a further seven hundred Papua New Guineans had joined the ranks.[27] Building on the creation of the Papua New Guinea Military District to administer the PIR in August 1963, the larger and more capable PNG Command replaced it January 1965. The creation of PNG Command cut the fourteen-year link between Northern Command and the PIR, and made the Army's forces in PNG directly subordinate to AHQ and of equal status to the Army's other geographic commands. The new size and importance of PNG Command was reflected in its being a brigadier's command, and Brigadier A.L. McDonald, later Chief of the General Staff and Chief of the Defence Force Staff, was appointed as the first commander. In keeping with Cabinet's emphasis on planning for PNG's future, McDonald's remit included creating a force that provided 'a basis for a future indigenous army'.[28]

The creation of a second battalion of the PIR (2PIR) in March 1965 marked a significant expansion of the Australian Army's combat power in PNG. Under the leadership of the former British soldier Lieutenant Colonel Donald Ramsay, 2PIR was raised from A and D Companies and support troops from the original PIR, now termed 1PIR.[29] The new battalion occupied the company outstation at Cape Moem, near Wewak, built during 1959 after the Manus outstation was closed. However, the outstation had only limited facilities, and the need to expand it to accommodate a battalion, support troops and their families meant that both the battalion and its barracks into which it moved were works in progress throughout 1965.[30] 2PIR had to settle in at Moem, raise new companies and create new administrative procedures for maintaining the battalion some distance from the PNG Command base in Port Moresby, all while providing a company for the Vanimo outstation and mounting patrols across the Territory. Indeed, both battalions faced a difficult period of rebuilding, as the transfer of so many soldiers away from 1PIR represented a blow to the capabilities and identity of the battalion.

Perhaps not surprisingly, as a result of the upheaval of the raising and the speed with which the expansion took place, it took time to forge 2PIR into a coherent unit. When the second CO of 2PIR, Lieutenant Colonel E. McCormick, assumed command from Ramsay in December 1967, he found a battalion that 'had problems', particularly in its discipline. The newly arrived RSM, Grahame Wease, similarly found that even after almost three years of existence 'the supposed specialist and support company [in 2PIR] were specialists in name only, well behind the standards of Australian battalions'.[31] At the same time, Wease believed the battalion to be 'gutless', as exemplified by thirty men falling out during the first parade he witnessed.[32] Drunkenness and disobedience were also concerns.[33] These issues were dealt with by the application of stricter discipline, and a 'fair dinkum' approach based on firm leadership. After eighteen months both Wease and McCormick reported that the quality of the battalion had turned around.[34]

Beyond the creation of 2PIR, PNG Command also gained a degree of self-sufficiency and greater capability with the creation of new support units and the expansion of old ones. For instance, a PNG Construction Troop was created from the PIR Pioneer Platoon in January 1965 and was eventually expanded to squadron size.[35] Similarly, other units such as PNG Workshop Royal Australian Electrical and Mechanical Engineers (RAEME), 800th Signal Squadron and medical, supply and provost units were created or expanded. Most of these units were based at Murray Barracks with HQ PNG Command and were administered by the similarly newly created HQ Murray Barracks.[36] When complete, these units made PNG Command capable not only of fielding far more combat troops but also of independently building roads and other infrastructure, of caring for sick and wounded and communicating with and coordinating its troops in the field. Completing the expansion in PNG Command's capabilities were

Figure 3.1 Taurama Barracks from Trig Hill. The Papua New Guinean married quarters are on the right (Australian Army Infantry Museum)

close links with a variety of units based in Australia. Certain units performed niche tasks, such as engineering construction squadrons, which were brought to PNG to complete particularly large projects, and RAAF transport aircraft, which were staged through the Territory as needed.

Most importantly, PNG Command relied on skilled Australian personnel at all levels to maintain its capabilities and lead its troops, and their numbers increased as the Army's forces in PNG expanded and became more capable. Between 1963 and 1965, the number of Australians posted to headquarters and support units rose from 40 to 60 per cent of the total number of Australian soldiers in PNG.[37] Given the educational limitations of many Papua New Guinean recruits, Australian soldiers were the only means by which to expand the support and headquarters units of PNG Command at this stage, and this represented an additional drain on the Army's resources. Such was the shortage of personnel that a suggestion in 1964 by the Administration that Army doctors be seconded to the Territory 'elicited smiles' from Army authorities, given that 'the Army was so acutely under-strength . . . that it could not meet its existing demands'.[38] The dearth of Australian personnel also served to accelerate the movement of Papua New Guinean soldiers into positions thought beyond them during the 1950s. In 1964 Papua New Guinean soldiers were posted to a unit other than the PIR for the first time when specialist soldiers, such as mechanics and signallers, were transferred from the PIR to HQ PNG Military District.[39] Many Papua New Guinean troops were also sent to Australia for training during this period, and around 150 were in Australia at the end of 1964.[40]

Reflecting the growing importance of the region in Australian defence considerations, Papua New Guinean units also trained more closely with other parts of the Australian Army throughout the 1960s compared with the previous decade. The first exercise involving both Australian and Papua New Guinean units occurred in 1963 with Exercise Long Hop along the Kokoda Trail, which saw SAS soldiers from Australia pitted against the PIR.[41] Papua New Guinean soldiers also served outside PNG for the first time during Exercise Crusader in July 1964, when a number were used as 'enemy' for Australian soldiers, a role they would perform on numerous occasions. In exercises in Australia and PNG, the PIR was reported as having performed well. The CO of PIR at the time, Lieutenant Colonel K. McKenzie, believed PIR soldiers were so effective as 'enemy' troops that 'the confidence of Australian troops began to suffer' and the Army decreed that the PIR was only ever to be used as 'friendly' troops in exercises.[42] Whether this was true or the hyperbole of a proud CO, from 1963 onwards exercises with the rest of the Australian Army came to be a common activity for the PIR.

Recruiting

Although the Australian Army sometimes struggled to provide skilled Australian officers and NCOs for PNG Command, the flow of fresh Papua New Guinean recruits to the Army was steady. In fact, the amount of willing and suitable Papua New Guinean recruits allowed PNG Command to expand far more quickly than planned.[43] In one half-yearly recruiting tour, for instance, 1342 applications were received and 205 men were enlisted.[44] The high numbers of potential recruits necessitated a change in the recruiting process from that of the 1950s. From January 1964, HQ PNG Military District assumed responsibility for all recruiting for the Army in PNG, finally relieving the PIR of this burden.[45] As part of this change, the PNG Military District Training Depot was created from the PIR training company that had existed at Goldie River since early 1955.[46] The following year the depot was renamed PNG Training Depot, under which name it continues to operate today. To all in PNG Command, the depot was known simply as 'Goldie', and was the first experience of military life for all new Papua New Guinean soldiers.[47] To sustain the PIR, two recruiting tours per year, in June and December, were implemented after 1964, and the time allocated for their training was cut from one year to six months.[48] As a result, the Army expanded the total number of recruits undergoing training in PNG Command from around 80 per year during the late 1950s to more than three hundred in 1964 and four hundred in the following year.

The need to provide a large number of new recruits who were healthy, intelligent and well suited to the Army also necessitated a more systematic approach to recruiting. Before the expansion one CMF officer, Major Don Barrett, had almost single-handedly managed PIR recruiting tours, ultimately recruiting some two thousand men for PIR.[49] However, Barrett represented the paternalistic belief held by many during the 1950s that intimate knowledge of Papua New Guineans born of long association with PNG was required to manage their recruitment and leadership.[50] The creation of a formation-level headquarters brought dedicated recruiting officers and attached specialist officers from Australia who relied not on a familiarity with Papua New Guineans but on professional recruiting practices.[51] Army psychologists were a key part of the recruitment process, bringing a more systematic and scientific approach to finding new enlistees.[52] In the absence of the indicators of suitability relied upon by recruiters in Australia, such as high school certificates, prior employment, literacy or even a common language, psychological intelligence testing was particularly useful for the PIR.[53]

The opening up of the previously 'restricted' Highlands region during the late 1950s, the availability of teams of recruiters and a larger recruit intake meant that for the first time a force truly representative of all districts in PNG could be contemplated. During the 1950s, only a very rough balance between Papua, New Guinea and the islands had been attempted, while no Highland soldiers had been recruited at all.[54] The Army embraced the possibility of recruiting a mix of groups from around PNG, both because of a desire to avoid ethnic tension and because of a vaguely defined objective of creating a 'national' army, and instituted a policy of representative recruiting. However, a number of negative consequences stemmed from this policy. The Army often had to accept recruits with lower standards of education or physical fitness than might have been the case had they been exclusively recruited in the more developed areas, such as the major towns and coastal regions.[55] Recruiting from across the Territory was also time-consuming and resource intensive. Although some young men applied directly to the PIR, most were recruited in their home regions by visiting recruiting teams.[56] Recruiting tours often lasted up to three months, and relied on chartered aeroplanes to visit most rural villages.[57] Moreover, the main recruiting team was often preceded by a lecture tour and preliminary checks on potential recruits. For instance, Major Geoff Payne, a psychology officer attached to a recruiting team in 1972, flew to all but two of PNG's eighteen districts between 8 May and 23 June, stopping in two or three locations each day.[58] The recruiting team travelled so widely that the 27-year-old Payne thought himself a 'tourist in the Army'.[59] Not surprisingly, after independence, the costly method of transporting recruiting teams across the country was discontinued, and potential recruits were expected to travel to central recruiting stations.[60] During the period of Australian colonial rule, however, the widely travelling recruiting teams made the PIR a common sight even in remote areas, and were a feature of Territory life.

The Administration was intimately involved in recruiting. Each recruiting team's chosen itinerary was discussed with civilian authorities before each tour, and district officers were tasked with 'sending out the word' to potential recruits in their areas so that there would be a pool of men on the day teams arrived. Local officials also accommodated Army teams during their stay, provided advice on potential recruits and passed on information about interested young men to the Army.[61] The Administration controlled the employment of Papua New Guineans in PNG Command in other ways as well. During the 1960s potential recruits were barred from enlisting in the PIR if they were already employed, and recruiters were told not to enlist a man 'unless he [brought] a letter from his employer to say that he [was] free to join the Army'.[62] For some civilians, the Australian Army was an unwelcome intrusion into their control over Papua New Guinean labour, as it offered an attractive alternative to plantation work. At least one plantation owner, angry at losing some of his labourers from the Kaviak region, wrote to the Administrator to 'protest strongly [the] mass recruiting of Kaviak labour for PIR as constituting unwarranted interference to a private business'.[63] No mention was made of the ability of Papua New Guineans to offer their labour as they chose.

Among those Papua New Guineans who tried to enlist, the rejection rate was high. Medical problems in particular disqualified large numbers of potential recruits. During one recruiting tour in June 1964, for instance, the attached doctor rejected twenty-nine applications out of a total of 223 on medical grounds, even after the applicants had been vetted before the final interview with the primary recruiting team. The most common problems were diseases of the heart, liver and kidneys, and poor eyesight.

Tuberculosis was also commonplace among potential recruits, and others were rejected on psychological grounds.[64]

While the PIR expanded, the first Papua New Guinean officers were recruited. Like PNG Command itself, these first indigenous officers were recruited both to provide manpower for Australia's defence and to prepare for the possibility of future independence. For the Australian Army the commissioning of indigenous officers offered advantages in leading Papua New Guinea troops, given their common background, and was thus a way to further ensure the stability of the force through a stiffening of well-educated, loyal and motivated Papua New Guinean leaders.[65] Shortly after the 1961 disturbance, Minister for the Army Joseph Cramer called for the commissioning 'of educated natives' so as to 'equip the Army in Papua and New Guinea for the role it will undoubtedly play in the development of the Territory'.[66] Equally, the experience of newly decolonised African nations was at the forefront of the minds of the Military Board, which believed that a principal cause of the 1960 mutiny in the Congo was the fact that 'at the time of independence there was not one native officer'. In 1965 AHQ argued that it was 'politically desirable' to fill subaltern postings with indigenous officers 'as quickly as possible', reflecting a growing sensitivity to independence.[67] By 1967, the board believed that officers should be commissioned many years before independence to ensure that they were 'well trained, responsible and loyal to their government aims'.[68]

Despite the importance attached to Papua New Guinean officers, the rate of commissioning was slow, primarily as the result of the paucity of appropriate candidates. In 1963, the first year indigenous officers were selected, there were only 397 Papua New Guinean men in total at high schools around the country, with just thirty graduates completing the highest level. Of these, the Army estimated that only six would be both suitable for service and interested in taking a commission. The Australian Army also had to compete with the Administration for this small, educated elite.[69] Colonel J. Pascoe, Area Commander PNG at the time, expressed concern about the lack of cooperation between the two bodies, complaining that the Administration acted as though it 'should have first pick and . . . the Army can have our ration from what is left'.[70]

COUNTERING THE INDONESIAN THREAT

From 1963, the Australian Army's expansion and recruiting efforts in PNG were oriented towards meeting a potential Indonesian threat along the border. No conflict eventuated, but hostile incursions were considered a distinct possibility by Army authorities, who feared that Indonesia might 'attempt to divert our attention and our forces by covert action against East New Guinea'.[71] There were certainly troubling signs at the time. Between May and November 1963, shortly after Indonesia took control in West Papua, Australian authorities reported twelve border-crossing incidents by Indonesian troops, police and officials. In addition, Indonesian aircraft had overflown PNG, and Indonesian troops had removed border markers. The Defence Committee recognised that there were probably a number of reasons for these incursions, not least the difficulty in identifying the border, which also led to an accidental crossing by a PIR patrol in October 1963. Moreover, locals paid little attention to boundaries imposed by outsiders and regularly crossed between Indonesian- and Australian-controlled territory. Nevertheless, given Confrontation and the conflict in Borneo, the possibility of Indonesian border crossings being the prelude to more aggressive action could not be discounted.

The difficult nature of the terrain near the border and each country's commitments elsewhere dictated that any Indonesian action would be small in scale. Defence planners assumed that Indonesia would use 'volunteers' to 'harass natives, engineer disputes' and possibly engage in raids in much the same way as it was doing in Borneo and Malaysia. There was little chance that small parties could be immediately detected in the jungle. Any larger incursion or build-up of troops would be more easily identified and countered, as it would involve a more significant build-up of troops in Indonesia and a long logistical tail. The Australian Army's peacetime task was therefore not to immediately halt these small incursions should they materialise, but instead to patrol the border and gather intelligence on Indonesian activity, while also training in the area for any escalation of hostilities.[72] The delicacy of the relationship also meant that, in proactively patrolling the border, Australia had to walk a fine line between deterring and provoking Indonesian action. In its strategic direction, the Defence Committee advocated 'avoiding action that would create an incident', while at the same time working to 'establish a definite, positively identifiable Australian Administration and civil police presence along the border area'.[73]

For all this, Australian defence planners considered 'overt Indonesian aggression' in PNG 'unlikely', and the Australian Army was by no means on a war footing.[74] Its disposition around the Territory was still firmly that of a peacetime force. Vanimo outstation, for instance, while close to the border was not intended as a defended company base similar to

Figure 3.2 Vanimo Company base, 1961. The small airstrip around which the original base was built was replaced by a longer strip, seen beyond the buildings (Australian Army Infantry Museum)

those in use by Australian and British forces in Borneo.[75] Indeed, with the company based there often depleted by patrols, Vanimo was largely indefensible in the event of concerted attack. This was brought home in 1963 when two unidentified patrol boats arrived offshore, much to the consternation of soldiers based there. Seeing the boats, the OC, Major Brian McFarlane, recalled thinking: 'Christ, if these are Indonesians, we've had it.' At that time the troops at Vanimo were armed only lightly, and PNG Command hurriedly flew up two 106mm recoilless rifles in response.[76] Luckily for the troops stationed at Vanimo, no further incidents took place. Ultimately, much of Australia's security in PNG rested on intelligence from a variety of national sources, including from the patrols mounted from bases such as Vanimo.

Had Australian patrols detected hostile infiltration along the border by Indonesia the contingency plan, Joint Service Plan Pygmalion, would have been implemented. This plan was developed alongside two others developed to defend against Indonesian action, Plans Spillikin and Hemley, which respectively covered defence against covert Indonesian action in Malaysia and more conventional responses to Indonesian aggression, including air strikes.[77] The first iteration of the plan was produced in

1964, and called for the deployment of the PIR and the SAS to the border area as a first response.[78] Two companies of the PIR would be employed in patrolling tasks, supported by an increased RAN and RAAF presence, while the remaining companies trained, refit and rested. This would allow a continuous Army presence in the area of operations. The SAS, at the time made up of a single company, would initially deploy to and operate from Vanimo, augmenting the PIR's long-range patrolling capability. A mainland-based infantry battalion and supporting units were to be sent to PNG only if the situation escalated or continued over a significant period, which would necessitate the rotation of the PIR battalions with Australian infantry.[79] As PNG Command expanded, Australian Army planners came to accept that two battalions on either side of the central range were necessary to sustain border operations adequately, given 'experience in PNG, contingency planning both during Confrontation and since, and a more detailed knowledge of the terrain'. This, in turn, reinforced the long-held assumption that a third battalion, based in Lae, would be required by PNG Command, to enable the battalions on the border to rotate out of the area of operations.[80]

In the broadest sense, Plan Pygmalion was a specific and fully fleshed-out version of the PIR's long-standing role of acting as the first line of reconnaissance and defence in the event of an invasion of PNG. The difference, however, lay in the shift in the tactical role of the PIR from a reconnaissance force not expected to engage in pitched battles with an enemy, to a unit that was expected to fight alongside Australian troops at every stage of a conflict. Indeed, Papua New Guinean troops were expected to form the main body of troops holding back covert incursions as Australian troops did in Borneo. While Australian-based units would reinforce it, the place of the PIR and later PNG Command in Plan Pygmalion was akin to any other Australian unit or formation, as demonstrated by the plan to rotate Papua New Guinean and Australian battalions in the event of a long-term conflict. Although there were political and legal limitations on where Papua New Guineans could serve, given New Guinea's position as a Trust Territory, in PNG at least, PNG Command's role from the mid-1960s was not defined by any perceived inherent capabilities of Papua New Guineans. Rather, in the event of conflict along the border, all similar units of the Australian Army were to perform much the same roles regardless of their composition.

Pygmalion drew on lessons from Australian and British experiences in countering Indonesian incursions.[81] Command, control and liaison with civil authorities in PNG were 'based on the experience of operations in Malaya and Borneo'.[82] Similarly, the role given to PNG Command within the plan had striking similarities to the operations that were being conducted in Borneo by the British and, between 1965 and 1966, by Australian forces. Operations in Borneo took place at company level or below, and troops conducted patrols out of small bases close to the area of operations.[83] Further, the PIR's training reflected the Army's Borneo experience. For instance, Exercise Badmash in late August 1964 was conducted from a patrol base in the Papuan border region by soldiers from C Company of the PIR, against 'guerrillas' from Administration Company.[84] Similarly, as will be discussed further below, regular patrols actively laid the groundwork for defeating any Indonesian attempt to subvert Papua New Guineans against the Administration by establishing 'contact with, and gain[ing] the goodwill of, the border people'.[85]

A closer examination of the large PIR training exercise Suitim Graun in December 1964 reveals just how the PIR was expected to fight. Conducted in the Papuan Western District, close to the border, the counter-insurgency exercise involved a platoon of men from 2RAR acting as guerrillas who had clandestinely landed on the Papuan coast with the goal of causing disaffection among local civilians.[86] In undertaking this role, the 2RAR soldiers were aided by a handful of PIR soldiers familiar with the area, as well as E. Sharpe, Assistant District Commissioner, who helped enlist the locals against the PIR. That this scenario imitated Indonesian raids that August against Malaysia was unlikely to be a coincidence.[87] Although not explicitly referring to Malaysia, the directing officer of the exercise and CO of PIR, Lieutenant Colonel McKenzie, believed that Suitim Graun offered an 'opportunity to rehearse for a state of affairs which appears the most likely background against which PIR, as a battalion, could become involved'.[88]

Exercise Suitim Graun therefore tested the PIR in the terrain in which it would be expected to fight against Indonesia, and among the population whose support it would have to enlist. It served to reinforce the importance of controlling population centres and confirmed the basic assumptions of the structure of the PIR, namely the focus on lightly equipped forces. Nonetheless, acknowledging the regiment's state of flux during its expansion, McKenzie felt that the exercise revealed some deficiencies in the PIR, particularly the technical skills of signallers and in the basic infantry skills of Administration Company, which acted as a rifle company during the exercise. Despite these problems, McKenzie was broadly happy with the battalion's performance, and was 'particularly pleased to see the standard of leadership displayed by three Pacific Islands

Figure 3.3 Papua New Guinean soldiers on patrol, Bougainville, 1968–69 (Peter Chard)

sergeants commanding platoons'. Having trained for Indonesian incursions in the border region, McKenzie believed his battalion 'ready for this kind of operation'.[89] This was probably a fair assessment, given the PIR's training in the terrain in which it was expected to fight, and its extensive patrolling experience.

PATROLLING

Patrolling was as central to the Australian Army's role in PNG as it was to the experience of serving there, and assumed a particular cachet during Confrontation.[90] It was, according to Brigadier Ted Diro, 'real duty'.[91] This was not mere bravado. Patrolling was essential to the detection of Indonesian activities along the border, and provided information for the Administration and the Australian intelligence services.[92] It was also excellent training for the PIR in the region it would fight in the event of war. In addition, the PIR was tasked with 'showing the flag' patrols to garner goodwill and reinforce the control of the Administration among local populations who would be useful during conflict.[93] Patrolling distinguished the PIR from units on the Australian mainland as it was, to a degree, 'semi operational'.[94]

Figure 3.4 Unloading supplies from an RAAF Caribou at Tapini, c. 1967 (Denis O'Rourke)

Papua New Guinean units planned their year around patrolling, with training, education and other activities fitting around the program.[95] Patrols usually occurred in platoon strength, although it was not uncommon for whole companies to go on patrol. The period a particular subunit was out in the jungle could vary between a week and months, and depended on the goals of the patrol, the terrain and the assets available in support. Patrols were closely coordinated with the Administration in a mutually beneficial arrangement that saw the Army gain guides and linguists, usually policemen, and the Administration enhance its own patrolling program.[96] Patrols took place in every district of PNG and, depending on the requirements and other commitments of the Army in PNG, there could be anywhere between twenty and fifty patrols a year.[97] As Confrontation reached its height, there was a three-fold increase in patrolling man-days, from 9575 man-days on patrol in PIR during 1964, rising to around 30 000 man-days the following year.[98] The capability of these patrols also increased with the use of fixed-wing aircraft to move troops and supplies to key airstrips and helicopters to supply them in the field.[99] However, each patrol was heavily dependent on the often-fickle weather, and a handful of Papua New Guinean soldiers remember being without rations owing to poor flying conditions.[100]

Ultimately, however, patrols were a matter of marching, often in very difficult country, which tested the officers and men tasked with carrying them out. The central border region is made up of a broad mountain range with peaks more than two thousand metres in height, while the flatter landscape towards the coast is defined by the Sepik River in the north and the Fly River in the south. Both rivers are surrounded by large swampy areas, while smaller rivers, fed by copious tropical rainfall, further break up the landscape. Patrolling therefore required a high degree of physical fitness; even the in-shape infantry trained for a month before heading out on patrol. Knee injuries, sustained in the mountainous terrain, were a common occurrence.[101] Equipment could be sorely tested as well, and soldiers often ended patrols with suggestions and complaints about the quality of Army kit. After one patrol in the mountainous border region, for instance, Major Harry Bell testily reported on the performance of a range of equipment including boots ('inadequate size range'), individual shelters ('badly leaking'), socks ('guaranteed to shrink') and torches ('A more useless piece of equipment is hard to imagine').[102]

The difficult nature of the terrain in much of PNG was compounded by the absence of detailed maps of large areas of the Territory. Major Peter Stokes, who led patrols in the border region during the early 1960s, remembered for instance that 'for the most part the maps were totally blank with grid lines and topographical symbols but no topography!'[103] Even in 1972, Second Lieutenant D.W. Simpson of 2PIR complained that 'maps were of little value ... [F]or every small stream marked on the map, there were at least 6–8 others in the same area.'[104] Moreover, in much of PNG the broken and densely vegetated country made distance as a measurement all but meaningless. As a result, the collection of topographical information to improve maps, estimate travel times and mark key areas was an essential part of patrolling, and patrols would report in minute detail on the 'going' in certain areas.[105]

Interaction with local inhabitants was an important, ubiquitous and often memorable aspect of patrolling. Collecting demographic information about communities and population centres before conflict broke out was essential to the PIR's wartime role of protecting and ensuring the support of civilian Papua New Guineans, and patrol reports were replete with sketches of villages and descriptions of their inhabitants.[106] Patrols also relied on locals for information about terrain and jungle tracks, which were the key topographical features in the otherwise impenetrable jungle. One patrol led by Second Lieutenant Bob Sayce in 1968, using maps that contained no topographical information about the area, cut days off its return time after being shown a quicker track back to its patrol base by local people.[107]

Troops also were under strict instructions to treat people they met with respect and not to damage property or steal from villagers. Incidents where property damage did occur were taken seriously by the Administration, as they 'could lead to open hostility during times of peace or war'.[108] In particular, soldiers were warned against 'fraternization with female natives', and patrols usually camped outside rather than in villages.[109] Despite this warning, some soldiers got into what was euphemistically termed 'trouble' with local women. Depending on the seriousness of the issue and the level of anger it generated, these soldiers were generally removed from the patrol and placed under arrest upon return to barracks while the patrol continued. In some cases, villagers might hide from patrols, either associating them with police and Administration, who were disliked for the control they wielded over villagers, or simply being afraid of the large group of strange men approaching the village.[110] In at least two instances PIR patrols contacted groups of Papua New Guineans who had never before seen a European.[111]

Relations with Papua New Guineans met in the course of patrols were generally reported as 'friendly'.[112] For their part, Papua New Guineans along patrol routes could make money or trade goods from patrols and find a source of employment as guides or recruits. Often, patrols were simply an object of curiosity for locals. Young men excited at the novelty of Europeans and Papua New Guineans in uniform accompanied one patrol for days. The officer commanding it recalled that 'one enterprising young man slept under my hutchie and every so often lifted my mosquito net just to look and check that I was real. They all thought our footwear was hilarious.'[113] The PIR also relied on local people for fresh produce to supplement their patrol rations. For this reason, patrol leaders carried coins (paper money having little value in remote areas); one officer complained about having to carry a sack full of shillings. However, in the more remote areas even coins had little worth, and 'the currency for carriers and guides, when you could find them, was salt, or coloured trade beads or tobacco'.[114]

Patrols were also important in exposing the Army to the breadth of PNG and its people, and vice versa. So-called 'prestige' or 'showing the flag' patrols, instituted by McKenzie, also had the express purpose of showing the Army in a good light. One such patrol in 1963, led by Lieutenant T. Holland, performed the Beating the Retreat ceremony thirty times, gave firearms demonstrations and displayed films. Holland believed

Figure 3.5 Village in Bougainville, late 1960s, described as 'a typical village at the start of the climb' (Peter Chard)

that around fifty thousand people in total saw the tour.[115] On a more practical level, patrolling in different areas with a subunit made up of a mix of Papua New Guineans was an opportunity for local knowledge to be diffused through the unit. In one case Private Moses Kiari, a Papuan soldier from the coast, was taught by Highland soldiers what could and could not be eaten while on a patrol that ran short of food in mountainous regions.[116]

Nonetheless, patrolling was first and foremost designed to prepare for possible conflict through training and intelligence-gathering, and clashes with Indonesian troops were an ever-present possibility during the early 1960s. Given the delicacy of the relationship with Indonesia, patrol leaders were instructed in the strictest possible terms to avoid incidents involving Indonesian soldiers or officials.[117] If confronted with aggressive behaviour, patrol leaders were instructed to retaliate 'with only such force as may be necessary to enable him to ensure the safety of . . . his patrol'.[118] Soldiers were ordered that they were to use their arms only if the patrol was directly threatened and there was no other course of action. Patrols were given ammunition 'sufficient to get out of trouble', and soldiers were not equipped to engage in protracted firefights, as machine-guns and other heavier equipment were left behind owing to their weight.[119] In one case, upon hearing of Indonesian soldiers in a village on the Australian side of the border, Lieutenant Colonel Ramsay ordered the patrol commander by radio to delay his approach until the Indonesians had departed. In doing so, Ramsay avoided a potentially volatile situation, in which, he admitted 'there could quite easily have been a firefight'.[120] On another patrol, soldiers were issued with large canvas signs with which to warn approaching Indonesians. This was recognised as somewhat absurd by one patrol officer, who later wrote: 'The safety of the soldiers holding erect no. 5 banner ("stop or we fire") whether exposed or not convinces me that the fifth warning should be delivered some other way!'[121]

PNG Command's patrols along the border were in keeping with the broader Australian approach to possible conflict with Indonesia. During peacetime, patrols were not intended to form a standing force to repel an Indonesian attack. Rather, they provided a medium for training, understanding the terrain and gathering intelligence. They were armed but, if attacked, they were to withdraw. Only once a conflict had begun were patrols to be offensive, with PNG Command deploying more heavily armed groups that would find and fight the enemy, as had been practised in Exercise Suitim Graun. In addition to being a vital part of the Army's operations in PNG, patrols were also greatly enjoyed by the soldiers who undertook them. For many of those who were interviewed for this book, patrolling was one of the most memorable aspects of service in PNG. Patrols were an opportunity to test skills, connect with the troops, act independently and see the country. So enthusiastic were some officers about patrolling that Father Ray Quirk described recent returnees as having an 'after-patrol look in their eyes':

> These patrols really started something with the young officers in the Unit. For a few weeks after they return from patrols, one has to be wary of them. Never be caught alone with them, otherwise you get a terrific earbashing. Maps are produced from back pockets, and spread in front of you, photographs appear from nowhere, and there is no escape. Three hours later one reels away, the mind numb and the body exhausted, having been submitted to the harassing ordeal of a day by day description of a six week patrol.[122]

The difficult strategic environment of the first half of the 1960s was the apex of Papua New Guinean units' importance to Australia's defence. Expanded in response to Indonesia, the PIR, and later PNG Command, formed the mainstay of Australia's forces in PNG, which was a far cry from the auxiliary role envisaged for the PIR during the 1950s. PNG

Command never went to war, but the Australian Army did not have to imagine what its wartime operations would look like in PNG, and although not combat, its patrols replicated many of the features of the operations it would have been called on to undertake in the event of war. PNG Command was experienced in operating in the jungle, working with local people, gathering intelligence about Indonesian activities and local conditions, and supporting its troops in the field. Equally importantly, the PIR could draw on the lessons learnt by Australian soldiers in Borneo to fill the gap between its peacetime training and the experience of war, and exercised closely with Australian troops. Ultimately, this capable force was an essential part of the Australian Army's order of battle during this period.

CHAPTER 4

FROM 'NATIVE' TO NATIONAL

PAPUA NEW GUINEAN SOLDIERS, 1960–75

At the same time as the PIR expanded, the place of Papua New Guineans within the Army underwent a profound transformation. By the end of the 1960s, the Australian Army no longer treated Papua New Guineans as simple 'native' soldiers who occupied subordinate positions as riflemen and junior NCOs, as it had during the 1950s. Instead Papua New Guineans served in headquarters units, fulfilled skilled technical roles and were steadily ascending the promotion ladder as officers and senior NCOs. These men formed a unique cohort of soldiers in Australian service. They joined for adventure or from a sense of duty, and left for family reasons, because of clashes with the Army or to seek other employment. Nevertheless, 'national' borders and residual prejudice limited their integration, so that although race came to define the place of Papua New Guineans within the Australian Army less and less during the 1960s, these men never occupied a position equal to Australian soldiers.

Increasingly 'exposed to the ebb of the colonial tide', the Australian Administration in PNG gradually but inexorably shifted focus from measured development to preparing for PNG's future as an independent state, as the result of international and domestic political change and a combination of a growing Papua New Guinean political voice and Administrators who increasingly understood that Australia's time in PNG was coming to an end.[1] By the mid-1960s, Papua New Guineans could watch any film, marry whom they wished regardless of race and were protected by law from discrimination.[2] The eight-fold increase in people attending some form of school to forty thousand by 1963 not only widened the opportunities available to Papua New Guineans but also helped create a nascent educated elite in the Territory.[3] In addition, the University of Papua New Guinea (UPNG) opened its doors in 1966 to its first Papua New Guinean students and provided a centre of debate about PNG's future. Finally, Papua New Guineans were granted increasing political rights, albeit still under the aegis of Australia. Indirect elections occurred in 1961, and the first general election for the House of Assembly was held in 1964.[4] Outside this forum, which was still dominated by the Administrator during the 1960s, Papua New Guineans also began to engage in the public debate over their future, and the first political party, Pangu, was founded in 1967.[5]

These shifts were felt keenly by Papua New Guineans within the Australian Army, given their position as employees of the Australian Government and their proximity to the centre of developments in Port Moresby. How these tendrils of change reached into the PIR is exemplified in the decision to end the ban on alcohol for Papua New Guineans after decades of prohibition. Papua New Guineans particularly disliked this law, as it was an everyday affirmation of the racial lines drawn by the Administration.[6] Within the Army, they were excluded from all social events that included alcohol and were instead relegated to separate messes or forced to attend 'dry' events. As a result of growing agitation for a repeal of a law seen by many – Australian and Papua New Guinean alike – as paternalistic, a committee of inquiry was set up within the Administration in 1962 to examine the alcohol issue, which was then debated widely by Christian missions, the Administration, expatriates and Papua New Guineans.[7] Ultimately, changing attitudes among Australians, in part owing to international pressure and example, moves to repeal similar laws applying to Indigenous Australians, and stronger and more articulate arguments made by Papua New Guineans, led to change.[8] Indeed, the end of prohibition in PNG occurred at the same time as the repeal of various discriminatory laws for Indigenous Australians, including that banning the consumption of alcohol.[9] By the end of 1962 Papua New Guineans could consume alcohol in licensed hotels and take beer home, and by November 1963 all restrictions had been lifted.[10] The relaxation of liquor laws did contribute to closer interaction between Papua New Guineans and Europeans in the Territory, although some of the latter resorted to other means, principally economic, to separate themselves from the former. The requirement that hotel patrons wear shoes, for instance, effectively barred most Papua New Guineans from drinking at these establishments during the early 1960s.

Figure 4.1 First integrated NCOs' mess after the end of prohibition for Papua New Guineans (Granter, *Yesterday and Today*)

As a result, segregation continued to exist, albeit in a social rather than legislative form.[11]

Australian Army authorities were largely optimistic about the effects of the end of prohibition. Major General Mervyn Brogan, GOC Northern Command in 1963, believed that it would boost morale among Papua New Guinean troops, as they would be able to share messes with Australians whereas before they had to be segregated.[12] Moreover, allowing soldiers to consume alcohol legally would end the danger of men secretly drinking to excess where they could not be monitored, or drinking hazardous illegal alcohol.[13] Ultimately, the end of prohibition in the Army came about uneventfully, in part because of pragmatic preparation by Australian officers. Wet canteens were set up in barracks to cater for the newfound freedoms of Papua New Guinean soldiers, creating a more controlled environment for drinking.[14] A handful of Australian officers also accompanied Papua New Guinean servicemen to pubs in Port Moresby in order to aid their introduction to alcohol.[15] Army Chaplain Ray Quirk argued that without the creation of a wet canteen the end of prohibition could have been 'a sordid affair', but owing to the Army's measures there was 'little problem with drunkenness'.[16] Nevertheless, alcohol-related discipline issues were certainly a problem within PNG Command after the end of prohibition. In 1967 for instance the Commander PNG Command, Brigadier Ian Hunter, complained that alcoholism was an problem among Papua New Guinean soldiers, and had at times led to domestic violence.[17]

DISMANTLING DISCRIMINATION WITHIN THE PIR

The Australian Army also made its own strides towards dismantling discrimination. These changes were the result of a growing acceptance of minorities in the Australian community, initiatives by Army authorities in Australia as directed by the government, and action by individual officers in PNG. The combined mess, for instance, was only legally possible with the repeal of prohibition by the Administration, but also relied on a recognition that Papua New Guineans could assume positions of responsibility as NCOs and manifest technical skill that, during the 1950s, had been seen as being beyond them.

The dismantling of discrimination in the Australian Army reflected a far wider effort on the part of the Australian Government to remove race-based discrimination from its policies during the 1960s 'on a quiet and gradual basis'.[18] Although in 1962 there was technically 'no bar to the enlistment or appointment of Australian Aborigines or non Europeans into the Australian Military Forces providing they meet the normal enlistment standards', the armed forces in PNG represented a specific exception. As set out in the 1951 amendment to the *Defence Act 1903*, the Australian Government was permitted to make regulations that pertained to 'native forces'. As a result, since the creation of the PIR and the PNGVR, recruitment was managed on the basis of race, with Papua New Guineans being allowed to join only the former while the latter was whites-only.[19] Papua New Guinean soldiers also received different pay and conditions to Australian soldiers. The provision to make specific regulations for 'native forces' meant that, while by the mid-1960s the last vestiges of discrimination within the Australian armed forces as a whole were removed, such as the requirement that naval officers be of European descent, structural discrimination against Papua New Guineans remained.[20] Ostensibly, this was to reflect the different level of development in PNG, particularly in terms of wages, which were to be kept 'in line with the principles applied to the Territory public service'.[21] The section of the Defence Act relating to 'native forces' remained in force until 1973, when the creation of the PNGDF – and therefore a different national pay scale – made it redundant.[22]

Although Papua New Guineans had to serve in PNG-based units, by the early 1960s there was a growing recognition that Papua New Guinean soldiers could take on positions of responsibility. From 1963 Papua New Guineans were posted not just as riflemen in the infantry battalion but also in more technical positions in headquarters.[23] There was also a concurrent growth in number of Papua New Guinean troops sent to Army technical schools on mainland Australia, from a trickle in the early 1960s to a flood by the end of the decade, further dismantling the barriers between Australian and Papua New Guinean.[24] By 1969 more than a third of Papua New Guinean troops had also been to Australia, particularly those who were in technical positions, and one in ten had been to Australia more than once.[25] In addition, in 1964 the Army allowed Papua New Guineans to enlist in the PNGVR, thereby removing the last vestige of discrimination based on race, at least within PNG.[26]

Even more significant was the Army's acceptance after 1960 that men of another race could command Australian soldiers within the PIR, which had particular implications for the commissioning of Papua New Guinean officers. Australian Army plans for the PIR always assumed that local officers would be commissioned eventually, but during the 1950s the Military Board felt that such appointments would be problematic while there was the possibility that Australians might serve under them.[27] Consequently, its policy was to ensure Papua New Guineans replaced all Australians in non-commissioned officer positions in the PIR before commissioning any of them as officers. By 1960, the Military Board sensed a shift in Australian soldiers' attitudes to other races, noting that 'a precedent has already been established with the appointment of an aboriginal officer to the ARA', and began the process of selecting Papua New Guinean officers shortly thereafter.[28] The pace of change was rapid. Although before 1962 the Military Board instructed that 'Pacific Island soldiers will exercise command over Pacific Island soldiers only', by 1964 Papua New Guinean soldiers were accorded the same authority as Australian troops, regardless of origin. Notionally, such changes opened up all positions within the PIR to Papua New Guineans, regardless of whether they commanded Australian troops.[29]

The increasing equality of the position of Papua New Guineans within the Australian Army in PNG was matched by improvements in service conditions. The monotonous food given to Papua New Guineans – mainly rice and meat – was improved, and the system of leave was reformed to be fairer to those who had to travel great distances to get home. Symbolic changes were also made to practices that emphasised the difference between Australians and their colonial subjects. For instance, Papua New Guinean soldiers were no longer required to wear uniforms when on leave from 1963, removing some of the potential for antagonism between civilians and soldiers, as occurred before the 1957 disturbance.[30] It also lessened the control exerted by the Australian Army over the private lives of soldiers. In many ways, these improvements were as significant as the changes to Papua New Guinean positions within the force, given the outwardly visible nature of uniforms and food as status symbols.[31] In Lieutenant Colonel McKenzie's opinion, these changes belatedly moved the PIR into line with the rest of the Australian Army. This was not before time, as he believed that 'some of the obvious cultural differences were used as an excuse to continue with man-management practices which had long gone out of mode in the rest of the Australian Army'.[32]

The role played by conditions of service in defining the place of Papua New Guineans in the Australian Army is most clearly illustrated in the provision of boots during the early 1960s. Like the end of prohibition for PNG as a whole, the introduction of boots marked an improvement in both quality of life and status. Papua New Guinean Thomas Posi, who joined the PIR in 1962, for instance recalled that 'we felt bad', as the absence of boots denied the fact that 'we are all human'.[33] Soldiers knew that the footwear policy represented a presumption of difference between Papua New Guinean and Australian, but also believed that they could not openly question their superiors. As Martin Takoin remembered, 'If you ask [about boots] they will ask you to resign and go. It was Army policy.'[34] By the 1960s, the view that Papua New Guineans were suited to bare feet was a minority one. More Australians felt uncomfortable with the inherently racist basis of the policy, especially as experiences on patrol unequivocally demonstrated that the absence of boots severely hampered operations as soldiers fell out of the march with injured feet. Consequently, many Australian officers pushed for their introduction, not least McKenzie, who considered the issue 'vital'.[35]

The first footwear trials were conducted in October 1962 during a patrol in the border region of Papua near Kiunga and Telefomin.[36] Professor Hirchfeldt from the University of Queensland was assigned to the PIR to assess the footwear needs of soldiers, who had on average much larger feet than their Australian counterparts. The trials quelled some grumbling among troops, but raised expectations that boots would be received shortly after. In the meantime, boots were issued to the police.[37] As in 1961, soldiers were angered by the apparent favouring of their rivals, and when no boots materialised after the trials, a small riot broke out at Taurama Barracks and a number of soldiers were discharged or fined.[38] It took another year for a canvas and rubber patrol boot and a leather everyday boot to be issued to Papua New Guineans.[39]

Despite the improvements in conditions of service and in the status of Papua New Guineans, a degree of discrimination remained in the Australian Army. The rejected application of Papua New Guinean J. Israel to join the ARA (as opposed to the PIR) in July 1965 is illustrative. At the time Papuans, like Israel, being Australian citizens by birth, were technically permitted to serve throughout the Australian Army, but were restricted from entering mainland Australia by the Migration Act, effectively limiting Papuans' citizenship to PNG.[40] The Departments of Immigration, Army and Territories discussed Israel's application at length, but he was ultimately denied his request. The reasons cited were the risk of upsetting the rationale behind lower wages for Papua New Guineans, since Israel would be paid at a higher rate than his fellow Papua New Guineans in the PIR, and the likelihood that even more applications would be received.[41] In his reply to Israel, the Minister for Defence, Alan Fairhall, argued that in keeping with the policy of developing a Papua New Guinean defence force it would not do for 'the residents of Papua and New Guinea to join other national armed forces'.[42] Fairhall's suggestion that, for Israel, the Australian Army represented a foreign force reflected a significant, but subtle, theme throughout the Australian Army's policies towards PNG.[43] Although technically Australian soldiers, they were perceived as Papua New Guineans, even before the nation of PNG was created. A further problem was the prohibition on sending New Guineans (protected persons under the UN Trusteeship requirements) to fight overseas, despite the desire of many Papua New Guineans to do so; as a result the Army would be forced to discriminate between Papuans and New Guinean enlistees, as the latter would be unable to serve overseas.[44]

The perception of PNG as a 'foreign' country was also present in the Army's policies towards classified information. As Papua New Guinean soldiers assumed positions in which they would have access to sensitive information, some in the Department of Defence also harboured doubts about their loyalty, given the possibility of future independence. In 1965 the Department of Defence decided on the code word 'Foxami' to mark those papers to which Papua New Guineans were to be denied access for security reasons.[45] Papua New Guineans were to be treated as foreign (rather than Australian) officers as 'it may be assumed that any loyalty of the people towards Australia will tend to diminish' as independence came closer.[46] The use of 'Foxami' over the more usual AUSTEO (Australian Eyes Only) was 'to avoid implications of racial discrimination'. However, this was problematic given that Papuan soldiers were Australian citizens, and hence no more foreign than Australians from the Northern Territory. Despite the concern of the Department of Defence about the security of sensitive information in PNG, Foxami seemed not to be widely used, particularly owing to the impossibility of ensuring that Papua New Guineans did not see sensitive material when there was no differentiation between them and Australians in headquarters.[47]

A PROFESSIONAL RELATIONSHIP

Despite the differential treatment of Papua New Guineans within the Australian Army, outright racism and discrimination between individuals was rare by the 1960s, particularly compared with the often-poor treatment of Papua New Guineans in the civilian community. Relationships between soldiers were less conditioned by casual racism, owing to the need for Australian soldiers to work closely, and effectively, with Papua New Guineans in the Army. Of course, absence of reports of racism is not necessarily evidence of the absence of racism itself, given the potential of individuals to refrain from mentioning what is often an uncomfortable subject. In addition, the highly structured nature of the military made the relationship between Papua New Guinean and Australian more opaque than it might have been in the civilian community, as different ranks did not mix. Nonetheless, there is evidence that the relationship between Australians and Papua New Guineans improved during the 1960s compared with the previous decade, which accords with the experience of Indigenous Australian servicemen during this period.[48]

Racism – casual or deliberate – continued to exist among civilians in PNG even as discriminatory laws were dismantled, as the habits of colonialism were slow to change. Terms such as 'native', 'boi' and 'bush kanaka', for instance, were still in use among members of the Administration well into the 1960s.[49] Many of the Australian ex-servicemen interviewed for this book believed that there was a far higher incidence of entrenched racism among civilians than within the Australian Army. Similarly, a survey of Papua New Guinean soldiers in 1967 suggested that most thought that there was still significant discrimination based on race in PNG outside the Army compared to within it.[50] Army Chaplain Ray Quirk complained in a newsletter to ex-PIR officers of the 'foolishness' of some Australians throughout the Territory, particularly 'johnny-come-latelys', who treated Papua New Guineans as people they could 'kick around'. Quirk was therefore pleasantly surprised when SAS soldiers stationed in PNG for Exercise Long Hop in 1963 quickly 'established a comradeship' with their Papua New Guinean counterparts. This relationship, Quirk hoped, would help in 'destroying the artificial superiority' felt by many Europeans in PNG.[51] In some cases, discrimination within the civilian community elicited indignation from Australian soldiers, as occurred in 1962 when Corporal Elau, a Papua New Guinean soldier, was removed from a commercial flight to Port Moresby in favour of a European member of the Legislative Council, thereby returning late from leave.[52] Similarly, Ken Swadling, an instructor at Goldie River in 1969, recalled a football match between members of the PIR and an expatriate team in which the European players 'made a point of stamping on their opponents' [unbooted] feet with their studded boots at every opportunity, as well as subjecting them to a vile stream of racist comments'. Racism was so prevalent in this game and others that the CO withdrew the team from competition for the rest of the season in protest.[53]

Of course, racism was not universal among civilians. The local Administration officer, for instance, condemned Corporal Elau's treatment as 'blatant disregard of business ethics'.[54] In 1964 a handful of Australian ex-servicemen in Papua New Guinea left RSL clubs in protest over a ban on Papua New Guinean ex-servicemen drinking there.[55] Nevertheless, casual and ingrained discrimination remained common throughout the colonial period. An Australian public servant with the Department of External Affairs, on visiting PNG in 1966, wrote that 'racial discrimination is practised by a large segment of the European community'.[56] Similarly, the UN Visiting Mission in 1968 remarked on a 'social separateness' between white Australians and Papua New Guineans, which had its origins in a disparity in pay, conditions and living standards.[57] Writing in the early 1970s, Wolfers argued that separation on the grounds of race remained in PNG, particularly in the continued use of the pejorative term 'boi', preference given to expatriates in stores, and the social exclusion of Papua New Guineans from pubs.[58]

Undoubtedly, Papua New Guineans were often treated as second-class citizens up to independence, albeit less obviously as time passed.[59] Throughout the 1960s there was also a growing Papua New Guinean resentment of their unequal position. Albert Kiki, as an outspoken proponent of Papua New Guinean equality for instance, condemned a 'white supremacy that was creating deep dissatisfaction' in PNG.[60] Outside their military tasks Australian soldiers were still active participants in the unequal race relations of civilian PNG. Most Australian servicemen in PNG employed domestic servants who were paid and housed according to a 'native' scale. Attitudes among some servicemen towards Papua New Guineans could also reflect the hierarchical nature of colonial society. When asked during a court martial in 1963 how he expected Papua New Guineans to address him, for instance, Second Lieutenant J.R. Elliot answered 'either as Sir or Master', and affirmed that this was common practice throughout PNG.[61] The term 'native' was also used by at least one officer to describe the Papua New Guineans encountered on patrol.[62] Interviewees recall that overt racist attitudes were displayed by a small number of Australian soldiers, but believed these to be rare exceptions to the rule.[63]

That the effect of prejudice among the Australian civilian population on Papua New Guinean soldiers worried the Australian Army suggests at least a different level of prejudice within the armed forces, if not its absence. During discussions on the commissioning of Papua New Guinean officers, the Military Board argued that the subordinate position of Papua New Guineans in the Territory was inimical to producing quality officers:

> The PNG environment is an environment of tutelage and patronage for the P[acific] I[slander]. The outward signs of his inferiority are visible everywhere. He is governed, he does not govern. This is not a good environment for a potential officer in whom self-reliance, a natural acceptance of responsibility, a natural assumption of the right to command are essential. Australia is incomparably a better officer producing environment than PNG.[64]

In this case, the Army believed that discrimination was detrimental to its task in PNG. Given the relative unfamiliarity of many Australian civilians on the mainland with other races, posting Papua New Guineans to the mainland also had its risks. Papua New Guineans were still being portrayed in the press in colonial, racial and paternalistic terms throughout the 1960s, and remained for many the 'fuzzy wuzzy angels' of the Second World War.[65] As a result, the Australian Adjutant General expressed the concern in 1965 that 'while internal Army discrimination is unlikely the civilian population in Australia may not be so tolerant' of Papua New Guinean officers compared with expatriates in PNG, and that this might place an 'intolerable' burden on him and his family.[66] In the event, no Papua New Guinean served long enough in Australia for their family to accompany them save for officer cadets, who were usually unmarried.

The Australian Army increasingly attempted to foster a strong working relationship among its soldiers in PNG throughout the 1960s. Following Administration practice, in 1962 the Military Board instructed that the term 'Pacific Islander' (shortened as PI) be used to describe inhabitants of PNG over terms such as 'native' and 'indigene'.[67] Although Elliot showed that this was not always followed, the change in language used by Major General Daly – who had a close relationship with the PIR over a number of years – is indicative of a wider shift in the Army's attitude toward Papua New Guineans. Describing the often-poor understanding by Australian officers of Papua New Guineans in the aftermath of the disturbance in 1961, Daly complained that they were 'inexperienced in handling natives'.[68] By 1967, however, officers with similar faults had become, in Daly's eyes, 'incompatible . . . with Pacific Islanders'.[69] Daly's comments not only show that even after this six-year period the relationship between Australians and Papua New Guineans still needed improvement but also reflect efforts to ensure a cordial working relationship in which Papua New Guineans were not 'handled' but with whom Australians instead worked together.

Australian and Papua New Guinean soldiers later recalled a firm professional relationship, given the necessity of working together in stressful situations such as patrolling.[70] Papua New Guinean officers were accepted as an important addition to the officers' mess, and the work day often ended with a drink and discussion to 'nut out problems' with the troops.[71] Similarly, Papua New Guinean NCOs remember a fruitful and friendly relationship their Australian counterparts, often as the latter prepared to hand over to the former in the process of localisation. Martin Takoin, for instance, recalled an older Australian sergeant, to whom he was understudy, regaling him with tales of the Kokoda campaign after a hard day's work.[72] Long hours, a challenging profession and a sense of professional camaraderie could result in strong bonds across ranks, and more than one departing officer remembered being escorted to his flight home by tearful Papua New Guinean soldiers.[73] Grahame Wease, the last Australian RSM in 2PIR, recalled an emotional farewell in Wewak, in which an entire company stood to attention as he boarded his plane. Before he departed, his batman handed him a coin, telling Wease: 'I've only got two dollars, but this is yours.' Wease still has the coin, and the moment remains a cherished memory of service with Papua New Guineans.[74]

With the close working relationships between them and Australians, former Papua New Guinean soldiers recall outright racism within the Army as rare. Ronnie Oiwelo, who worked closely with Australian soldiers during his training to become an Army clerk, spoke of a 'friendship with the Australian people... [they] were very very nice to us. We worked together, like sit and drink together tell stories about [our] job, and to me, like, they were very good.'[75] For Oiwelo and others, the professional rewards of training with Australians was an important and positive aspect of the relationship; Papua New Guineans, like their Australian counterparts, were professional soldiers, and took pride in their service and careers. However, positive memories of the relationship are also coloured by comparisons between the well-organised PNG Command under Australians, and the travails of the PNGDF after independence.[76] Discipline, in particular, was remembered as far stricter and more effective under Australians whereas the problems of the PNGDF after independence and today are attributed to its absence.[77] Although the fact that the interviewer was Australian could have distorted their answers, many former soldiers were willing to report cases of structural inequality while simultaneously viewing the personal and professional relationship in a positive light.[78]

Nonetheless, as Daly's comments on the compatibility between Australians and Papua New Guineans suggest, even during the 1960s, this relationship was sometimes marred by distance between the two groups. Papua New Guineans were largely treated as equals in a professional sense by the end of the 1960s, yet the 'social separateness' identified by the United Nations in 1968 also existed in the Army.[79] On a professional level, the relationship was often clouded by the distance of rank, which made interaction between Australian and Papua New Guinean troops in different positions unlikely, and in some cases was actively discouraged in the interests of discipline.[80] The profound difference in culture could also play a role. One study of national servicemen posted to PNG as teachers during 1972 found that negative perceptions of Papua New Guineans tended to increase marginally during their period of service, as these men came to know Papua New Guineans.[81] Among those in the sample, favourable attitudes towards Papua New Guineans were also inversely related to satisfaction with Army life, a tendency in keeping with more recent experiences of US troops engaged in cross-cultural teaching activities.[82] Although not necessarily indicative of the attitudes of all Australian soldiers in PNG, the increase in the racist perceptions is not surprising given the general or limited knowledge of Papua New Guineans before posting to PNG.

As with the attempted introduction of the 'Foxami' code word, the knowledge that independence was a possibility, however distant, also coloured the position of Papua New Guineans within PNG Command. Ted Diro, for instance, believed that the PIR was always seen as a separate unit, and independence was never far from the minds of Australians when discussing its role and the soldiers within it.[83] Nevertheless, a sense of separation has also been seen as a positive: many Papua New Guinean soldiers viewed Australian officers and senior NCOs as impartial, given their position outside any tribal tensions among soldiers.[84] It is doubtful that this preference for officers who were removed from Papua New Guinean tribal issues would have been expressed had the relationship included overt racism.

PAPUA NEW GUINEAN MOTIVATIONS TO SERVE

Although by the mid-1960s Papua New Guineans enjoyed an improving position within the Australian Army, better conditions and a closer relationship with Australians, as Israel's case showed there also remained clear limitations on their position within PNG Command. Yet recruits were plentiful throughout the period of Australian rule, and service in the Army was considered an elite occupation. In joining the Army in such high numbers, young Papua New Guinean men were motivated by the financial and educational advantages of service, the perception of the PIR as an avenue for adventure and a sense of duty. A survey of high school students in 1969 found that the occupation of 'soldier' was on average the fourth most desired profession, after doctor, priest and agricultural officer.[85] That the Army expanded at a pace far higher than anticipated during the 1960s is testament to this popularity. Recruiting team visits to villages around the country were usually well attended, and a great many young men would turn out either to undergo tests or simply to watch the proceedings alongside other interested people.[86] Willing young men far outnumbered the places for them within the PIR. On a 1964 recruiting tour in the Highlands, 118 men were interviewed as part of the pre-selection tour, but just twenty were sent to the main recruiting assessment station at Mount Hagen. Of these, only ten were accepted. This process of pre-selecting men and sending only the best to be assessed was repeated in twenty-nine other centres in PNG during that tour.[87]

Many Papua New Guineans enlisted for financial gain, and recruiting pamphlets emphasised the financial benefits of joining the Army.[88] By the mid-1960s, the wages of a newly joined Papua New Guinean private were $117.50 per annum, rising to $497.50 after five years service; sergeants

Figure 4.2 Papua New Guinean recruit sleeping quarters, Goldie River,
c. 1962 (Australian Army Infantry Museum)

could earn more than ten times the basic entry pay of a private. In addition,
there were significant allowances for married soldiers and those with
trade skills. For all soldiers, basic necessities, such as accommodation and
rations, were provided in addition to wages. In this way, a soldier earned
far more than the minimum wage for Papua New Guineans (between $52
and $65 per annum in 1966), and a private with five years service and
trade skills could earn as much as a civilian teacher: between $650 and
$960 per year.[89] In addition, a soldier's life provided opportunities for
advancement by providing men with a general education and, in many
cases, transferable technical skills. As discussed further in chapter 5, most
Papua New Guinean soldiers keenly embraced education as an avenue
to social mobility, status and increased pay.[90] It is likely that the Army
added to the repertoire of marketable attributes among these men and
provided them with both proof of their ability to potential employers
and general skills they could take home after serving.[91] In addition, the
general education that all Papua New Guinean soldiers received could not
have but helped them in a country with a poor literacy rate.[92]

Nevertheless, Papua New Guineans did not join the Army purely for
financial reasons; many enlisted out of interest in and identification with
the institution.[93] Some Papua New Guineans, particularly those who

joined during the 1950s, did so after hearing their fathers' or relatives' war experiences either with the NGIB or the PIB, or as a carrier. Some prospective recruits had family already serving.[94] Men such as Caspar Kakar joined because he had seen newspaper articles depicting the work done by the PNG Division of the RAN, but was later persuaded to join the Army.[95] Others joined after seeing the PIR as teenagers, as it patrolled through their village, or because they grew up close to a barracks.[96] Jack Kukuma, for instance, played football with Australian engineers in Popondetta before joining.[97] Around 7 per cent of new recruits had had experience with the extremely popular cadet movement, begun in 1960 and run by the Army, and the first eight Papua New Guinean officers had been in the cadets.[98]

The possibility of adventure was also a factor for some.[99] On arriving in Port Moresby, one young man was so taken in with the new sights that he believed the town 'was Australia'.[100] Others signed up for the status that being a soldier conferred, with its uniforms, weapons and access to technology. The Pipes and Drums were especially attractive to young men, and the band was used on some 'prestige' patrols for this reason.[101] A recruiting film produced in 1973, written by an Australian captain and narrated by Papua New Guinean Lance Corporal Michael Pissa, demonstrated the way in which the PIR was marketed to Papua New Guineans, both through the film itself and in its depiction of the PIR's 'prestige' activities throughout PNG. Pissa told the audience of his reasons for wanting to join the PIR after seeing an Army display in Mount Hagen:

> . . . we saw the pipes and drums of the Pacific Islands Regiment. It was the first time I saw the pipe band, and the first time I saw soldiers also. When I went back to school I promised myself that one day I would join the Army and become a piper. This idea excited me, even though I knew life in the Army would not be the same as life in the village.[102]

Despite the position of Papua New Guineans as colonial subjects, one of the motivations for enlistment was a sense of service or duty. Papua New Guineans had complex layers of loyalty, and could concurrently have obligations to kinship groups, support Papua New Guinean independence, and also serve Australia and the Queen.[103] As Lovering points out in his study of Malawian soldiers in the KAR, in the context of colonialism these overlapping loyalties could be seen as 'politically unproblematic' by indigenous soldiers.[104] In one survey of fifty-five Papua New

Figure 4.3 Warrant Officer Osi Ivaroa, recruiting poster. Caption translates as 'Strengthen your country. See a recruiting officer immediately' (Chalkies Association)

Guinean other ranks in 1970, for instance, the chance to defend the country and its people and to serve 'Queen and country' were among the most common reasons to join the Army, although these sentiments might have been developed after enlistment.[105] Papua New Guinean nationalism was a vague conception during the early 1960s, and there is the possibility that soldiers' memories have been shaped by PNG's later independence. A number of minorities, such as the Kamba in Kenya and Māori in New Zealand, embraced their 'martial' status for the prestige and material benefits it promised, yet race or ethnic identification were not referred to by Papua New Guinean soldiers when explaining their reasons for enlisting.

Army recruiting made use of these multilayered identifications, referencing both service of Australia and Papua New Guinean statehood. One recruiting poster drew on the well-known face of Warrant Officer Osi

Ivaroa, the PIR's longest serving NCO, first Papua New Guinean RSM, and recipient of the British Empire Medal. In the poster, Osi replicated Lord Kitchener's famous finger pointing in posters of the First World War, calling on young men to see the Army recruiting officer. Under Osi's stern visage are the words 'Strongim kantri belong yupela', which translates as 'Strengthen your country', and an exhortation to see an Army recruiting officer immediately. Here, the Australian Army drew on Osi's long service in the Australian Army, for which he was widely known, to promote the national characteristics of PNG Command.

PAPUA NEW GUINEAN LIFE IN THE AUSTRALIAN ARMY

The more than two thousand Papua New Guinean men within PNG Command during the late 1960s was a young cohort, almost three-quarters of PNG Command being younger than twenty-four in 1969.[106] By 1973, 70 per cent of the soldiers in the Command had less than four years of service and fewer than 10 per cent of those in rifle companies had served more than eight years.[107] In all, a quarter of Papua New Guinean soldiers were married, a proportion shaped by the ban on marriage for soldiers in their first four years of service (a practice applied to Australian soldiers as well). Of those soldiers who had signed on again after their initial four-year enlistment had expired, almost half were married, and of these 40 per cent had children.[108] Reflecting the wide recruiting policies of PNG Command, the origins of Papua New Guineans were incredibly diverse: by one count 206 different languages were spoken in PNG Command. All men spoke Tok Pisin, most spoke English and a quarter spoke Motu, PNG's third most spoken language. Each of the other 203 languages were spoken by no more than 8 per cent of soldiers, some being known by only a handful of men in the force. As a result of this linguistic diversity, most likely unmatched by any other army in the world, all soldiers were fluent in two to three languages, with some speaking four or five.[109] By the late 1960s all Papua New Guinean soldiers were taught English during their time with the Army, although proficiency varied. Soldiers in technical and senior positions and those with long service tended to speak the language more fluently, but the language of the average soldier and of most orders and instruction remained Tok Pisin.[110]

Compared with that of the 1950s, the force of the 1960s was 'more homogeneous' in education and prior employment. As the decade progressed, an increasing number of young men enlisted straight from school, and the education level of the average Papua New Guinean soldier rose with each intake.[111] Largely, this was the result of the significant improvements in education in PNG from the late 1950s, which created a larger cohort of educated young men. This in turn allowed the educational preconditions for entry into the Army to be raised.[112] Combined with the classes given by Army teachers, the high education level of Papua New Guinean soldiers marked them out from the rest of the population, and by 1969 almost three-quarters of all soldiers had received at least seven years schooling in total.[113]

Papua New Guinean soldiers were therefore an educated and wealthy elite in PNG, and saw themselves as such.[114] Fewer than 94 000 of the Territory's 1.6 million people were employed across all industries, and the relatively high pay of soldiers differentiated them even within this small group.[115] Moreover, their position as soldiers, with particular skills, access to technology and visible military symbols, also contributed to their status. Nonetheless, there is no evidence that Papua New Guinean soldiers converted their elite status into political ambition during Australian rule as voting rates suggest that Papua New Guinean soldiers were not necessarily more politically aware or active than civilians.[116]

Although they were not overly political, as noted in previous chapters Papua New Guinean soldiers were more active in pursuing their interests when their perception as an elite *within* PNG was not met. Pay and conditions were an important part of many soldiers' decision to enlist, and not surprisingly, these were 'the major source of dissatisfaction', surpassing discipline and the difficulty of the military life as causes for concern.[117] Of the seven soldier protests in PNG during the 1960s, of which the 1961 disturbance was by far the largest, four had their origins in pay, while a further disturbance concerned a promised, but undelivered, period of rest and relaxation.[118] That the police often received pay and improvements to service conditions before the Army did not help matters. In 1968 taunts by police that 'you dress for show, we work for dough', reflected the intensive competition between these two institutions, both of which saw themselves as *the* elite in PNG.[119]

Yet the difference in the reaction of Papua New Guinean soldiers towards different types of discrimination conforms to the apolitical nature of many military strikes, mutinies and disturbances in the colonial world and indicates where Papua New Guineans drew the boundaries of acceptable treatment.[120] When all Papua New Guineans were discriminated against equally, Papua New Guineans were less likely to protest. Similarly, in situations in which soldiers had no specific grievance, they were

Figure 4.4 6 Platoon, B Company, PIR, 1961 (Australian Army Infantry Museum)

unlikely to react violently. As discussed above, the prohibition of alcohol for Papua New Guineans, despite being a glaring symbol of inequality and paternalism, did not elicit a strong reaction among Papua New Guinean soldiers against the Australian Army, or Australians in general. When Port Moresby erupted into days of rioting following a rugby match in 1968, soldiers simply returned to barracks, and were roundly praised for doing so by their commanding officer.[121] This is not to suggest that inequalities between Papua New Guineans and Australians were not a point of contention: among educated and professional Papua New Guineans, 'equal pay for local people doing the same work as Europeans' aroused the 'strongest opinion'. Instead, it was their status relative to other Papua New Guineans that caused the most severe disaffection among soldiers.[122]

Although the figures were distorted by the absence of any retiring soldiers from the statistics, PNG Command being a young force, the discharge patterns do suggest that discipline remained an issue in the late 1960s.[123] After their initial four-year enlistment period, around 25 per cent of Papua New Guinean soldiers during the late 1960s were discharged, either involuntarily or of their own free will.[124] Among the 239 soldiers discharged over the two-year period between 1966 and 1968, the most common reason was disciplinary (seventy-eight), followed by 'retention not in best interests' (fifty-four). Of those leaving voluntarily, forty had finished their engagement, and a further thirty-three left at their own request before their time had expired.[125] Compared with Australian soldiers, proportionally more Papua New Guineans were discharged for disciplinary reasons or 'for other reasons indicating a failure to make satisfactory adjustment to the system'.[126] Army researchers found that those soldiers discharged on disciplinary grounds 'were found to be more intelligent than that group of soldiers that was not discharged', suggesting that 'the brighter a soldier is, the more likely he is to conflict with the "system"'.[127] Soldiers still serving, meanwhile, believed that their fellows left as a result of poor pay, family matters and strict discipline, rather than ill-discipline or unsuitability, suggesting more about their views of the pitfalls of Army life than the reasons behind discharges.[128]

All soldiers retained strong links with their families, home regions and culture and overwhelmingly returned to their home regions after discharge. The type of employment found by soldiers after leaving PNG Command was diverse, but often not directly linked to the skills they had learnt while serving. Of 224 former soldiers sampled in one study, forty-one were drivers, while seventy-one were subsistence farmers, twenty-seven were plantation workers, the rest being employed in a variety of jobs including firemen, a minister and a 'guillotine operator'.[129] Nonetheless, studies of the employment of ex-servicemen conducted at the time did not, and could not, assess the degree to which service in the Army influenced a former soldier's approach to civilian life, values and outlook. Almost all of the Papua New Guinean ex-servicemen interviewed recalled their service favourably. However, as the majority of these men had long careers in the Army, this is not necessarily representative of all soldiers. Nonetheless, surveys taken in the 1970s did indicate that whatever the reason for their discharge, most of those who had left the Army still held it in high esteem.[130]

The place of Papua New Guinean soldiers within the Australian Army reflected the degree to which it engaged with and built on the development of PNG. During the 1960s, Army authorities accepted that Papua New Guineans were not simple 'native' soldiers but instead were people who could occupy positions of technical skill and responsibility. As a result, the Army implemented its own changes alongside those of the Administration. In some cases soldiers were more inclusive than civilian society: when RSL clubs in PNG refused Papua New Guinean veterans entry, it was the sergeants' mess at Taurama Barracks, only recently integrated, that welcomed them on Anzac Day.[131] When asked about racism in the

Australian Army, Ken Swadling acknowledged that there were exceptions to this inclusion, but argued that the Army's need for a coherent and efficient team necessitated a close relationship:

> In my 20 years in uniform I never observed or experienced racism within the Australian Army. I've seen racism by soldiers towards non-soldiers, but never between soldiers. The reason for this was very simple: if you're in combat you depend on your comrades around you to help you stay alive and they depend on you. It doesn't matter what the colour of their skin is.[132]

Diverse in their backgrounds, motivations and experiences, the Papua New Guinean soldiers who comprised PNG Command were young, ethnically and linguistically diverse, increasingly educated, proud and with strong links to home. Their loyalties were complex, given their position as both Australian soldiers and potential future Papua New Guinean nationals. Undoubtedly Papua New Guinean troops were an elite within the Territory, and participated in the Australian Army to serve their own educational, financial and personal ends. Nevertheless, although legal discrimination was undone during the 1960s, the place of Papua New Guineans within the Australian Army was still framed and limited by Australians' sense that Papua New Guineans were foreign. Bureaucratic inequality remained even after legal discrimination had been removed, and Papua New Guineans were always considered separate from Australian soldiers owing to their race or, later, their future nationality.

CHAPTER | 5

'A NEW TASK'

LAYING THE FOUNDATIONS OF A NATIONAL ARMY, 1966–71

Brigadier Ian Hunter took over the growing PNG Command in April 1966 from its first commander, Brigadier A.L. McDonald. At this time PNG Command was still expanding rapidly and had recruited more than four hundred men over the course of the year; by late 1967 it contained 2216 Papua New Guineans and 367 Australians.[1] Clear in his vision for PNG Command and outspoken, Hunter was a energetic force behind the development of this newly expanded formation, but on arrival in PNG, Hunter 'found the Force was unsettled, as it tended to lack direction, motivation and co-ordination'.[2] Teething problems played a role, but the threat that PNG Command had been preparing to meet was also, slowly but clearly, dissipating. By August an agreement ending Confrontation with Indonesia had been signed in Bangkok.[3] Between 1966 and 1969, as the likelihood of renewed tensions lessened, the Department of Defence gradually downgraded its assessment of PNG's strategic importance from 'vital' to merely 'significant'. As a consequence, Australian defence planners were increasingly vague about PNG's strategic importance and the future defence needs of the Territory.[4] Hunter neatly encapsulated the challenge facing his command in a 1967 conference with the Chief of the General Staff (CGS):

> In the earlier confrontation [sic] situation, and before Vietnam
> assumed its present importance, Australian members in the
> Command could see their task in relatively simple terms of preparing
> their troops for war. This situation has passed and staff members

Figure 5.1 Brigadier Ian Hunter and Lieutenant Colonel Donald Ramsay, discussing the building of Moem Barracks, Wewak, c. 1966 (Sinclair, *To Find a Path*)

have found themselves faced with a new task, one which the Australian Army has had limited experience, in a time-frame which they have reason to believe is limited, against a background of changed Australian priorities.[5]

This 'new task' was one of forging a military force that represented and served PNG, which Hunter championed enthusiastically. Whereas at the beginning of the 1960s PNG Command focused on defending Australia, by the end of the decade independence was the primary driver of the force's activities. Although Australia's defence remained important, by 1969 Hunter reported to the *Age* newspaper that the purpose of PNG Command was to 'create a national army before there is a nation'.[6]

Hunter, like others in PNG, reacted to a growing momentum towards Papua New Guinean independence. The thawing of the relationship with Indonesia, alongside broader international and domestic pressures, allowed PNG's political future to be seriously discussed in Canberra and Port Moresby for the first time. Up to 1966 the measured economic and educational development advocated by successive Ministers for Territories Paul Hasluck and Charles Barnes had continued. However, the creation of a Select Committee on Constitutional Development within the House of Assembly in Port Moresby that year, led by PNG's future Governor-General, John Guise, pushed a reluctant Department of Territories for Australian leadership, if not a decision, on PNG's future.[7] Barnes held that the Australian Government should provide broad guidance only, believing that PNG and its people were still unprepared for independence. Nevertheless, he took the matter of PNG's 'ultimate status' to Cabinet, marking the first time that this body had explicitly addressed the issue of PNG's political future.[8] In March 1966 Cabinet discussed three options for PNG: complete independence, integration within Australia as a state and finally 'association' with Australia, which could range from Australia retaining some powers of government, such as defence, to treaties binding the two nations together.[9]

In fact, Cabinet adopted a fourth option, and 'decided against making, or so much as attempting to make, a decision' on the future of the Territory. Instead, it called for 'as much flexibility . . . as possible', noting that 'it will be necessary to avoid both formality and precision in what is said to the Committee [on Constitutional Development]'.[10] Simultaneously, the Australian Government moved to discourage the idea of statehood, which had the effect of alienating some Papua New Guineans, as it gave lie to the idea that it was only development, and not race, that separated PNG and Australia.[11] The government's decision to maintain flexibility set the tone for the next four years; some form of self-government was probable in the short to medium term, but when and in what form was left open-ended.[12] Even in 1970 only 11 per cent of Australians believed that independence would occur in five years or less, although more than 42 per cent expressed no opinion at all.[13] In the interim, the Administration, and by implication the Army, was to maintain its measured and gradual development.

THE ARMY THREAT

The end of Confrontation and the possibility of independence spurred discussion about the role, shape and size of PNG Command, exposing the divergence in opinion between civilians and the Australian Army in both PNG and Canberra that had once been kept in check by the risk of war with Indonesia. As Hunter admitted, during Confrontation 'there was no question of acceptance of the Army; now, with cessation of threat, some reservations have arisen within certain sections of community'.[14] Following the détente with Indonesia, the Administration, Department of Territories and concerned civilians questioned the suitability of what they perceived as an expensive force that too closely followed the Australian Army's structure and had a propensity for instability, as the disturbances had supposedly showed. The questions raised in the course of these debates were often valid, particularly those relating to the size and cost of the force. However, PNG Command was still not considered as part of the Australian governance of PNG or of a future state, but was, according to Daly, 'looked on as something different', a fact demonstrated by its complete absence from the annual Administration reports.[15] Any concerns cannot be separated from this disconnect between the Army and the Administration and between their parent departments, which represented at times an 'ongoing feud' that coloured discussions between the two sides.[16]

Central to the criticism of PNG Command were recurring strikes and riots among Papua New Guinean soldiers, all of which were linked by civilian commentators to the two disturbances in 1957 and 1961. In August 1966, for instance, a violent dispute broke out between police and soldiers outside a Port Moresby theatre.[17] The brawl was probably sparked by taunts traded between the two groups but, like the 1961 disturbance, had its origins in soldiers' anger over the pay compared with that of the police. These tensions simmered for the next three years, with a further, but largely peaceful, strike over pay occurring in 1969, for which the Army discharged sixty men. As had occurred after the disturbances, the Administration kept close watch on those who were discharged.[18] As before, a significant part of the problem was the lack of information given to soldiers as the decisions worked through Canberra bureaucracy, while the pay increases for the police, being the responsibility of the Administration, were announced relatively quickly.[19] However, where before Department of Territories officials saw riots by soldiers as a challenge to Australian authority, now they saw them as threatening PNG's future stability as an independent nation. In response to the 1966 disturbance J.L. Legge, the Department of Territories' Defence liaison officer, argued that 'it was doubtful whether [the PIR] could be relied upon' in the event of general unrest throughout PNG, making reference to 'armed forces taking over control from established government' in newly decolonised countries.[20] Secretary George Warwick Smith agreed with his junior, and explicitly linked 'the recent unrest among members of the PIR' with 'the number of instances during the past ten years in which the armed forces have taken over control from the established government in developing countries'.[21]

As noted previously, while evidence of continued discipline issues, and potentially failures of leadership, earlier protests represented an appeal to authority rather than its rejection.[22] Moreover, the seven disturbances among soldiers between 1957 and 1970 paled in comparison against similar incidents among police, which were largely ignored by those claiming that the Army represented a threat to the stability of PNG.[23] Between 1960 and 1968, the Administration recorded fifteen police riots, including a mutiny in one of the riot squads charged with quelling civilian disturbances. In 1966 alone, the Police Commissioner admitted that 195 members of the RPNGC 'have been before a court on criminal charges', in addition to normal disciplinary tribunals. In the same period, just fifteen soldiers were convicted in civilian courts, although some discipline problems would have been dealt with internally. In the words of the Director of Military Operations and Plans, the 'Secretary External Territories' criticism of the PIR based on the disturbances certainly looks tame alongside the police'.[24]

The concerns within the Department of Territories reflected a more public debate then taking place in newspaper opinion columns, academic journals and public forums, in which PNG Command was seen as a threat to civilian government in light of coups and military-led violence in other decolonising states.[25] Basita Heatu, the pseudonym of a Papua New Guinean teacher, wrote in the journal *New Guinea* that the Army did not have a clear role in PNG and that, as well as encouraging a belligerent attitude towards Indonesia, it was also as capable of attempting a coup. In sum, Heatu argued, 'the army is probably the biggest single threat to the peace, security and development of the country'.[26] The following year another Papua New Guinean, Kokou Warubu, voiced similar concerns in *New Guinea*, asking his readers 'isn't an army likely to be one of the most divisive forces in a country such as ours? Hasn't it proved so elsewhere. The record seems fairly clear.'[27] Similarly, in an article in *People* entitled 'Who could take over New Guinea', Australian journalist David White raised the possibility of PNG following the path of such countries as Kenya, Burma and South Vietnam, where the military had taken power.[28] As part of a three-part series in the *Canberra Times* in 1969, UPNG academic Alan Gilbert argued that too much attention and money was being lavished on the military whereas too little support was being given to the police.[29] Events in Africa, Gilbert argued, demonstrated that 'the early government of a newly independent nation is likely to fall victim to military officers' ambitions backed by the weapons of the Army'.[30]

Hunter was not blind to the possibility of further disturbances among soldiers in PNG during this period, but believed that the worst that could be expected was a strike or soldiers joining civil unrest, rather than a full-blown coup. To this end, PNG Command developed a contingency plan in 1966, designed to forestall, limit and halt 'military unrest involving Pacific Islands soldiers'. The plan detailed the action to be taken if strikes, riots or mass disobedience were expected among soldiers, and drew heavily on experience of the previous disturbances. Officers and NCOs were to avoid trouble by maintaining a clear picture of morale in the ranks, securing important areas such as the motor pool if trouble broke out, and calming the situation. Force was not to be used, and weapons were not to be carried. If struck, Europeans were to 'smile, not hit back' as 'Our hold is a moral one . . . a situation of European vs PI must be avoided'. As far as possible, Australian personnel were to make use of Papua New Guinean officers and NCOs to quell any trouble.[31] A second plan, codenamed 'Kwik Start', was formulated 'to isolate PI soldiers from civil disaffection occurring in the Port Moresby area'. In the event of strikes or riots, soldiers were to be moved out of Taurama and Murray Barracks and were to be told that the movement was part of a short notice operational readiness exercise.[32]

Critics of PNG Command, however, claimed to see evidence of the Army's potential to usurp civilian government. The civic action program was the object of particular criticism. Begun by Hunter in 1967, civic action capitalised on PNG Command's patrol program to provide infrastructure, training and medical aid directly to Papua New Guinean civilians. Where possible, all regular patrols included a civic action element alongside their training and information-gathering activities. For example, when C Company 1PIR conducted a counter-insurgency exercise in northern New Britain in 1968, it finished its training with the construction of two bridges, improving the road from Rabaul.[33] It was Hunter's aim to 'give full credit' for civic action to the Administration. The program also had the support of the Administrator and was discussed in a conference with all district commissioners at Taurama Barracks in April 1967 without controversy.[34] The benefits of patrols like this were two-fold. First, the Australian Army added to the capability of the Administration's works department, a role that it would continue after independence. Concurrently, these patrols aimed at improving relations with the community, demonstrating to Papua New Guineans that the 'Army [was] something belonging to them', while demonstrating to the soldiers that they served the people.[35]

Civic action also complemented the more general assistance the Army provided to the Administration. Often at short notice, the Army offered manpower, transport and expertise. One of the largest examples of these efforts was the deployment of troops from 1PIR to the Highlands to combat an influenza epidemic that broke out in 1969 and killed around two thousand people. During the crisis the Army mounted patrols to remote regions, supported by RAAF transport aircraft, providing inoculations to thousands of Papua New Guineans.[36] Similarly, the RAAF airlifted food into the drought-affected Highlands in 1972.[37] PNG Command provided aid to the Administration in other, smaller, ways, such as in April 1968 when 1PIR was involved in the search for a lost Canadian woman on the Kokoda Trail, having been called in by the Administrator after twenty-four hours of a police search. The strengths that PNG Command brought to the operation demonstrated its broader civic role in the Territory, particularly as the police had 'pitifully inadequate equipment', lacked operational rations and camping gear, and possessed 'completely inadequate footwear and clothing for the conditions in which they were operating'. The woman was eventually found by a soldier of Major Michael Jeffery's C Company, but died shortly after of exposure and exhaustion.[38]

Given the relatively routine nature of military support to the Administration, the Department of Territories was not informed about civic action. As a result, the first Canberra heard of the program was from a short Australian Broadcasting Commission report. This elicited a terse demand for information from Warwick Smith, who feared that the Army would 'encroach' on the Administration's role in the Territory and usurp the civilian government by offering a more attractive source of authority to the police and kiaps.[39] Given that he had approved the Army's civic action plan, Hay did not share his superior's view that PNG Command might be positioning itself as an alternative government.[40] Despite Warwick Smith's concerns, the civic action program remained. In January 1969 the debate over civic action spilled into the public domain, sparked by comments made at a Youth Conference in Port Moresby by Dr Ron Crocombe, director of the Australian National University's New Guinea Research Unit. Echoing Warwick Smith, Crocombe argued that civic action could undermine the Administration in the Territory by presenting a competing authority to the people, as had occurred in newly decolonised nations. Others, such as UPNG academic Professor Charles Rowley and Vincent Eri (later a Governor-General of PNG), held similar views, and the issue also received attention in the Australian Parliament.[41]

There was no evidence to suggest that the Army was supplanting the Administration, intentionally or otherwise, especially given the intimate involvement of Administration officials in the civic action process, from approving the recipients of aid to accompanying the patrols. Moreover, unlike police, magistrates and kiaps, who were responsible for enforcing the Administration's (sometimes unpopular) policies and laws, PNG Command had never been used as an instrument of colonial control, and had far less opportunity to arouse the ire of civilians in its day-to-day activities. There was also no evidence that Papua New Guinean civilians viewed the Army as anything other than an arm of the government, and that is how troops presented themselves. If the Army did indeed command greater respect than civilian authorities, Crocombe and others failed to question why this might be, or whether this was indeed cause for alarm. Potentially, other influences were at play as well. As historian Robert O'Neill pointed out in 1971, the Vietnam War had a negative effect on the discussion, as 'opponents of the war in Vietnam were in a mood to damn the methods of counter-insurgency which include civic action'.[42] Moreover, residual colonial fears of 'arming the native' might have an influence on anxieties about the Army. Although it was never stated explicitly, criticism of 'the Army' in PNG clearly referred to 'Papua New Guinean soldiers'. No concerns were ever voiced about the possibility of a coup in Canberra; Papua New Guineans were the issue.

The power of the perceived twin threats of unreliability and the potential for a coup were demonstrated in the negative portrayal of the Army in a short booklet published by the Administration in March 1967 entitled 'The Government in Papua New Guinea'. The booklet aimed to help Papua New Guineans 'understand better some of the major political developments currently taking place', but caused outrage among members of the Army in the Territory, and in defence circles more generally.[43] Purporting to discuss the key pillars of a democratic government, it was overwhelmingly disparaging when it came to defence forces, telling readers:

> In some countries where the people did not watch carefully that their government worked well, and where the elected members could not govern properly, the government has been taken over by the Army . . . in places where this happens, the boss of the Army becomes a dictator and the ordinary people do not have any say in running their country. This has happened in many new African countries.[44]

Figure 5.2 1PIR marches through Port Moresby, late 1960s (Australian Army Infantry Museum)

Hunter wrote of his 'considerable concern' about this presentation of the military, believing that it 'fails to recognize the Army as an essential and lawful element of the community framework, and represents it only as a potential danger to democracy and to the rights of the individual'. By linking the military to the creation and maintenance of dictatorships, Hunter argued, the booklet portrayed it 'as basically undemocratic, power-centred and in short undesirable'. Reflecting the strategic context in which these debates took place, Hunter went so far as to suggest that communist sympathisers could manipulate this idea to subvert Papua New Guineans, arguing that such actions were the 'common and well-documented practice of communist and subversive organisations in emerging countries'.[45] Although the link to communism was perhaps far-fetched, Hunter's anger was reasonable, given that the Administration had traduced the Australian Army and Australian soldiers by discussing the Australian Army *only* in terms of its potential threat to the government. He was not alone in his outrage, and the matter was met with consternation in Parliament, among defence officials and in the press.[46]

The booklet furore was a particularly sour note in the relationship between PNG Command and the Administration. In the end, the debate over the booklet was resolved only in October 1967 at the ministerial level. Although both Ministers Barnes and Fraser supported their own departments, it was agreed that the booklet would be rewritten and a second booklet discussing the Army in PNG be published, which it was in 1969.[47] The omission of the Army in a book ostensibly about PNG as a proto-nation captures the casual and ingrained disregard of the Administration towards the Army, despite the former's role as the precursor to an independent PNG defence force. Leadership on independence was an Administration and Territories responsibility; that they did not engage with the Army on the issue of defence, and viewed it simply as a threat, was a particular failure.

HALTING THE EXPANSION

The public and private discussions on the future of PNG Command during 1966 and 1967 represented the first, informal, skirmishes on the issue of the force's place in an independent PNG. From late 1967, the Australian Government increasingly took a role in the planning of PNG Command, whereas previously it was content to issue broad direction on armed forces in PNG. Although the Army previously devolved planning for the PIR to Northern Command and then PNG Command, it was no stranger to this level of strategic and political direction. However, what was novel was the involvement of other government departments not usually associated with defence, most notably the Department of Territories.

In October 1967, the Ministers and Secretaries of Defence, Territories and the Army (Fairhall and Hicks, Barnes and Warwick Smith, and Fraser and White) met to discuss the future of the Army in PNG in response to the changed strategic circumstances and the disagreements between the Army and Administration.[48] While the assembled men found common ground on the need for PNG Command to 'conform with the general economic and political development of the Territory', significant differences remained. Barnes believed that 'the Army had been a little too sensitive' about the booklet issue, and reiterated his belief that there was a strong possibility of an Army takeover in PNG, citing the 1961 disturbance as an example. This equation of a riot over pay – an example of a force 'not under proper control', according to Barnes – with the potential for a military coup demonstrated a blinkered view of the issue, given the difference in intent between an industrial strike and coup, as well as the far greater level of organisation required of the latter. It also denied any role the Administration might play in either causing or preventing violence, placing responsibility squarely at the feet of the military. Barnes also displayed a disregard for the coordination between PNG Command and the Administration that he advocated during the meeting. When Fraser expressed concern about the limited number of officer recruits and the slow rate of commissioning in response to Barnes' emphasis on developing a loyal military, he was met with an equivocal response by both Barnes and Warwick Smith, who believed that the Administration should have priority in recruiting educated Papua New Guineans. This prompted a frustrated Fairhall to point out 'that the Army's problems regarding officers could become Territories' problem if it were not solved'.[49]

Despite these disagreements, Territories and the Departments of Defence and the Army agreed that the future of PNG Command should be examined cooperatively, in the form of a joint Cabinet Submission. For its part, the Army agreed that a review of the pace of expansion was necessary, given the change in strategic circumstances in relation to Indonesia and the focus on Vietnam; it had previously gained approval for a postponement of the end of the expansion period from 1968 to 1970 owing primarily to shortages in manpower caused by the Army's other commitments.[50] Over the protests of Territories, the JPC took responsibility for the research that formed the basis of the submission, given the wider strategic implications of the discussion.[51]

Although the resulting report's discussion of the role of PNG Command in the context of PNG's future was significant, particularly given the consultation with the Department of Territories, its vision for the force differed little from that set down in 1963. Regarding the Command's structure, the JPC maintained that the long-planned but as yet unraised third battalion was still required to maintain the operational flexibility and capability of the Army in PNG but called for its creation to be again delayed, to 1972, 'to avoid saddling a future government... with a defence force it could not afford', although it offered no indication of how an affordable defence force might be achieved.

The JPC disagreed with Territories' barely hidden fears about the threat posed by Papua New Guinean soldiers; although the report discussed the potentially high cost of the force, readers were left in little doubt that its production was the result of Territories' concern 'about the threat to internal security which a force insufficiently imbued with a sense of loyalty to the civil power would represent'. In response to concerns about instability, the Army warned against too rapid an expansion and the dangers of poor policy decisions by the PNG Administration and any future government. The answer, the JPC argued, was a measured expansion and a focus on education, which would create a force that was cognisant of its role in supporting a democratic government. Finally, in recognition of the rapidly evolving political and strategic situation, the JPC called for another, more comprehensive review not later than mid-1970.[52]

Conservative and undertaken to mollify the Department of Territories, the report pleased few observers. The Directorate of Military Operations and Plans (DMO&P) was strongly critical that the JPC had even mentioned the potential for PNG Command to be a threat to internal security, arguing, that it was 'miles ahead of the ideals being promoted in any civilian organisation of TPNG'.[53] This was not an unreasonable assertion, given the levels of organisation, education and training within the Army; it also ignored that civilian institutions were not heavily armed. Hunter also took umbrage at suggestions of instability, arguing that problems often had their origins in policies outside PNG Command's control, such as pay.[54] Not surprisingly, the review also did little to answer the concerns of Barnes or his department, renamed 'External Territories' in January 1968. Reflecting the fragility of the previously agreed joint approach, Barnes petitioned Cabinet in August 1968 for a halt to the still continuing expansion, making particular reference to economic considerations and 'past instances of disaffection in the PIR over pay and conditions of service', instances that he argued held implications for 'the reliability and stability of the force'.[55] Indeed, Barnes went as far as to argue that the Army should 'restrict to a minimum the [Army's] strength at Port Moresby, which is the main centre of political activity and unrest'.[56]

Because of these disagreements, the Minister for Defence agreed that further interdepartmental discussion was a waste of time, and supported Barnes' submission to Cabinet suggesting a halt to the expansion.[57] Although acquiescing, Prime Minister John Gorton was not interested, believing that it was 'such a minor matter that it cannot take a high priority'.[58] Cabinet would arbitrate between the two departments, but the direction of the future PNG defence force was still largely to be left in the hands of public servants. Presented with Barnes' arguments and recognising that continued expansion was not absolutely necessary in the current strategic climate, Cabinet agreed to maintain the PIR at its current strength in September 1968, until the Defence Committee completed a further review.[59] This was a turning point for the Australian Army in PNG. Although PNG Command filled vacancies in its units, rationalised

Figure 5.3 1PIR band trooping the colours, 1968 (Australian Army Infantry Museum)

others, and replaced Australian soldiers with Papua New Guineans, its structure and size was largely to remain the same until independence.

In these discussions and elsewhere in government, there was a growing acceptance that PNG Command was the foundation of a future defence force, rather than simply an important part of the Australian Army's order of battle. After a visit to PNG in 1969, the Secretary of the Department of Defence, Henry Bland, argued: '[W]e must see it not as a part of Australia, nor anything resembling an extension of Australia. For our purposes, the Territory should be seen as a country of South East Asia.'[60] Bland praised the way in which the 'PIR belong[ed] to the Territory' in its outlook, not least through civic action, but he also argued that before the military in PNG could be independent it needed to be simplified, particularly through the unification of the three services. Bland also stressed the importance of accelerating the replacement of Australian personnel with Papua New Guineans. As a considered examination of PNG Command from a broader perspective than had hitherto been attempted, Bland's findings were influential in Canberra, and helped spur a forward-looking approach that focused on independence.[61] As part of this, a PNG Command Planning Cell was set up in 1969 to plan for a force 'appropriate to the needs of an emerging Nation'.[62] The cell shortly produced its own report, which in turn informed the broader studies being completed in Canberra, and would continue the important role played by the command in advising on its own future.[63]

This shift towards the conception of PNG Command as the precursor to a Papua New Guinean defence force was cemented in the completion in 1970 of the review called for in 1968 by Cabinet. This review explicitly referenced the term 'defence forces' for the first time when referring to PNG Command. Raising the possibility of a homogeneous defence force unlike the three-service structure then employed in Australia, the JPC envisaged a force of three small battalions of infantry with three companies each, ten patrol boats, and an air wing of seven aircraft expanding to more than twenty aircraft in the long term. In 1970, as in 1963, three battalions were to provide a unit for Papua, one for New Guinea and a reserve, reflecting the assessment that small raids over the border were the most likely threat, as they had been during Confrontation just a few years earlier.

Although the JPC called for consultation with Papua New Guineans on defence matters for the first time, the question of whether PNG needed a force of the size proposed – or indeed any defence force at all – was left unanswered.[64] No official government statement was made on the requirement for a defence force; Australian officials dealt with the issue only obliquely, generally assuming that Australia would leave PNG with some sort of conventional force. Bland for instance argued that 'an obligation rested on the Australian Government to provide a defence force for a country on the way to independence' just as it would provide a police force or education infrastructure.[65] In public, Labour MP Kim Beazley argued in 1969 that it would be 'disastrous' for the Australian Government not to provide a defence force, as this 'would mean that if on independence Papua–New Guinea wanted an army, it would have to go through the painful process of creating one.[66]

A 'SEED BED OF NATIONALITY'?

As the commander of PNG Command, Hunter could advise on but not directly partake in the discussions of his command's future. Nonetheless, while the force's future was debated in Canberra and in the press, Hunter set about preparing his forces for a place in an independent nation, working independently and within his own resources on this 'new task' of creating a national army. The result was a force that, after 1966, emphasised some national, Papua New Guinean characteristics, through the systematic recruitment of a demographically representative force and the intensive education of Papua New Guinean soldiers. Although these initiatives were in keeping with the broader policy shifts in regard to PNG, the Australian Army instituted them independently, a feat made all the more remarkable by the lack of interest within the Administration.

Hunter was keenly aware of his force's place in PNG's future, and laid out his plan for PNG Command at the annual CGS conference in July 1967. There, he set PNG Command squarely against the background of the Territory's development, arguing that the Army was 'not immune' from the change occurring around it. In examining what kind of military should be developed in this context, Hunter did not take for granted the proposition that a PNG defence force should wholly reflect Australian structures and doctrines or the idea that the force should be decided on purely economic grounds. Instead, he believed that the future of the military in PNG depended on the strength and stability of the state it served. Given the development of a Western-style democratic government, Hunter reasoned, 'we have no choice but to seek to develop the form of army most appropriate to the desired political aim – a Western type army'. In regard to the size of the defence force, taking note of the British experience in Africa, Hunter recognised that the choice was between 'a modern army of a practicable size and diversity', which would allow any Papua New Guinean Government 'the options of reducing, maintaining or . . . increasing' the force, or 'something else, thus effectively reducing the options available'.[67] This aligned with Bland's ideas on the Australian obligation to provide the structures of state in PNG.

Hunter could only note the issues surrounding the structure and size of a future force, but he could influence the character of the troops who would compose it. He believed that the process of creating a loyal and efficient military rested on the men who comprised it, arguing that 'the three elements of the problem – developing an effective army, producing the right manpower and improving Army/community relations – have the one common factor: the Pacific Island soldier himself'.[68] By focusing on the Papua New Guinean soldier and 'working through him', Hunter, and his successor Brigadier Ralph Eldridge, hoped to create the foundations of a national army.[69] With this approach, Hunter shaped PNG Command during his time as commander into a force that was oriented towards independence, despite its position as part of the Australian Army, re-purposing policies that pre-dated public debate on PNG Command to reflect the new emphasis on independence. Hunter's ideas formed a blueprint for later Army thinking: it was here, rather than in the rush before independence a handful of years later, that the composition of the PNGDF was begun.[70]

A crucial part of forming a national army was the policy of balancing ethnicities. Although this process had begun in 1951 as a structural response to the tribal tensions first encountered during the Second World War, as noted above, the idea that a demographically representative PNG Command would encourage loyalty to the PNG nation – as opposed to *wantoks* or the PIR – was not raised until early in the 1960s. The PIR education officer, for instance, wrote in 1962 that ethnic diversity provided a strong base from which to create a sense of national identity. Given the organisation's unparalleled diversity relative to the Administration or police, he argued that 'PIR is probably the best "seed-bed" of Nationality in Papua and New Guinea'.[71]

How a demographic mix within PNG Command was to be achieved was never explicitly stated. Certainly, efforts were made in recruiting, as noted above, while at Goldie River there was a deliberate policy of mixing ethnicities within subunits, and each soldier's origin was taken into account when he was later posted.[72] However, Major Dennis Armstrong, one of the psychologists charged with managing the demography of PNG Command, reported in 1968 that while Hunter was quite emphatic in his desire for a representative force, 'actual policy on balancing or stabilizing the size of national sub groups is not completely clear'. One option was that PNG Command recruit equal numbers of men from all ethnic groups in PNG, regardless of the total size of each. The second approach was to match the proportion of each group in the Army with PNG's demography, such that some ethnic groups would be larger than others.[73] Essentially, the tension was between ensuring that no one group in the Army grew too large and making the force representative of PNG as a whole. No policy decision was articulated, but the demographic composition of PNG Command and the PNGDF shows that the second option was favoured.

The process of balancing different groups in PNG Command was made more difficult by wastage and promotion; men might be recruited in demographically proportionate numbers, yet at higher levels the balance was impossible to maintain. Consequently, PNG Command was never entirely representative. The promotion of men on the basis of merit, although fair to the men and advantageous for the Army, meant that the demographic balance between regions was not maintained after initial recruiting, and some regions were over-represented at senior NCO level. Eastern Highlands province, for instance, had only 7 per cent of the sergeants and warrant officers it should have produced if rank was apportioned on a demographic basis, while, in contrast, the Gulf region had fifteen men in this category when it should have had just four. Combined with the low numbers of Highlanders in the Army, the lower rate of promotion resulted in far fewer NCOs from this group across the Command compared with other regions. The study that compiled these results put the variation down to the level of 'Western acculturation'; those areas that had had greater contact with the Administration, and therefore higher levels of education, development and access to skills and trades, were more likely to be promoted.[74]

The idea that the PIR was 'headed for rapid de-tribalisation' as a result of the management of the force's demography, as Major Harry Bell asserted and Hunter hoped, was optimistic.[75] As discussed in previous chapters, although tribal loyalties did not play a significant role in the disturbances, they were nonetheless important to Papua New Guinean identity.[76] Soldiers retained strong links with their home region, returning there during leave and after discharge, suggesting that the Army's program of integration did not remove all *wantok* ties.[77] The informal institution of the 'lain boss' within the PIR – based on the practice of an indigenous leader within labour lines on plantations and among wartime carriers whose unofficial authority ran parallel to that of the Army – was the most important part of this undercurrent of tribal loyalties within the Army. Discussing the RPNGC, Clive Moore argues that indigenous police were able to pursue their own agendas, which were 'well disguised' from their officers, suggesting that ethnic ties and structures among Papua New Guinean soldiers might have been invisible to Australians.[78] Under the system, soldiers would defer to these men, whose authority was based not on rank but on tribal standing. One study of almost three hundred new recruits in 1973 found that 'local group loyalties do appear to exist' among Papua New Guinean soldiers, but that these were not extreme and were 'context bound', implying that not all situations within the Army were governed by such links.[79] Instead, the role played by *wantoks* was that of a support network to which a soldier might turn during a crisis, or within which particular issues considered outside everyday military tasks were decided and acted upon.[80] One Australian recalled that a soldier's *wantok* might decide 'who would take their discharge this year and who would ... be recruited this year'.[81]

Papua New Guinean soldiers had a dual sense of loyalty both to their home regions and to the Army. Brigadier Ron Lange, CO 2PIR between 1971 and 1973, argued of Papua New Guinean soldiers that 'when in uniform, they were PIR'.[82] Yet these soldiers also had close ties with their villages and language groups. The colourful tribal dance and cooking competitions that were a feature of 2PIR battalion birthdays, for instance, suggest that while regional identities were important to each soldier, they were nonetheless manageable. In this case, soldiers would group together on *wantok* lines during special occasions while happily coexisting on an integrated basis for the remainder of the year.[83] Papua New Guinean soldiers held similar views about layered nature of loyalties in PNG Command. Martin Takoin, a Papua New Guinean who enlisted in 1965, agreed that the *wantok* system was 'strong', but it was 'not [present] on duty'. Soldiers in his group at recruit training nominated one man in the group to take the lead in ensuring that recruits mixed together, while at the same time Takoin continued to see himself as a member of his own village and ethnic group.[84] Moses Kiari, a private in C Company 1PIR in 1969, agreed that while there was enmity between Highlanders and coastal men, their tasks as soldiers made cooperation vital. According to Kiari, '*wantoks* were no help in combat'.[85]

The experience of the PNGDF after independence is further evidence that *wantok* links were not in the process of dissipating during the 1960s and 1970s. Factionalism within the military in PNG increased as the funds and leadership provided by Australia dried up, and partisanship within the PNG Government saw the PNGDF neglected. According to May, a 'hint of regionalism' remained within the force in the years after independence, as the problems of wastage and demographic balance were exacerbated by a lack of resources. This does not mean that the policy of managing the ethnic balance was not successful. Even in the face of the Army leadership's involvement in politics and the various crises facing the PNGDF in the 1980s and 1990s, the incidence of ethnic tension within the PNGDF remained similar to that in the 1960s and 1970s; it was present, but did not affect the everyday management of the PNGDF.[86]

TALKING THE ARMY OUT OF A POLITICAL FUTURE

While the policy of ethnic balance addressed the composition of PNG Command, an education program laid the foundations for a force that served PNG above all else. The program was a significant commitment by the Australian Army, as by the end of the 1960s one in twelve Australian soldiers in PNG were from the Royal Australian Army Education Corps (RAAEC), making it the second largest corps there after the infantry.[87] In fact, after 1966 the Australian Army was the third largest educational institution in PNG after the state and mission schools. In the Army, education was overtly aimed at preparing for independence, as well as improving the general level of schooling among soldiers. Commenting on the scale of the education program in 1971 and in particular the civics courses taught to Papua New Guineans, O'Neill remarked that 'one cannot help but be struck by the unique experience of seeing an army striving hard to talk itself out of a political future'.[88]

Despite improvements in PNG's education system throughout the 1950s and early 1960s, and despite a consequent rise in the educational qualifications of Papua New Guinean recruits, the overall level of education within PNG Command remained low by the mid-1960s.[89] According to the Secretary of the Army, in 1961 'only a limited number of recruits [had] reached 3rd class standard education, i.e. the equivalent of a nine year old child', and many of these men remained in the ranks many years later, having received little education in the interim.[90] A significant problem was that after recruit training, soldiers received little opportunity to attend educational classes. The PNG education officer, Captain L.V. Sweeney, complained that what Papua New Guineans had learnt during training was prone to 'deteriorate into a wistful desire on the part of most students', which was compounded by 'an unwillingness on the part of most Europeans to render any assistance'. In 1963 more than three hundred Papua New Guinean soldiers still had no education at all, usually because they had enlisted before the increase in educational standards.

Sweeney pushed for general education, which he hoped would lay the foundations for a national military by creating an 'efficient fighting force' as well as establishing 'a Nation out of a hotch-potch of peoples'.[91] With the support of the CO of PIR, Lieutenant Colonel McKenzie, Sweeney proposed to the Military Board in 1963 that the number of Army educators in PNG be increased.[92] AHQ agreed to expand RAAEC presence in PNG, from three to eleven officers and warrant officers, with two more on the raising of 2PIR in 1965. However, the small size of the RAAEC necessitated an 'Australia-wide' recruitment drive to find 'the right chaps to fill some of the junior postings', but this seems to have been unsuccessful.[93] A fortuitous answer to the manpower problem was provided by the introduction of national service by the Menzies Government at the end of 1964, under which a number of trained teachers were conscripted each year. Major Henry Dachs, Sweeney's replacement as Education Officer in PNG in 1965, championed the use of national servicemen, and a team from the RAAEC examined the issue in early 1966. The first twenty-five national servicemen were sent to PNG shortly after.[94] Roger Jones, Assistant Director of Army Education between 1967 and 1969, supposed that the speed of the decision was the result of the progression of Brigadier A.L. McDonald to Deputy Chief of the General Staff (DCGS) after serving in PNG between 1965 and 1966. McDonald would have been well aware of the educational requirements of PNG Command and, as DCGS, in a position to address the issue.[95] Whatever the reason, these men arrived in time to substantially enhance Hunter's ambition to form a national army from Papua New Guinean soldiers.

Ultimately around three hundred national servicemen teachers served throughout PNG Command, alongside a number of regular education officers and NCOs.[96] In accordance with National Service provisions, these men completed their training as teachers at university or a teaching college, followed by a year of classroom experience. In addition, Army selection committees were careful to choose men who were happy to work with Papua New Guineans and accepting of other races.[97] With the arrival of these men, PNG Command had enough trained men to send teachers to every base and outstation in PNG. Between thirty and fifty National Service teachers were posted to PNG on each rotation. In 1969, for instance, around eight to ten RAAEC personnel were posted to each of the two battalions, five to Goldie River Training Depot, and seven to the new base and future officer training centre at Lae. In addition, Murray Barracks Area, in Port Moresby, received around fourteen teachers, reflecting the size of the base and its centrality to the Army in PNG.[98] The arrival of National Service teachers allowed for the ongoing education of Papua New Guineans until the end of conscription in 1972, after which the number of RAAEC personnel in PNG fell drastically, from more than fifty to just ten.[99]

By 1968 each Papua New Guinean spent a minimum of six weeks per year in classes, in addition to recruit training, and weekly lectures and discussions.[100] The curriculum was based on the Australian Army Certificate of Education (AACE) course, which had three levels soldiers could attempt, and they were placed in classes that matched their abilities.[101] Soldiers could also choose between a range of subjects, such as general science, social studies, bookkeeping, Australian and Asian history and economics.[102] Soldiers seeking promotion, however, were required to reach particular levels of education, as in Australia.[103]

Figure 5.4 2PIR soldiers with Sergeant Greg Ivey, 1969 (Greg Ivey)

In the classroom, Papua New Guinean servicemen were both students and soldiers. The fifty-minute classes of around twelve to fifteen students were not military in focus, and were taught by civilian-trained teachers.[104] Moreover, in such places as Murray Barracks, classes consisted of a diverse range of soldiers from different support or headquarters units.[105] However, students remained under military discipline in class, unlike in civilian educational institutions. One teacher remembered that 'this certainly meant a captive and co-operative audience. Each class would be marched in and sat to attention. The NCO would say "Your class, sir," and the lesson would begin.'[106] Nonetheless, Papua New Guinean soldiers were enthusiastic learners, and were cognisant of the role that education played in their future and their privileged position in PNG society.[107]

The curriculum taught to Papua New Guinean soldiers was based on Australian courses, modified to suit PNG, although former RAAEC personnel disagree as to how well adapted the courses were to Papua New Guinean students.[108] As Phillip Adam argued, a great deal depended on the skill of the teacher in communicating information across the cultural divide, and there was 'a fairly variable result in that regard', such that he believed that 'some of us were better at doing that than others'.[109] Reflecting the Army's tendency to rely on the skill of Australian officers and NCOs in getting to know the needs of their troops, rather than on developing systematic training, none of the former RAAEC personnel interviewed recall any instruction as to how to relate the course material to Papua New Guineans.

The program of general education was aimed at improving the reasoning of the average soldier, and Hunter's goal of ensuring that this was properly directed in service of a democratic government was achieved through a 'civics' program.[110] Civics classes were largely in the form of lectures and discussion classes developed by a psychologist from the University of Queensland and administered to individual units.[111] Sixty periods per year were allocated by PNG Command to civics and ethics classes, compared to 270 for general education. The civics lecturer, usually a member of the RAAEC, focused on the history of PNG and Australia, forms of government, domestic and international politics and the role of the soldier. Topics included a comparison of the democratic (Australian) and totalitarian (Chinese) systems, the United Nations and PNG's independence. The important questions facing PNG Command in the context of PNG's development were also addressed, in lectures such as 'What are the duties of a soldier-citizen?', 'Who controls the armies? Who does a soldier represent?' and 'What does the army give to the community?' The lectures were compulsory for all soldiers not engaged on official duties, and had at least one discussion period afterwards. These periods were taken by infantry officers, usually at the platoon level, and were far more relaxed than education classes, soldiers being encouraged to debate issues and ask questions of their officers.[112] Education, in particular civics, also complemented the national focus of the Army's policies of demographically representative recruiting and civic action.[113] During their education, soldiers were taught about the diversity of PNG while also having a chance to see it first hand, both in the mix of backgrounds in the barracks and on patrols around PNG. Similarly, the discussion classes as part of the civics program offered a chance for soldiers to talk through issues with Papua New Guineans from all areas of the Territory, a rare opportunity outside UPNG.

In reaching all Papua New Guinean soldiers, the general education program was a success, and PNG Command was far more highly educated than the remainder of the Papua New Guinean population. Papua New Guinean soldiers also embraced the program at the time, and all interviewed for this book fondly remembered it almost fifty years later. In creating a body of men loyal to the elected government, the effects of the education program and its civics course are harder to assess. PNG

Command certainly contributed to Hunter's goal of giving each Papua New Guinean soldier 'a firm, logical and reasoned basis for his behaviour'; given the emphasis on civics, most soldiers would have been taught, at least, of their role in civil–military relations and in an independent PNG. The Army certainly believed that education played a central role in preparing PNG Command for independence, and stressed this point in public and in its planning.[114] Moreover, in contrast to the Administration's 'half-hearted' efforts at political education, the Army civics program was far more comprehensive.[115]

Former national service teachers point to the absence of a military coup in PNG in the years after independence as evidence of the success of the education program.[116] The reality is more complex than this. As is discussed further in chapter 7, the PNGDF after 1975 was probably unable to conduct a coup successfully, given its small size, technical limitations and the nature of PNG's geography. The strength of government institutions and public opinion might have also played a role. But the PNGDF was also *unwilling* to conduct a coup, and senior officers, not least Diro and Lowa, retired early to join civilian politics, showing that, among them at least, the principle of the separation of the military and government had been internalised.[117]

The second half of the 1960s was a watershed period for the Australian Army in PNG, as the changed strategic situation and looming independence spurred discussion on the future of the force. Reflecting the long-standing civilian suspicion of Papua New Guinean soldiers, the often-heated discussion of the Army's future in PNG revolved around the potential for a Papua New Guinean defence force to threaten the stability of the nation. These public debates and bureaucratic tussling had a strong influence on the Army's activities, as they prompted a re-examination of the structure and cost of PNG Command, as well as a closer coordination between the defence group of departments and the Department of Territories. However, although the resultant reviews focused on the structure of PNG Command, it was the Army, specifically PNG Command, that changed its tasks to take into account the new context in which it operated. PNG Command's education program and attempts to maintain a diverse and representative force, in addition to the commissioning of officers and civic action, were its own initiatives. Aspects of this new task were used to answer critics, particularly the education program, yet the sheer scope of that effort, and the fact that it had its origins before the acrimonious debates that followed the end of Confrontation, suggest that the Australian Army in PNG had engaged with its position in PNG not just as part of Australia's defence but also as a forerunner to a PNG defence force.

The period between 1966 and 1970 was also the last time in which the Army in PNG would believe it had the luxury of time. From the first plan for the PNGDF in 1970, the measured and slow process of building a loyal and stable institution quickly gave way to preparations for independence in the immediate future. Commenting in 1969, just four years before self-government, Eldridge asked 'the $64 question': 'How long will we have? All that I can do is pluck at a figure and keep an open mind and be flexible.'[118] Ultimately, the Australian Army had just five years to create the PNGDF. Much of this process would rely on the work done during the late 1960s to create the basis for a 'national army'.

CHAPTER 6

THE 'BLACK HANDERS'

AUSTRALIAN SOLDIERS AND THEIR FAMILIES IN PNG

Australian soldiers who served with the Army in PNG were sometimes given the sobriquet 'black handers'. Although the origins of the term are opaque – explanations range from a reference to the Sicilian mafia, the symbols on stop signs in Port Moresby and the skin colour of Papua New Guineans – 'black hander' denoted a self-identified distinctiveness among those who were posted to PNG, as a result of the particular requirements of service there and the sense that the PIR and PNG Command were unique postings with their own challenges and rewards, both for soldiers themselves and the families that often accompanied them. There was some truth to this, particularly as after the disturbances the Australian Army in PNG sought a particular type of officer who was suited to working with Papua New Guineans, while service life in tropical PNG undoubtedly was more difficult than a posting to Sydney or Melbourne.

Perceptions of service in PNG among Australian soldiers were mixed, and depended on the time period during which a soldier was posted there. In the 1950s the Army's disregard for the PIR helped shape the perception that PNG was a backwater, and it was justifiably considered professionally and socially removed from Army life in Australia. Northern Command complained that the situation for many officers posted to PNG during the regiment's first years was 'most upsetting, particularly in an isolated unit such as PIR' as they believed that officers from the same commissioning cohort would hold lower ranks as a result of posting to

PNG.[1] Moreover, few Australian soldiers knew much about PNG and its people during the 1950s. The Territory figured little in the lives of most Australians and, as a result of a bipartisan approach within government, rarely entered the political forum.[2] Sergeant Bill Guest, sent to the PIR in 1951, recalled for instance that he 'didn't know what PIR was or what it did, and everyone else seemed as much in the dark'.[3]

These attitudes changed by the 1960s, as PNG increased in strategic importance and the PIR expanded. Brian McFarlane, who served with the PIR as a captain in 1963, was 'very grateful' for missing much of the short-lived 'pentropic' organisation experiment: 'There wasn't anything much happening in Australia at the time and I've always felt that I was very lucky to be in PNG where there were things happening and where we felt as if we were doing something useful.'[4] However, with Australia's involvement in Vietnam, such attitudes changed again. Not only did the war consume Army resources but also it attracted the attention of career-minded officers for whom a position in a combat unit was perceived as the key to advancement and, in many cases, professional satisfaction. As a result, McFarlane argued, 'When Vietnam became hot, everybody really wanted to go'.[5] Similarly, Graeme Manning, whose period of service in PNG as a major – from 1964 to 1967 – straddled the deployment of combat units to Vietnam, believed that during the Vietnam War 'PNG posting became less attractive than it had been previously'.[6] The then Lieutenant Albert Jordon was more blunt, recalling that 'we were pissed off that we were sitting in Papua New Guinea when the war was in Vietnam'.[7] Papua New Guinean officers also wished to serve in Australia's major South-East Asian war. Many, including the future chief of the PNGDF, Ted Diro, felt that they were wasting their training in peacetime PNG.[8] Although no Papua New Guineans were permitted to serve there, the length and size of Australia's commitment meant that most regular officers were sent to Vietnam at least once.[9]

For a short time after the Australian withdrawal from Vietnam in 1972, PNG service once again offered a posting where, as McFarlane believed, 'things were happening'.[10] However, with the approach of independence, PNG no longer represented a long-term career opportunity for ambitious officers. After Papua New Guinean independence in 1975, service with the PNGDF became a posting to a foreign military outside the 'normal' career path of the Australian Army. This was an opportunity for a different experience, but could also remove an individual from the Army's main foci.[11]

Overwhelmingly, Australian personnel viewed their service in PNG as professionally rewarding, a time when they were often given significant responsibilities and greater autonomy compared with service in Australia. Bruce Selleck, a platoon commander and company second in command in 1PIR from 1973 to 1975, for instance, remembered PIR as offering a 'unique command experience', arguing: 'It was a peacetime army in Australia...PNG was an overseas posting with different and varied challenges...I recall others in the main being of the same opinion.'[12] Adrian Clunies-Ross, a infantry officer, remembered that although he would much rather have been posted to a regular battalion, when he reached the PIR he realised that 'there were certain advantages in being there, and it was quite interesting'.[13] Young officers were often sent on long patrols with only a senior NCO for guidance, encouraging a level of self-sufficiency that they were unlikely to experience in Australia. Even in Vietnam, few infantry officers received such a degree of independence from higher authority.[14] Dick Flint, adjutant of the PIR from 1957, argued that the PIR was a 'great training venue for young officers who were given sometimes impossible tasks with no good maps, poor communications, no proper resupply organization'. In the event of trouble, Flint remembered, 'the man on the spot fixed it as best he could without a superior within sometimes hundreds of miles'.[15]

At more senior levels, PNG's isolation, self-sufficiency in capabilities such as training and, for a time, the tense situation on the border with Indonesia, offered significant opportunities for Australian officers to hone their skills. The tasks that the Army performed there could range from organising the patrol program and outstation rotations to search and rescue and preparing to deploy in aid to the civil power. Moreover, even after the creation of PNG Command in 1965, battalion COs had a significant degree of latitude to develop their command as they saw fit.[16] Importantly, the two PIR battalions were additional opportunities for service as a CO, given that there were only nine other battalions even at the height of the Vietnam War, and usually far fewer.

However, some officers believed that despite the professional benefits of serving there, PNG had a detrimental effect on their careers, particularly as officers without any knowledge of the PIR regarded service in PNG negatively.[17] Murray Blake felt that service in PNG was less useful professionally as the experience was not with Australian soldiers.[18] Ian Gollings, a company commander with 2PIR in 1968, argued that among those who served there, PNG was seen as a 'great joy' and a rewarding posting but to those who did not, it was seen as 'a bit of a joke'.[19] The perception that 'black handers' considered themselves aloof from other officers certainly did not help improve opinions of PNG service. After his first posting to PNG during the early 1960s, Stokes believed that one negative aspect of service there was the development of 'a sort of clubbishness amongst "black handers" which became very boring to those who didn't serve there... [M]any of us became somewhat divorced from the real world of the Australian Army.'[20] As rewarding as service there might have been, Manning felt that time spent in PNG did 'nothing for me... in the profession of arms'.[21] Similarly, Brock felt that 'service in PNG was not particularly valued' by the Australian Army, and believed that although many of the officers who served there were competent, few achieved higher rank.[22]

The poor perception of the effect of PNG service on careers, although a minority view, does accord with scholarship on the harmful professional effect of service in areas considered on the periphery of a Western military's role, such as foreign advising or secondment. David Moore and Thomas Trout have termed this the 'visibility theory of promotion', arguing that that performance 'is not sufficient to explain the promotion process'. Instead, the degree to which an officer's achievements are *visible* to authorities helps define the success of an individual's career.[23] In this way, as Morris Janowitz argues, contacts such as those built at military academies can forge successful careers as these institutions are at the centre of military life.[24] Equally, those on the periphery of the collective identities created at such military foci could, as a result, see their careers suffer.[25] Of course, the influences shaping a soldiers' professional life are varied, including education, seniority and whether a soldier has seen combat.[26] Moreover, when an officer serves in the military is of vital importance, as promotion is accelerated during times of expansion and war.[27] There were certainly advantages to certain career paths in the Australian Army; officers who had graduated from Royal Military College (RMC), Duntroon during the 1960s, for instance, were more likely to go on to higher rank than their counterparts from Officer Cadet School (OCS), Portsea.[28] Nevertheless, as will be seen, the careers of officers sent to PNG during the 1960s show that in regard to that posting at least, there were no disadvantages for the officer corps as a whole. The perception of PNG as a backwater suggests instead that the negative perceptions of the 1950s took time to dispel, and that the Army, despite its efforts there, nonetheless saw PNG Command as secondary to its other commitments, particularly Vietnam.

Selecting the 'definite type'

The posting of officers to PNG during the PIR's early years was marked by the absence of any specific selection policy. The first cohort of seven Australian soldiers sent to PNG in 1951 included just three men who had served with the PIB or NGIB, including the acting CO, Major Shields. Many of the men who were posted to the PIR during the 1950s had also seen service in PNG, although most had little direct experience of working with Papua New Guineans and could not speak Tok Pisin.[29] The first CO, Lieutenant Colonel Sabin, for instance, had no opportunity to serve in PNG, having been taken prisoner by the Japanese in Malaya during the Second World War.[30] Moreover, the quality of those men sent to serve under Sabin sometimes left something to be desired. Looking back after his term as CO, Sabin recalled that 'several Australian members were quite unsuited to the task and returned to the mainland. Others were not trained or sufficiently experienced for their posting and made the burden heavier for those who were conversant with their duties.'[31] Lieutenant Colonel N.P. Maddern, CO of the PNGVR and HQ Area Command, similarly suggested that the PIR received 'undesirables' in the form of 'those with poor service records and marital troubles'.[32] Finally, Daly, writing after the 1961 disturbance, believed that the officers sent to the PIR in the early 1950s were 'by no means the best available'.[33]

The Army's lack of concern about the quality of officers sent to PNG was matched by the inadequate trickle of men to the PIR during the early 1950s, leaving the regiment consistently undermanned. Such was the shortage that Major General Seacombe, GOC Northern Command, complained to his superiors in 1952 that 'there are only 4 effective officers out of an establishment of 14, and there are 6 WOs or NCOs deficient'. Of these, Seacombe noted that 'Lt Ward . . . had to be brought out of New Guinea, and Captain Beacroft is suspect [sic] of TB'. Seacombe lamented that it 'would appear that I have placed higher priority on the raising and training of this Unit than has been warranted, otherwise I feel that the Army Headquarters would not have allowed the present situation to occur'.[34] The hard-won lessons of other colonial armies that good officers were essential to the effective management of indigenous troops seems to have been overlooked by the Army during the 1950s.[35]

In mid-1957 the Director of Army Psychology found that although the Administration and senior Army officers agreed that careful assessment of men for posting to PNG was necessary, 'as far as can be ascertained no specific procedure has been applied to the selection of either officers or other ranks'.[36] An Army-wide officer shortage certainly contributed to this problem; however, the perception that the PIR was a simple unit that required no particular energy or skills to lead also influenced who was sent there. The decision to have warrant officers, rather than lieutenants, command platoons in the PIR was symptomatic of the belief that the PIR required instruction rather than leadership. Only in 1957, after six years of working in PNG, did Northern Command, under Daly's leadership, recognise that 'the knowledge and the responsibilities required of a platoon commander are in no way reduced by the command of native troops as opposed to Australian troops. Rather they are increased.'[37] Certainly, not all officers sent to the PIR during the 1950s were of poor quality. Some, such as CO Lieutenant Colonel Bert Wansley, would return to PNG later at higher positions. Nevertheless, the Australian Army's posting policy, such as it was, reflected a view that although the PIR was important in the defence of PNG, it was on the periphery of the Army's other activities, and hence a low priority for quality officers and men.

The two disturbances laid bare the consequences of the PIR's manning deficiencies, and forced the Army to consider the quality and quantity of the officers it sent to the unit. After the 1961 disturbance, Daly placed the blame squarely on the shoulders of inadequate Australian officers, who often did not speak the language and were clearly out of touch with their troops. Of the six 'contributing factors' Daly later put forward to explain the Army's failures, five related to the quality and training of Australian officers posted to the PIR, many of who had 'little prospect of advancement'.[38] Both the Administration and Department of the Army agreed with this assessment. As a result, the Army placed far greater store in the selection of quality officers for service in PNG. The Army was less concerned about building up a cohort of senior Australian NCOs, as 'very few of them are in executive positions' and therefore had less influence on the PIR. Daly was not suggesting that Australian NCOs did not have an important role to play but, as they were being gradually replaced by Papua New Guineans, a cohort of these men was thought unnecessary.[39]

Daly emphasised that the officers sent to PNG should be 'of a definite type' and that 'the PIR officer must not only be a good officer, he must, in addition, be capable of understanding the native mentality and in order to do this he must have some affinity towards him'.[40] In choosing the right officers for service, the Army emphasised experience with Papua New Guineans over specific training for the role, aiming instead to choose efficient, enthusiastic and self-reliant officers who would learn on the job. Coupled with appropriate experience, it was hoped that these qualities would create a body of men capable of working well with Papua New Guineans. The emphasis on individual initiative and familiarity with Papua New Guineans over training can be seen in the process by which Australian officers learnt Tok Pisin while in PNG. As Bell noted, after the debacles of 1957 and 1961, an 'increased emphasis was placed on Pidgin-speaking capacity', but it was 'the improved motivation of officers [that] produced the linguistic improvement, rather than any official Army policy'.[41] Only short and rudimentary introductory courses were offered to officers arriving in PNG; a more common approach to learning Tok Pisin was to send new arrivals on patrol with their platoon, to facilitate understanding of Papua New Guinean soldiers.[42]

Determining an individual's willingness to serve with Papua New Guineans was a crucial part of the selection process. Many soldiers were asked by Army selection boards about their views of Papua New Guineans. Although the type of questions varied, few servicemen remember the questions being subtle. Ray McCann, who served in PNG as an engineer officer, recalled feeling 'bemusement about the "innate superiority of the white man" question' during his appearance before a selection board, while Mike Dennis was asked, before his posting as a platoon commander in 1969, whether he thought 'black people had smaller brains'.[43] According to Cliff Brock, a company commander in 1PIR, such questions might have been intended to offer soldiers unwilling to serve in PNG a chance to opt out.[44] Conversely, some servicemen were also chosen because of their civilian experience in PNG or with Indigenous Australians, often as children.[45] The Army was also cognisant of the challenge of serving in an isolated and foreign environment, rating PNG alongside Antarctica with regard to difficulty of service.[46] Reflecting the unique requirements on men working with other cultures, psychological testing for PNG was also similar to that conducted with men serving with the AATTV.[47]

The demand for officers during the expansion and in the lead-up to independence made the selection process imperfect, particularly as the need for officers with specialist skills led to an influx of men without prior experience in PNG. This was especially the case at higher ranks, where there were fewer individuals from whom to choose. In non-infantry positions that did not require an officer to work closely with Papua New Guineans, such as at headquarters, or that required particular technical skills, such as signalling, compatibility with Papua New Guineans was a secondary consideration to filling a vacancy.[48] In addition, the demands of Vietnam was a significant restriction on who was sent to PNG. The most glaring example of the officer shortage was the Army's difficulty in raising the proposed third battalion of the PIR. In 1967 the Minister for the Army, Malcolm Fraser, argued that the unit had not yet been formed in part owing to the drain caused by Vietnam on manpower and the difficulty in 'providing European staff of the right calibre'.[49] Two years later, Brigadier Eldridge, Commander PNG Command, reported that as a result of Vietnam 'the standard of officers has reduced'.[50]

After the 1957 disturbance, the CO of the PIR was granted the power to send home those men who were deemed unsuitable for service in PNG, but had not otherwise failed as officers. In a sign that leadership in the PIR was beginning to be accepted as different from that in Australian units, an officer's return to Australia was considered 'no slur on the officer at all or a black mark in his book'.[51] There were other, less official, means by which an officer could be returned to the mainland, and while some officers were explicitly returned to Australia owing to their poor performance, others were quietly 'transferred', and a number of interviewees recall servicemen being sent back to Australia before their tours had been completed.[52] Without access to personnel files, the reasons for the early return of officers and men are difficult to ascertain. Often, other soldiers themselves did not know: Ross Eastgate, a Signal Corps officer in PNG Command in the early 1970s, remembered that sometimes 'people simply weren't there'.[53]

The final stage in ensuring a flow of suitable officers to PNG was returning for a second tour those men who had displayed an aptitude for working with Papua New Guineans. In a continuation of the process of returning unsuitable officers, COs could also recommend that some officers who had served time in PNG not be posted there a second time. In August 1961, for instance, four officers of eleven who had recently completed a tour of duty with the PIR were marked 'further service with PIR not recommended', although the reasons for this recommendation were not given. Clearly, however, such suggestions were subject to the requirements of the service, as at least one of the four returned to HQPNG Command as a captain two years later.[54]

The process of careful selection and management of officers for PNG service took time to implement, but was ultimately largely effective. A close examination of the careers of two cohorts of officers serving in PNG from 1960 and 1966 demonstrates that not only were selection and management policies implemented but also they created a strong group of officers equal to any in the Australian Army. The careers of each group, of thirty and fifty-three respectively, can be followed through the *Army List of Officers of the Australian Military Forces* (commonly referred to as the *Army List*).[55] As a comprehensive guide to all officers in the Army published annually during this period, the *Army Lists* contain the name, date of birth, date and place of posting, date of substantive rank, and corps of individual officers, and can be used to trace their career trajectories. The 1960 and 1966 groups of officers represent the Australian Army in PNG at two different points: before the changes brought about by the 1961 disturbance, and just after the creation of PNG Command and 2PIR, when these changes could have been expected to take effect.[56]

The extent of the Army's post-1961 policy of returning officers with experience in PNG was reflected in the growth of the number of men with prior PNG service between 1960 and 1966. In 1960, no officer then in the PIR had previously served in PNG. By 1966 at least five of fifty-three officers had prior experience in the PIR (the two COs, two majors and a captain). Considering that, of the second group, thirty-seven men were lieutenants who would not have had a prior opportunity to serve in PNG, this is a significant change. Around four or five years elapsed between the end of an officer's first tour in PNG (on average three years in duration) and his return. As a result, only one officer, Donald Ramsay, was present in both 1960 and 1966, as a major and later as CO of 2PIR. Half of the 1960 group (fifteen of thirty) had been posted back to PNG by 1968 and 1969. Included in this number was the CO of PIR in 1960, Lieutenant Colonel J. Norrie, who would return to lead the PNGDF to independence as Commander PNG Command. The proportion of officers who returned from the 1960 group was particularly high among lieutenants, of whom ten of fourteen returned. Although the 1966 group contained three future COs of the PIR (R. Lloyd, L. Lewis and R. Lange), the number that returned was proportionally far lower than the 1960 cohort: only thirteen of its men returned to the PIR before independence, usually between 1970 and 1972. By this time, there was a larger pool of officers from which authorities could chose, as well as a growing body of junior Papua New Guinean officers.

There is no evidence that officers who served in PNG in 1960 and 1966 were of different quality from those who did not. In contrast to the 1950s, the officers sent to PNG during the 1960s were typical Australian Army officers. When compared to officers who did not serve in PNG, neither the 1960 nor the 1966 officer cohorts differed in the pace with which they reached higher rank.[57] A significant number of the junior officers in the 1960 cohort would also go on to senior ranks: one would become a major general, three brigadiers and three full colonels, and twelve would be promoted to lieutenant colonel. Of the remaining twelve, two had left the Army by 1964 and another two by 1969, leaving only eight men who did not ascend to a rank higher than major. Compared with other junior officers commissioned around the same time, soldiers serving in PNG achieved slightly higher final ranks, although given the small size of the group this might not be significant.[58] Although the infrequent and incomplete production of the *Army List* after 1980 makes tracing the 1966 group more difficult, their careers seem to have followed 'normal' paths. In both groups there was little difference between the ranks achieved by those officers who returned to PNG for a second or third posting and those who did not.

An examination of the senior officers in the Australian Army after 1970 is further evidence that officers sent to PNG included high achievers. Of those who served in the PIR at junior and field ranks during the 1960s and 1970s, at least six became major generals and at least eleven became brigadiers; this number is almost certainly low, given the lack of a nominal roll for PNG Command and the difficulty in charting individual careers without access to personnel files.[59] At one stage, men with PNG experience made up a significant portion of the senior rank cohort: in 1988 three of the fourteen Australian major generals then serving had been posted to PNG. One former CO of 2PIR, Michael Jeffery, later became a major general, Deputy Chief of the General Staff, Governor of Western Australia and Governor-General of Australia. A further indicator of success is the ascension of officers with PIR experience to command of battalions of the RAR, which were, and are, prestigious and sought-after positions for infantry officers. Between 1970 and 1990, the period in which those who had served as junior and field officers in PNG could expect to reach lieutenant colonel rank, at least seventeen former PIR officers commanded a battalion of the RAR, out of a total seventy-two men, thereby making up almost a quarter of the COs in the RAR over a twenty-year period.[60] Indeed, at least one former PIR officer held a battalion command each year during this entire period. This is in addition to the six lieutenant colonels who commanded either of the two battalions of the PIR after 1970, all of whom had previous PIR experience. At the higher and more prestigious ranks of the Australian Army, therefore, those with PNG experience were well represented, suggesting that, at the very least, many of those who served in PNG were considered good officers.

Figure 6.1 Port Moresby street, 1968 (Frank Cordingley)

'IT WAS A TOUGH PLACE TO LIVE IN'

A soldier's professional life was only one aspect of living in PNG. These parts of a soldier's experience were not quarantined from his professional career; instead, the financial, social and psychological effects of living in PNG were a central aspect of the experience, alongside more military tasks such as patrolling and training. Some of these issues were mitigated by improved pay and conditions, as well as the growth of the Territory and its amenities during the 1960s and 1970s. However, the burden on families caused by isolation, the climate and foreign cultures remained a challenge throughout the period Australians were stationed there. David Butler, second in command of the PIR in 1965, recalled that he 'enjoyed every minute of it, [but] oh hell, it was a tough place to live in'.[61]

PNG, unlike many other Australian overseas postings, was deemed 'accompanied', meaning that wives and families lived with soldiers. During the post-war period, the establishment of relatively large permanent armed forces, the rise in the birth and marriage rates and the drop in the average marrying age helped change the demography of the armed services throughout the Western world, and families became the norm among servicemen down to relatively junior levels, whereas before the war they had been rare.[62] Australia was no exception.[63] The peacetime stationing of Australian forces overseas meant that for the first time, large numbers of Australian military families were posted overseas. Wives accompanied service personnel overseas *en masse* from 1947 following their husbands in the Australian contribution to the British Commonwealth Occupation Force, Japan.[64] From 1951 until independence in 1975, service wives and children were present in PNG, living on bases and in Port Moresby town. The only other substantial posting of families overseas occurred in Malaya from 1955, when families accompanied the battalion deployed with the Far East Strategic Reserve.[65] Throughout the period discussed in this book, almost all of the families of Australian servicemen overseas were divided between Malaya and PNG.[66] Although PNG was an Australian Territory, the two were considered similarly foreign; the Army believed that service there was 'more akin to serving in say Malaysia rather than . . . serving in a mainland command'.[67]

Military wives and families were therefore an important part of military life in PNG. By the mid-1960s, 51 per cent of Australian officers and 69 per cent of other ranks in PNG were married (with a total of 63 per cent across the force).[68] This was a higher percentage than in the Army at large, reflecting the almost complete absence of Australian soldiers below the rank of sergeant in PNG, which made the force more mature, more likely to contain career soldiers and more likely to be married. In 1966–67, for instance, the Army was made up of 43 548 servicemen, of whom 15 435 were married (35 per cent) and 9528 were posted overseas. More than 1400 family members lived with servicemen overseas.[69] The lack of junior enlisted personnel also explained the difference in marriage rates between officers and other ranks, as there were still a large number of junior officers, most of whom were single. Families were present at the four principal barracks in the Territory, Murray and Taurama in Port Moresby, Moem in Wewak and Igam in Lae. Soldiers serving at the two outstations, on Manus Island and at Vanimo, were unaccompanied owing to the bases' remoteness and small size.

Given the number of accompanied soldiers in PNG, any exploration of the personal lives of many soldiers is therefore inseparable from a discussion of families. Moreover, as American historian Donna Alvah argues in regard to the US military during the Cold War, wives were seen by military authorities, and the soldiers themselves, as an important auxiliary to the military's core functions. They not only supported their husbands and managed the home but also strengthened bonds between servicemen in the social sphere and acted as a conduit between the civil and military worlds.[70] Australian wives had a similar role, and were conceptualised

Figure 6.2 Moem Barracks, late 1960s. Australian and officer quarters are on the left, Papua New Guinean married quarters on the right, and the barracks themselves are in the centre (Chalkies Association)

as sources of moral and material support for their husbands. Equally, unhappy and unsupported wives were recognised as having the potential to depress morale. For instance, the Secretary for the Army argued in 1961 that the youth of many wives and their frequent separation from their husbands in 'unfamiliar and trying conditions' led to 'domestic tensions which place added stress on the serviceman'.[71]

Living in PNG was certainly challenging for soldier and spouse alike. The first and often most confronting aspect of living and working in PNG was the tropical climate: high temperatures and, in the wet season, cloying humidity and heavy rain. Indeed, the first 'blast of hot air' when stepping off the aeroplane in Port Moresby was seared into the memory of most of those who were sent there. The humidity meant that many types of food with which families had been familiar in Australia were hard to obtain, expensive and spoiled quickly. In Port Moresby, for instance, a single lettuce could cost a pound in 1958, which was almost ten times the price in Australia.[72] At Moem Barracks in Wewak, most food was delivered every six months, and stored in large freezers from which families and troops were provisioned.[73] In the tropical environment malaria and other diseases were prevalent, necessitating the weekly spraying of houses on the bases, and poisonous snakes and insects were common in gardens.[74]

The hot and humid climate, moreover, often made a mockery of a sense of decorum. Stokes remembered the problems associated with keeping uniforms tidy, writing sarcastically: 'Starching was a good idea because it didn't breathe, and after two or three applications it got stale and smelled offensively, which in turn served to ensure young officers didn't get too close to each other.'[75]

The poor quality and quantity of much of the accommodation in PNG ensured that there was often no refuge from the climate and other annoyances. A perennial shortage of married quarters in PNG meant that the period a family waited for a 'call forward' from Australia could be weeks or months. Movement was then organised and paid for by the Army, and household items, from clothing to cars, were shipped up later. As married quarters were allocated on a points system based on the number of dependants, years of service and time on a waiting list, those who were forced to find accommodation off base were predominantly younger soldiers and their wives.[76] The married quarters themselves were often shoddy, particularly during the regiment's early years.[77] The home allocated to Kathleen Holding and her husband Fred in 1952, for instance, was 'really just a kitchen, a bedroom and a sitting room alcove with walls of tarred paper and a tin roof over the top. The whole structure was raised on stilts . . . the houses were flimsy and hot.'[78]

The provision of married quarters and other accommodation was an important morale issue for the Army, not just in PNG but also throughout Australia. However, the Army had trouble persuading the government of this, given the cost of constructing them.[79] At the beginning of the 1960s, the situation was so bad that a Department of the Army report stated that the 'grave shortage of married quarters' was 'perhaps the most demoralising factor of service in this area'.[80] PNG was not alone in this: 2RAR suffered from a shortage of married quarters in Malaya in 1955.[81] Although Cabinet approved the construction of additional married quarters in 1961 and 1964, by 1967, Hunter was forced to complain that the shortage of quarters was 'aggravating and is posing a serious morale problem particularly as many of the officers and other ranks being posted to the Command have endured long separation resulting from service in South Vietnam'.[82]

For single or unaccompanied servicemen, accommodation in the first years of the PIR was also primitive, with many single soldiers living in tents.[83] Stokes remembered the single officers' quarters in 1960 as poor: 'Living conditions were such that a prisoner to-day would get a better deal . . . The ablution blocks were of algae coloured, tinea coated concrete with occasional hot water bursting forth from recently installed solar panels which were no good during the cloudy season when hot water was most needed.'[84] However, McFarlane, who arrived in PNG three years later, believed that the setting of the single officers' quarters, 'amongst prolific tropical ferns and shrubs', made for 'a pleasant scene'.[85] Similarly, national serviceman Lieutenant Ted Clark described his stay at Goldie River, during which he had his own room in a new barracks and was treated to films at night near the river, as 'like living in paradise'.[86] The pace of construction during the 1960s ensured that where there was accommodation, it was often new. These barracks were expensive at the time, but the economic problems of PNG after independence has meant that they are still in use.

Living in an isolated and undeveloped posting made pay and conditions of service in PNG contentious issues, particularly for those men who had to support a family. During the 1950s servicemen were granted allowances to compensate them for service in the Territory, with a lieutenant receiving £275 per annum on top of his base pay. This, however, was a third less than their counterparts in the Administration or the Commonwealth Public Service at that time.[87] This amount was also small when considered in the light of the potential added costs of living in PNG, such as expensive imported food, the need to send children to boarding school in Australia or to rent housing outside the barracks if no married quarters were available. Jenny Ducie, who joined her husband Ron in Port Moresby in 1961, complained about the 'paltry' wage given to young officers with families: '[T]he financial penalty for being a married Second Lieutenant with a wife unable to work were severe. As one senior officer explained "lieutenants are not meant to be married".'[88]

In keeping with the Army policy of selecting from the most appropriate personnel to be posted to PNG, pay and conditions were gradually improved throughout the 1960s. By 1968, servicemen received allowances for clothing, food, children's education and 'living out' in rental accommodation.[89] Servicemen were also given an allowance for learning Tok Pisin. Whether for professional or financial reasons, a number of Army wives also supplemented their income in PNG by working. Some women were even employed by the Army, or at the base primary school. This employment also had the added effect of linking wives and their families to the wider civilian world within the Territory.[90] However, the peculiarities of PNG could always impose a financial burden unlike that in Australia; one peculiar problem was the increasingly frequent need to entertain Australian politicians and dignitaries visiting PNG.[91]

The unique aspects of working in PNG and with Papua New Guineans could take a toll on servicemen and their families. Working with Papua New Guineans could be more demanding for Australian officers than working with Australian troops, as they had to work more closely with them, learn another language, familiarise themselves with a foreign culture, and devote weeks to patrolling the remote jungle.[92] Such were the effects of these stressors that Minister for the Army Joseph Cramer wrote in 1961 of 'a disturbing incidence of physical and nervous disorders among European members serving in the Territory. These are, without doubt, due to the abnormal stresses and pressures which stem from the exacting and demanding nature of the duties inherent in this type of service.'[93]

Life in PNG could impose a mental strain on families, just as it could for soldiers. Just being in PNG could be stressful: Anne Eastgate realised how demanding life in Port Moresby as an army wife was only when she had returned to Australia.[94] Wives were often alone, for large parts of the day and for longer periods when their husbands were on patrol or posted to a six-month outstation rotation. Scheduled radio contact between Port Moresby and the outstations was possible for wives, but anyone with a radio receiver could hear the conversation. During periods of heightened tension with Indonesia, however, radio contact was halted.[95] For the most part, this meant that women had to manage a household and care for children by themselves. With husbands constantly away, poor hospitals and family thousands of kilometres away in Australia, family illness and pregnancy could also be significant problems.[96] In addition, prolonged absences and difficult living conditions often led to domestic tensions. Occasionally this isolation could threaten a family's security. In 1956 an officer's wife awoke one morning while her husband was away on patrol to find a Papua New Guinean soldier in bed with her. She was rescued by neighbours who heard her screams.[97] Similarly, Maureen Glendenning wrote of 'having a few prowlers', and Anne Eastgate recalled having someone try to break in to her house.[98]

THE ARMY COMMUNITY

In such circumstances Australian servicemen and their families in PNG turned to a strong Army community for support, relaxation and entertainment. This community was a structured one with an unofficial hierarchy among wives based on the rank and position of the husband. At its head was the wife of the CO.[99] Diane Lewis, wife of Laurie Lewis, CO of

2PIR in 1974, believed that 'the CO's wife and the officers' wives [were] responsible for the welfare of the wives and their families'.[100] Wives were an essential part of the Army's management of family problems. For instance, after her home was flooded while her husband was on outstation duty, Lynette Horton, the 21-year-old wife of a national serviceman with the RAAEC, turned to the CO of 1PIR at Taurama Barracks. She remembered: 'I arrived at [Lieutenant Colonel Ron] Lange's office calm and collected but then burst into hysterical weeping and scared the poor man half to death. Like all good men in a crisis – he called his wife!' After being comforted by Mrs Lange, Lynette was sent home in the company of a handful of Papua New Guinean soldiers who helped her clear the house. When her husband Kevin returned from Vanimo, the pair were given a married quarter.[101]

Although the military community provided support, its small size could also be claustrophobic. Bev Hartwig, an RAN officer based at Manus Island during the 1970s, recalled that everyone had to 'get on'.[102] Among the soldiers and families in Wewak, Lae and Port Moresby, the same applied, as families lived cheek by jowl and domestic problems were readily apparent to neighbours.[103] Wives and officers took an active role in ensuring that the community was harmonious, leading 'to a situation where officers' wives were discussing the private matters of other ranks and their families'.[104] In some instances, other families could consider the CO's wife 'dictatorial'.[105] For some younger wives, the hierarchy could be stifling, particularly for those few who accompanied national servicemen. Some remembered being looked down upon by the Regular Army wives.[106] Sometimes social problems became official issues. Brian Iselin, a movement sergeant in 1969 and therefore privy to most of the departures and arrivals in the Territory, believed that some soldiers were returned to Australia as the result of extramarital affairs. Iselin argues that adultery was seen as 'both a morale and a moral issue' given the small size of the community.[107]

For soldiers, particularly those without families, the officers' and sergeants' messes were an important part of social life in PNG.[108] Brock, having been part of the mess culture of both the British and the Australian Armies, argued that even after an officer left the mess to start a family, it remained at the heart of Army life: 'It was like a home that when you married you left, but you still belonged to.'[109] After the end of prohibition in 1963, Papua New Guinean soldiers joined the mess and participated in the range of activities there, from formal dining-in nights to the end-of-day drinks at the bar.[110] However, some of the mess activities, with their origins in traditions dating back to the Napoleonic era, seemed old-fashioned and ritualistic to newcomers, particularly those without a stake in the system, such as national servicemen: one joked that mess nights were 'Monty Python-esque'.[111] Nonetheless, although some regulars were suspicious of the short-service national servicemen in the mess in PNG, particularly given that many had received quicker promotion, most were quickly integrated professionally and personally.[112] As John Kelly argued, their background 'didn't matter: they served'.[113]

Given the limited social outlets in PNG, the Army community worked hard to provide its own entertainment. The younger officers and NCOs, usually unmarried, formed social groups among men of similar rank and age, often frequenting the Port Moresby pubs in their leisure time. For more senior officers, wives played an important role in the creation of a community beyond the mess, acting as facilitators by organising social events, clubs and other activities. Indeed, such was the importance afforded Army wives that Northern Command argued in 1950 that the position of CO in the PNGVR and the PNG Military District should be held by a married officer owing to the social obligations required of him.[114] Younger men and family men could be divided by rank, age and marital status, but both groups mixed in certain social gatherings. For instance, at Christmas unaccompanied and single soldiers were divided equally between family dinners, giving them a sense of home during the holiday season.[115]

The Army community was very active, and social life 'was rather hectic'.[116] The calendar included parties, barbeques, excursions and films. There was a heavy drinking culture among soldiers and their wives, as in Australia as a whole during this period. Alcohol was available at the mess bar, and at parties most imbibed liberally.[117] Peter Murray remembered, for instance, that PNG was 'the sort of climate where men are inclined – and some women – to drink too much'.[118] Major Don Gillies complained in 1971 that 'drunkenness is rapidly becoming a major disciplinary problem'.[119] Nonetheless there does not seem to have been the same problems caused by alcohol as there were among Australian troops in Vietnam, presumably owing to the absence of the stresses of continual combat, the older average age of Australian soldiers in PNG, the presence of families, and being under the aegis of Australian laws.[120]

Like countless soldiers before them, servicemen in PNG took advantage of their overseas posting to 'see the world'. Around Port Moresby, soldiers and their families visited the coastal village of Hanuabada, built on stilts north-west of the town, and travelled to the foothills of the Owen

Stanley Range. In Wewak, one young national serviceman and his fellow sergeants went 'on weekends ... to town, to the villages and wherever the roads would take you. Several times we would arrive unannounced at a village.' Exploring relics of the Second World War was also popular, particularly as some training exercises traced the course of wartime engagements.[121] In 1966 a member of the RAAEC, Warrant Officer Dan Winkel, organised tours around the Territory using DC3s rented from Trans Australia Airlines and flown by pilots of the RAAF. These flights were initially organised for national servicemen, but were open to all members of the Army.[122] These trips visited most parts of PNG, including the famous Goroka Show in the Highlands and battle sites of the Second World War. For many soldiers, particularly national servicemen, such outings were remembered as the highlight of their postings.[123]

Sport was also an important part of Army life in the Territory. One sergeant recalled that he 'got out through sport', using the field as a way to escape the frustrations of Army life.[124] The Australian Army, in turn, saw sport as 'an integral part of military training and complementary to the general programme of physical fitness training'.[125] By the mid-1960s every Wednesday afternoon was devoted to sport, and Army teams played in local competitions. Teams were mixed race by the late 1960s, and it was not unusual to have only one or two Australians in a team otherwise entirely composed of Papua New Guineans.[126] Officers and men were similarly mixed within sporting teams, the idea being that rank was left on the sidelines. Some soldiers complained, however, that senior officers took sport too seriously, and that a soldier's sporting prowess might be taken into account during the posting process.[127]

Sport was also seen as a way to foster links with the civilian community. The Boroko Hash, for instance, drew on the long tradition of the Hash House Harriers, a running group that originated in colonial Malaya. This included a strong social element; some joked that the event was simply 'an excuse for a drink'.[128] Other Papua New Guinean and Australian wives entered the Port Moresby netball competition, which was organised by the Army Wives Club. The competition reflected the nature of the Army community, as the impetus came from Australian wives while the Army supported it with free transport and facilities.[129] Other Australians preferred to wager on sport. A keen follower of horse-racing, Chaplain Ray Quirk recalled how he ran bets among Australian soldiers exercising on the Kokoda Trail in 1963, noting the incongruity of finding 'slips with two bob each way bets in strange places' along the trail, when forward elements of the PIR left their bets for those following behind.[130]

Figure 6.3 An Army rugby team, 1968 (Australian Army Infantry Museum)

'OF THE SAME COMMUNITY, BUT NOT OF THE SAME FAMILY'

It is axiomatic that interaction with Papua New Guineans was a unique feature of service in PNG. On mainland Australia, the Army was over-whelmingly European in origin, and the military families living on and around the country's military bases were overwhelmingly Anglo-Australian.[131] In Malaya, from 1955, Australian military families lived and worked among a foreign culture and people, and Australian troops cooperated and occasionally socialised with Malays, but not as part of the same organisation. Only in PNG, after the racial barriers were dismantled during the early 1960s, did Australians serve with large numbers of non-Europeans regularly, and have the opportunity to socialise with them. This was an evolving relationship. Army wife Diane Lewis recalled that, during her first posting in 1955, association with Papua New Guineans 'just wasn't thought of', but by 1974, 'as women and kids, we would all mix, just as you would anywhere'.[132] However, for all the social, non-professional relationship between Papua New Guineans and Australians, the two groups were still not completely integrated. In the words of Bert Wansley, they were 'members of the same community, but not of the same family'.[133]

Structural factors, particularly rank and pay, helped limit the social interaction between Australian and Papua New Guineans. As platoon commander Lieutenant Peter McDougall recalled, 'Professionally my relationship was that of "masta" (Platoon Commander) with my NCOs and soldiers. We did not mix socially apart from special occasions.'[134] As Australians were always given the rank of sergeant or above, this precluded almost all informal social interactions with Papua New Guineans below that rank, which the Army enforced. RAAEC Sergeant Phil Adam, for instance, recalled being admonished by regular soldiers for visiting the other ranks' mess.[135] There were exceptions, but relations between Australians and Papua New Guineans could also have an element of paternalism. Stokes recalled that as a lieutenant, when prohibition for Papua New Guineans ended in 1963, 'us younger officers were quick to take some of the younger native Sgts and Cpls in hand and take them into the lounge of the top pub where we could keep an eye on them'. Nonetheless, he pointed out that 'the race segregation [in PNG] was nothing like what I had to experience in the southern states of the USA a year later [on exchange with the US Army]'.[136]

Australian dominance of the relationship could be stifling for Papua New Guineans. In the mid-1960s, one battalion CO took it upon himself to decide what were appropriate living standards for the wife of a young Papua New Guinean officer, who was moved from accommodation in Wewak to lodgings in the base with another family, so as to better reflect what he considered the proper place of an Army wife.[137] Families of Papua New Guinean other ranks accommodated on base were subject to equally restrictive direction by Australian authorities, such as house inspections to ensure that quarters were kept clean. Papua New Guinean Thomas Posi, after moving into married quarters with his wife at Goldie River in 1966, saw this as an unfair imposition on civilian wives, who were forced to live 'under pressure [of] military rules'.[138] Similarly, Australians dominated the Army Wives Club in PNG. Contact between Australian wives and those of enlisted men was encouraged through the club, usually run by the wife of the Australian CO at each base, which encouraged 'both expatriate and indigenous wives to meet and learn about each other's cultures'.[139] The Wives Club met weekly to 'assist local indigenous women adapt to the rapidly changing society into which they were moving . . . [H]ealth hygiene, nutrition, budgeting, sewing were all subjects taught and

discussed.'[140] The Wives Club was part of a network of similar organisations catering for the wives of police, missionaries and plantation workers,
but often served to reinforce traditional women's roles as homemakers
and childbearers.[141]

The gulf between Australians and Papua New Guineans was evident
when Stephanie Lloyd, wife of company commander and later CO 2PIR,
Major R. Lloyd, organised a season of basketball among Australian and
Papua New Guinean military wives in the mid-1960s. This team played
other women's teams around Port Moresby and also provided umpires
for games. Only when a number of Papua New Guinean wives sat down
to take the umpires' exam did it occur to Lloyd that some of the women
could neither read nor write. Instead, they had been coached by those
Papua New Guinean women who were literate, and completed the exam
by whispering their answers to the examiner, who then wrote them down.
In another instance, the whole team was invited to an end-of-season lunch
at Government House with Lady Cleland, wife of the Administrator and
patron of women's basketball in the Territory. Lloyd recalled that despite
'explaining to our players how special it would be – the big house, the
beautiful gardens, the delicious feast', none of the wives were ready when
the truck arrived to take them to the party: 'Some were gardening, or
lazily boiling clothes in outside coppers. No one was smiling, [or] waiting
in excitement as we expected.' The wives were persuaded to attend, after
'lots of cajoling', but remained 'silent and sultry' at the bottom of the
gardens of Government House. Eventually, the situation was explained
to Lady Cleland, who sent lunch down to the Papua New Guinean women
while 'the others' – presumably the European wives – ate in the 'big house'.
According to Lloyd, this episode 'was just another of the unpredictable
turn of events in our close involvement with Pacific Islander wives'.[142] At
the very least they revealed a lack of understanding of these women, and
spoke to the depth of the (often unrecognised) gulf between Australian
and Papua New Guinean.

Different scales of pay and conditions helped to cement the distance
between families in PNG, as Papua New Guineans could not afford to
maintain the same lifestyle as their Australian counterparts.[143] Discussing
the hospital needs of the expanded PNG Command, Brigadier A.L. Mac-
Donald noted that as the Army was 'not obliged to pay for the hos-
pitalisation of dependants', the decision of which of the two types of
ward in Port Moresby a member of a military family would enter if they
fell ill 'would be a matter of choice and financial capacity'. Essentially,
MacDonald argued, this would result in European dependants using the

better equipped, 'intermediate wards', 'while non-European dependants would, in general, select the public wards'.[144] As in the civilian community, Australian and Papua New Guinean family accommodation was separated, living on different areas of the base. Papua New Guinean quarters were also different, usually being smaller, with kitchen and toilet facilities shared among a group of families.[145] Papua New Guinean officers, however, were granted the same married quarters as Australians, in the same area.[146]

Service in PNG also saw Australian soldiers interact on an everyday basis with civilian Papua New Guineans. Even enlisted soldiers could employ a 'wash iron boy' to take care of the laundry.[147] For those in married quarters, a 'haus boi' or 'haus meri' lived in a small room at the back of the property. They slept on a rough bed, and their employers were not required to provide food. Some Australians felt uncomfortable about the low pay given to servants, but were told not to 'rock the boat' by others who had been in the Territory longer.[148] Despite their position, the pay was far higher for Papua New Guineans than they might receive elsewhere. Moreover, Papua New Guineans could also become quite close to their families, and strong friendships could form. Children were also conduits of contact between Australian families and Papua New Guineans. Within Taurama Barracks, children attended the same primary school by the end of the 1960s, and came to know each other well.[149] Brian Iselin's four-year-old 'was better than both [parents at speaking Tok Pisin] as he mixed with the garden boy and house boy. We often found him squatting up at the house boi's hut discussing the world's issues!'[150] Indeed, Don Gillies remembers that by the end of his posting to PNG his 'kids spoke like locals', but Francis Tilbrook worried that his children were 'starting to go a bit native', given the amount of time they spent with Papua New Guinean children on base.[151]

As another indication of the relationship, sexual encounters between Australian servicemen and Papua New Guinean women appear to have been uncommon, although there are few archival and oral sources on this delicate subject. Prostitution was illegal in PNG for the period of colonial rule, as it was throughout Australia until the end of the twentieth century, although this did not necessarily preclude the practice.[152] Like their fellow soldiers in Vietnam, there is evidence that Australian servicemen visited brothels in PNG. One Australian engineer was reported by the provost detachment in Lae for visiting a Chinese club and a euphemistically termed 'private house', necessitating a 'short arm inspection' upon return to Port Moresby.[153] Winkel also reported that Australians visited

Figure 6.4 Taurama Primary School children, c. 1970 (Chalkies Association)

a brothel named Madame Phu's in Port Moresby.[154] Nonetheless, given that PNG was under Australian law, the number of visits to brothels in PNG was probably far lower than in Vietnam, and the very few cases of sexually transmitted infections in PNG during the late 1960s supports this contention.[155] Moreover, national serviceman Norm Hunter believed that talk of prostitutes in Hanuabada village in Port Moresby was 'as much legend as reality'.[156]

Romantic relationships between Australian soldiers and Papua New Guineans also seem to have been rare. Before 1962 sexual relationships between Australians and Papua New Guineans – of both sexes – were illegal.[157] Even after these laws were repealed, the Australian community still frowned upon such unions.[158] Indeed, throughout the 1950s and into the 1960s, the three Australian services actively discouraged their servicemen from marrying non-European women.[159] In a policy approved by the Minister for Defence as late as 1966, the difficulties of marrying an 'alien' were to be emphasised to soldiers hoping to marry, and although there was no legal barrier to marriage, 'the fact that Asian marriages are permissible should not be made known'.[160] Australians and Papua New Guineans could work together, but for them to live together was too much for the Australian Army of the 1960s.

The social and professional experiences of Australians who served in PNG reflect the Australian Army's perception of units in PNG and the Papua New Guineans who composed them. Although some soldiers saw PNG as a backwater, the fact that those men who were sent to PNG were of the same high quality as those posted elsewhere demonstrates the increasing integration of PNG Command into the Army's order of battle during the 1960s. Moreover, the success of the officer selection process shows that the Australian Army had internalised the need for quality officers after the disturbances. Equally, the distance between Australians and Papua New Guineans within the Army, and their perception as foreigners, is more readily evident in their social relationships. Papua New Guineans and Australians certainly did mix but, as Bert Wansley pointed out, they were never considered wholly integrated or equal. During the 1960s and early 1970s Australian servicemen and their families, unlike any other period before or since, lived and worked alongside a large number of people from a foreign culture, in the same organisation. However, although Australian families looked to each other for support while isolated in PNG, Papua New Guineans were only on the fringe of this community.

CHAPTER 7

'A DIFFERENT WORLD'

THE RUSH TO INDEPENDENCE,
1970–75

When Papua New Guinean Brigadier Ted Diro took command of the PNGDF on 17 September 1975, a day after independence, he found the young force 'like a different world'.[1] The organisation he led – the world's newest defence force – was based on the two battalions of the PIR, supported by air and naval elements, and administrative and logistics troops. As with Diro himself, who had been commissioned at OCS in 1963, had served as an Australian officer and had only recently relinquished control of 1PIR, the colonial legacy and the Australian Army's long experience in PNG was plain to see in the structure and role of the PNGDF, as was the Australian-led process of decolonisation.

Although having 'attempted to stand against the tide of rapid decolonisation' in the Pacific throughout the previous decade, the Australian Government ended its colonial rule in PNG hastily.[2] After 1972 Papua New Guineans became increasingly involved in deciding the direction their country would take after independence, but Australia alone defined how and when it quit PNG.[3] During the period 1970 to 1975 the gradualism that had for so long shaped the policy of the Australian Government towards PNG, evident in the paternalism of Minister for Territories Paul Hasluck and the measured economic growth championed by his successor Charles Barnes, was done away with. In the place of these policies came a pragmatic and focused program of decolonisation, the object of which was viable independence in the short term above all else.[4]

Figure 7.1 Colonel Ted Diro (left) hands over 1PIR to Lieutenant Colonel Ken Noga, 1975 (Sinclair, *To Find a Path*)

By 1970 the Australian Government under Liberal Prime Minister John Gorton had accepted that independence in the short term could not be avoided.[5] The government's change in attitude towards PNG was in part the result of a break by the Labor Opposition Leader, Gough Whitlam, from the decades-long bipartisan support for PNG's gradual development as a precondition for self-government or independence. Whitlam's agitation, combined with domestic and international pressures, helped make independence a fact, with only the form to be decided.[6] As a result, when the Labor Party was elected in December 1972, PNG's path towards independence was largely set, although Whitlam did accelerate the process.[7] The Gorton Government laid out plans for the transfer of power to a self-governing PNG in 1971, but the progression to independence was made possible by the Papua New Guinean elections of April 1972, which saw election of a coalition led by Michael Somare.[8]

However, even shortly before independence, attitudes outside the Australian Government towards this watershed event were mixed. Domestically, most Australians remained largely indifferent to PNG affairs. Among those interested Australians polled in 1971, a large proportion felt that independence should come after five years at the minimum, given PNG's limited development.[9] Some Papua New Guinean politicians, particularly in the Pangu Party led by Michael Somare, pushed for speedy self-government and greater Papua New Guinean control over government functions.[10] In contrast, other Papua New Guineans, particularly in the Highlands, hoped for a continuing relationship with Australia.[11] Regardless of the range of opinions about independence in the first years of the 1970s, few in Australia or PNG thought independence would come as quickly as it did.[12]

The Whitlam Government's policy of immediate independence fit neatly with that of the Somare Government and helped drive the pace of decolonisation.[13] Government functions were incrementally delegated to PNG from 1972, although Australia retained oversight through the Administrator and reserved responsibility for foreign affairs and defence until March 1975.[14] Although slowed by protracted discussions over the constitution, independence came on 16 September 1975, eleven years after the first elections in PNG, and just three years after self-government. Throughout this period, Australians dominated the decolonisation process, forming policy overwhelmingly without direct Papua New Guinean input before the election of the first PNG Government in 1972. Only for the last three years before independence were Papua New Guinean politicians, public servants and ordinary citizens invited to participate.[15] Australians set the tone, too. Nelson, present at UPNG during this time, captured the irony of the situation in that the colonial power, not the subject people, were more likely to 'make effective use of suppressive, racist colonialism to justify their own withdrawal'.[16]

As independence approached, Australian and Papua New Guinean authorities sought to place PNG in the context of the wider decolonised world, and investigated the experiences of new nations, particularly in Africa.[17] During the 1970s, for instance, the Australian Government asked for advice from the United Kingdom in transferring defence powers.[18] Similarly, Papua New Guinean members of the PNG House of Assembly sent some of their number on a study tour of former British colonies.[19] Some attempt was made by the Defence Department to draw on the experience of constructing independent military forces in decolonising countries, but a lack of available information meant that little came of this initiative. The department's long experience in PNG and of its defence also no doubt played a role in persuading it that it had the information it needed.[20]

Parallel to political considerations, the diminished strategic importance of PNG relative to the early years of the Cold War played an important role in bringing about independence. The Australian disengagement from the Vietnam War and the abandonment of the associated policy of 'Forward Defence' in favour of what would eventually be termed 'Defence of Australia' changed Australia's views of PNG.[21] The reach of modern weapons lessened PNG's utility as either a barrier or a base for operations, while the Australian Government increasingly wished to distance itself from the overseas deployments that had characterised the defence policies of the 1950s and 1960s.[22] These changes were clearly and unequivocally laid out in the 1973 Strategic Basis Paper, which abandoned the long-held belief in PNG's strategic importance, instead conceptualising it simply as an area of 'abiding' but not 'vital' interest.[23] Although Australian planners agreed that it was desirable to ensure that the new nation remain friendly and free from the influence of hostile forces, the possibility of PNG being invaded or subverted was no longer the existential threat it had been considered to be during the Second World War or the first decades of the Cold War. Consequently, Australia was willing to relinquish control over what had only a few years previously been considered a key pillar in its defence and a likely third theatre of conflict after Vietnam and Malaysia.[24]

The possibility of instability of PNG was yet another factor in the haste with which Australia pursued decolonisation. Tribal violence was on the rise in the Highlands, while in Port Moresby and other urban centres the crime rate was growing.[25] Secession and protest movements in New Britain and Bougainville, discussed further below, also worried an Australian Government placed in an awkward position as it strove to ensure PNG's security at independence while also attempting to avoid incurring political and financial costs as it did so.[26] Whitlam's Defence Minister, Lance Barnard, for instance, stressed to Papua New Guinean ministers 'the difficulty for Australia, both locally and internationally, should Australian Servicemen become involved in internal security situations'.[27] In Nelson's words, the involvement of Australian personnel, particularly soldiers, in quelling Papua New Guinean violence 'would have resulted in a wave or public revulsion within Australia and opprobrium across the globe'.[28]

Although there had been some Papua New Guinean voices in the debate over the Army in the late 1960s, Papua New Guinean politicians became officially involved in discussions on defence only from 1972 with the election of a Papua New Guinean government, when Australia encouraged the appointment of a defence spokesman. Michael Somare, leader of the Pangu Party, initially took the position himself, handing over to Albert Kiki the following year.[29] Kiki's appointment was somewhat ironic, given his intimate involvement in the PIR disturbance of 1957 and his prior criticism of the Army. By 1974 Papua New Guinean political and public service representatives were involved in consultations on the nature of the defence force, while Papua New Guinean officers were also involved in planning for the PNGDF.[30] The purpose of such involvement was twofold: to garner Papua New Guinean views, and foster a familiarity with the particular issues and challenges of defence.[31] Nonetheless there was some anger among Papua New Guinean civilians participating in this process, who believed that they had lacked an authoritative voice in the defence discussions up to 1972.[32] Coupled with the culture of antipathy between the Administration and the Army in PNG, the absence of Papua New Guineans from the planning process before 1972 occasioned a limited pool of knowledge regarding the military among Papua New Guinean civilians, for which blame can be shared between all Australian departments, civilian and military.[33]

For their part, the Army and the two other services fell in line with government-set timetables as they were implemented and changed throughout the short progression to independence during the 1970s. There was no one moment during which the Army was told to prepare for independence. Rather, it had been doing so gradually for a decade, creating new policies and adapting old ones, such as in education, as the discussion of PNG's independence gathered momentum. The decision to halt the expansion and plan for a defence force was taken during the 1960s, for instance, before a timetable for independence had been set. Even by the 1970s, the timetable remained vague, and in 1971 both the Minister and the Secretary of Defence believed that the absolute earliest independence would arrive was 1976.[34] The Army, like all other areas of the Australian Government concerned with PNG, had to be somewhat flexible in its planning.

INTERNAL SECURITY: 'NOBODY COMES OUT SMELLING LIKE ROSES'

In contrast to much of the colonial experience in Africa, the military in PNG became closely involved with internal security only as independence approached, having never been used as an instrument of colonial control.[35] Surprisingly, given the long-standing suspicion of the military within the Administration and Department of External Territories, it was civilians who were the most vocal exponents of the Army's involvement in internal security, whereas the Army was deeply troubled by the possibility of soldiers being used to quell domestic unrest. Two crises in particular, on Bougainville and New Britain, worried the Administration and the Australian Government sufficiently to investigate the use of PNG Command to support the police, a practice then known as 'aid to the civil power'. On Bougainville in 1969, the need to requisition land for a township and port facilities for the as yet unbuilt copper mine at the centre of the island caused anger among Bougainvilleans, who felt they had been neither consulted about nor fairly compensated for the use of their land. Locals clashed with police in August when they attempted to halt building work. The tension on the island attracted a great deal of press coverage, and the Australian Government considered, but did not approve, the use of the PIR to support the police.[36] The situation calmed enough for Army involvement not to be necessary, but tensions continued to simmer after independence, culminating in a protracted, complex and deeply divisive conflict during the 1980s and 1990s.

Shortly after the first clashes on Bougainville, the Administration was faced with unexpected trouble in New Britain among the local Tolai people. A political group known as the Mataungan Association (meaning 'alert' or 'watchful'), embarked on an anti-government campaign sparked by a combination of lingering anger over land title disputes and dissatisfaction with the operation and composition of the Rabaul council, which had had its area of control expanded.[37] Crowds of Tolais organised by the Mataungans staged protests in September 1969, which were confronted by a thousand police flown to New Britain from around PNG after local officers proved unable to quell the unrest. Their arrival brought the situation under control and enabled arrests, trials and a commission of inquiry. However, violence flared up again in December, culminating in an attack on Administrator David Hay and other officials during a visit to the troubled province. Hay feared that protests could escalate into widespread violence, and requested that soldiers be made available to aid police if the situation deteriorated.[38]

In response to these events, the Defence Committee urged caution and stressed that the deployment of troops should be the government's last resort.[39] Minister for Defence Malcolm Fraser considered the issue to be serious and was reluctant to support any call-out before the legal aspects of such a move were completely clear and the matter had gone before Cabinet. However, he was overruled by other members of the government.[40] On 19 July 1970 the Governor-General, the ubiquitous Paul Hasluck, was directed to sign an Order-in-Council granting the Administrator the power to call out the three services in PNG if the police lost control or looked to be close to doing so. Approval from the relevant ministers was required, but the Administrator could issue a call-out without reference to Canberra and seek approval later if the situation seemed dire.[41] In the event, troops were not deployed, as police eventually controlled the situation on New Britain. However, the use of the Army was considered highly likely throughout the period of the crisis; soldiers of 1PIR were at one point issued orders to proceed to the island, and were told to stand down only as they were about to board trucks to take them to waiting aircraft at Port Moresby airport. The Order-in-Council was retained in case violence resumed, but was ultimately rescinded ten months after it was signed.[42]

As it had little experience in aid to the civil power, the Australian Army was thrust into an unfamiliar role by the unrest in 1969 and 1970. Even as internal security operations were mooted as a possibility by the late 1960s, the Army refrained from preparing for aid to the civil power.[43] It was only after the Bougainville protests that Eldridge, as Commander PNG Command, took it on himself to begin training for internal security, some months before an official instruction from Canberra to do so.[44] No Australian manual or doctrine existed for aid to the civil power, and PNG Command was instructed to use the British manual *Keeping the Peace* as the basis for training.[45] However, there was still some confusion about the role soldiers could play, and whether they were required to use only their normal arms – their rifles and bayonets – rather than police riot gear, and this delayed training with the police.[46] The PIR had completed basic aid to the civil power training only around the time of the New Britain crisis; however, by June 1971 the situation had improved, and troops had been trained in legal issues, cordoning, the treatment of civilians, the use of gas masks, and crowd dispersal.[47]

The doctrine for aid to the civil power called for minimum necessary force. After the Governor-General had issued a call-out, the military would deploy forces to trouble areas alongside police. A magistrate would accompany soldiers and give final permission for action if he believed that the police were unable to contain the situation.[48] The magistrate's presence provided a second layer of civilian control, as well as an additional legal safeguard for the soldiers. Once given permission to act, the officer in charge would again order the crowd to disperse. If this failed, the same officer would order a single soldier, identified by number to conceal his identity, to shoot at a selected ringleader, identifying the target and the number of rounds to be fired. No indication was given in *Keeping the Peace* of whether this was specifically to kill, but officers were told that 'fire must be effective'. This action would be repeated until the crowd had dispersed.[49] One former PIR officer bluntly stated that a soldier's role in civil unrest 'was to shoot and kill people – end of story'.[50] The use of deadly force rather than a show of force, such as firing over the heads of protestors, was seen as a sharp but controlled response consistent with the idea of the military as a last resort: violent, but final. It also was intended to ensure that soldiers, not trained in police work, were employed under an officer, in a controlled situation and according to their existing skills and equipment. Aid to the civil power doctrine, and the Australian Army's understanding of its role, called for soldiers to act as the state's last resort, figuratively and literally standing behind the police with overwhelming force, should unrest prove beyond the control of civilian authorities.

Although the Army's own doctrine was clear, there was confusion concerning the legal standing of soldiers involved in internal security.[51] There were no legal provisions for the military to be involved in the regulation of civilians, such as arrest, cordon and search, or roadblocks, as these were police tasks.[52] More importantly, an Interdepartmental Committee on the internal security issue found that 'the present legal rights of a soldier are no more than those of a private citizen. Therefore if a soldier takes action involving the use of force, he could be liable for action in the civil courts', a situation that understandably worried the Army.[53] Indeed, the position of soldiers in aid to the civil power operations was clarified only in the early 2000s.[54]

Despite being later presented as keen for the role, the Australian defence community, from the minister to junior Army officers, were extremely reluctant during the 1970s to become involved in internal security tasks.[55] Wilton and Daly, the Chairman, Chiefs of Staff Committee and CGS respectively, expressed deep reservation about using the Army in internal security situations. Fraser and senior members of the Department of Defence shared these views.[56] Similarly, Brigadier Eldridge was adamant that the PIR should be used only in the direst of circumstances and that it should act with the absolute minimum of force.[57] Peter Stokes, OC Administration Company of 1PIR at the time of violence in New Britain, remembered that Eldridge instructed his officers that, if deployed, the PIR was 'to be absolutely confined to key point security with extremely rigid rules of engagement which almost amounted to "surrender if you have to but don't shoot anyone"'.[58] When ordered to stand down shortly before they were due to travel to the airport to board aircraft to New Britain, many Australian officers expressed relief that they would not be put in what they saw as a situation from which few would emerge untarnished. Colonel Ron Lange, CO of 1PIR at the time, likened aid to the civil power to cleaning a sewer: it was a job that had to be done, and done professionally, 'but nobody comes out smelling like roses'.[59]

Papua New Guinean soldiers held more varied views on their involvement in internal security.[60] For some, the opportunity to be deployed represented a change from training, and the possibility of 'active' service was met with interest.[61] Others recognised that the situation was a complex one, and regarded it in the same way as Lange: as an unpleasant task that they were nonetheless required to perform as professional soldiers.[62] However, there was concern among both Australian and Papua New Guinean soldiers that involvement in aid to the civil power could erode the strong and relatively uncontroversial relationship the Army had with the Papua New Guinean public. Civilian views in PNG were also mixed and, as the Defence Committee pointed out, public opinion was dictated by the seriousness of the situation and the type of force used, rather than the use of the Army *per se*.[63]

The origins of the New Britain and Bougainville protests in regional, rather than national identification and the potential for PIR involvement also raised concerns about the reliability of PNG soldiers. In particular, some in the Army and the Administration feared that the hundred or so Bougainvillean soldiers in PNG Command might not obey orders in the event of a deployment of the PIR on aid to the civil power operations there, and some advocated leaving them behind.[64] However, although the performance of Papua New Guinean soldiers was not tested in an internal security situation, it is doubtful whether they would have shirked their duty in the heat of the moment. Soldiers had rarely disobeyed orders *en masse* while on exercises or patrols. As noted in previous chapters, those instances where soldiers had challenged military authority, such as during the disturbances, were the result of a specific set of grievances, usually pay and conditions, which the soldiers saw as being outside their normal duties. Moreover, the diversity of Papua New Guineans in the Army precluded support for the Mataungan Association or protesters in Bougainville spreading throughout the military.

The Army was also proactive in addressing any possible disaffection, and officers met Bougainvillean soldiers and arranged talks by Administration officials. In September 1969 four Bougainvillean soldiers were sent to tour the island and report back to their fellows, suggesting an internalisation of the lessons of the disturbances, in particular the need for the Army to explain a given situation clearly to the soldiers to forestall trouble.[65] The Australian Army understood that while links with family and community were important enough to necessitate a trip home for some Bougainvillean soldiers, they were malleable enough to allow soldiers to act professionally in the interests of the Army. In this case, the Army accepted and worked with the soldiers' links to their home, using them to defuse the situation.

DEFINING THE PNGDF'S ROLE

The role the PNGDF would play in an independent PNG was decided by Papua New Guineans, as part of the creation of a national constitution. From 1972 this fell under the purview of the Constitutional Planning Committee (CPC), a body composed of members of the new parliament and other nominated Papua New Guineans. The CPC's powers were extensive and, as Downs notes, 'almost overnight the CPC came on the scene as a third party to the talks taking place between the Somare Government and the Australian Minister for External Territories'.[66] Its discussions were shaped by the limited time before independence, which compelled the constitutional role of the defence forces to fit with their existing capabilities and size. For instance, the CPC could not realistically recommend that PNG dispense with a defence force, or that it be combined with the police, as this would necessitate substantial structural changes. At the same time, the suspicion of armed forces that had been present among members of the Administration and public were plainly evident in the CPC's deliberations on the PNGDF.

The absence of any direct threat after the end of Confrontation made the PNGDF more difficult to justify, as the force seemed to be without a clear purpose. To critics, the proposed defence force was too small to resist or deter a full-scale conventional threat should one materialise, while at the same time large enough to be an expensive burden on the PNG state.[67] In a 1974 address to the House of Assembly as defence spokesman, Kiki neatly encapsulated the problem with this argument, pointing out that while the idea of external defence 'still conjures up in many people's minds the kind of major invasions which this country experienced in World War II', outright invasion was not the only threat, and as a result could not form the sole basis for PNG Government thinking.[68] Rather, as the Confrontation experience had demonstrated and as the Australian Army was acutely aware, the intricacies of international relations could create a situation in which small-scale incursions occurred for the purposes of diplomatic posturing. In 1966, for instance, Australian troops were engaged in combat operations against Indonesian soldiers in Borneo while Australian diplomats worked in peacetime Jakarta.

Planners in Australia and PNG considered a capable defence force to be 'valuable insurance' for the range of possible threats short of outright invasion, and a means through which PNG could demonstrate its willingness to defend itself and its interests.[69] The idea that leaving PNG without a defence force would place too great a burden on the new nation if it ever needed a military in an emergency also seems to have been a consideration.[70] According to Kiki and the government he represented, PNG accepted the need to 'deter possibilities of small-scale infringements of our sovereignty which could disturb the peaceful lives of our people or involve external pressures on the country to abandon the pursuit of its national aims and interests'. The Somare Government was also keen to ensure that PNG had an alternative to relying on Australia or some other power to deter or defeat even a small incursion, making the defence force both a symbol of a modern state and a means by which to secure PNG's new independence.[71] Conversely, fostering the PNGDF also served Australian interests, as it tied PNG closely to Australia while also encouraging PNG 'towards self-reliance and to political and administrative solutions of its difficulties'.[72]

More contentious was the issue of the PNGDF's role in internal security after independence. Given how close the Administration had come to deploying the PIR to New Britain, and considering the likelihood of continued violence, protest and crime, both Australian and Papua New Guinean authorities believed that the PNGDF should act as a force of last resort should the police prove unable to contain a crisis. However, any involvement of the PNGDF in internal security fed into ongoing fears that it might assume a political role after independence. To this end the CPC was adamant that the PNGDF become involved in internal security only in the direst of situations.[73] For their part, the Army and Department of Defence maintained their aversion to being involved in internal security. However, again illustrating the disconnect between civilian and Defence views of the military, External Territories complained that the Army envisaged a 'more restricted participation in [internal security] roles than considered desirable'.[74]

The possibility that the PNGDF might mount a coup, or otherwise disrupt PNG's fledgling nationhood, worried the CPC.[75] In its discussion of 'disciplined forces', the CPC explicitly placed the PNGDF against the large number of coups around the world in the preceding decade. Given what it saw as the frequency of military coups in newly decolonised nations, the committee believed that 'it would be folly to ignore entirely experience elsewhere' and that 'we would have failed in our duty had we neglected to give very serious consideration to the role of the Defence Force'.[76] As the PNGDF had been an integral part of the Australian Army for decades, the CPC argued, it had 'no real link' with PNG and its people, a questionable assertion given the Army's role in civic action and efforts to ensure an ethnic balance.[77] That the CPC did not state what it believed was a 'real link' with the community suggested that the position of the PNGDF as a well-trained, educated and wealthy elite – and an armed one at that – was the problem, rather than an absence of interaction with the Papua New Guinean public relative to other government institutions.

It is difficult to see how the PNGDF's elite status could have been changed. Any reduction in training or education would make the force next to useless. In many ways, the military had to be an elite in PNG, given the low rate of education and employment throughout the Territory. Moreover, the PNGDF's high pay was closely tied to that of the police and public service, both of which remained uncontroversial. Any reduction of wages, moreover, had the potential to cause the very unrest that the CPC was anxious to avoid. If there was a tenuous link between the military and civilians, a lack of understanding of the Army, at least in part stemming from a long-standing suspicion of the Papua New Guinean soldiers dating back to the 1950s and a sense that the Army was outside the government of PNG, as it had been with the Administration, was partly to blame. The CPC's view of the PNGDF as a potential threat therefore created an odd situation, in which PNG's own representatives accepted the long-standing Administration position that there was something inherently unstable about Papua New Guinean troops, which had its origins in the racially based views of soldiers held by colonial authorities during the 1950s and early 1960s.

Nevertheless, clearly resigned to the material fact of the PNGDF's existence, and aware of Kiki's arguments about the necessity of a defence force to respond to a range of contingencies short of large-scale invasion, the CPC envisaged the force as one focused on external threats, while attempting to curtail its involvement in domestic affairs. Its recommendations, which were almost verbatim incorporated into the Constitution, envisaged a four-fold role for the PNGDF.[78] First, the force was to defend PNG and its territory. Second, it was to assist PNG in fulfilling its international obligations. Only third on the list was the role of assisting civilian authorities in the event of a natural disaster, internal security crisis or other national emergency. Finally, in an acknowledgement of the capabilities of the force and its position as one of the few truly national institutions, the PNGDF was to engage in nation-building tasks.[79] Overall, these roles reflected not only the grudging acceptance of the PNGDF at independence but also the continuing suspicions about its potential political role.

STRUCTURING THE PNGDF

While the role of the PNGDF was decided with Papua New Guinean input, Australians overwhelmingly directed its structure, albeit limited by a lack of clear guidance as to the timing of independence. The Army had little notion of when it would be required to have 'finished' the PNGDF, such that in 1971 Brigadier Eldridge reported to the CGS, Lieutenant General Daly, that his command laboured under 'extreme difficulties' owing to 'indecision in Canberra' over the structure of PNG defence forces and a 'disinclination to set a time frame for planning'.[80] Nonetheless, although planned by Australians in a timeframe that did not allow for substantial changes, the PNGDF that was created was not wholly unsuited to PNG's needs, as some have suggested. The force used as its starting point a structure that had proved capable during Confrontation and was oriented towards patrolling and low-intensity fighting, which matched the type of conflict the PNGDF would be expected to face in the future.

Close coordination with civilian departments differentiated discussions about the structure of the PNGDF from the Army-only planning of the 1960s. Building on the first blueprints for the defence force, from 1971 planning was conducted by working groups of the Departments of Defence and External Territories, with other bodies, such as the Army or the Administration, being co-opted as partners when necessary, or asked to provide background information for their parent departments.[81]

Forming the basis of the discussions was a series of seventeen individual investigations, conducted by groups from various departments as needed, ranging from analyses of communication, equipment and training in the PNGDF to the employment of Papua New Guineans in civilian defence positions and the future defence relationship.[82] In order to manage these wide-ranging studies, a PNG Defence Coordinating Committee (PNGDCC) was created in 1972 under the direction of Minister for Defence David Fairbairn.[83] The interdepartmental nature of these efforts was not the only change in the planning process. Within the Australian defence establishment, the Department of Defence's leadership in the planning of the PNGDF reflected its growing power over the service departments, which would eventually be formalised in the amalgamation of the Army, Navy and Air departments in the Tange reforms of the late 1970s.[84]

Despite the Defence Committee directing that 'planners should not be burdened with preconceived ideas', Australian defence authorities envisaged few radical changes to the PNGDF, and the force ultimately reflected decisions made in successive plans for the expansion of the PIR during the early 1960s.[85] This frustrated representatives of the civilian departments charged with managing PNG's independence, who felt that the proposed force was unsuited to PNG's needs and, more importantly, was too costly for a new nation with a restricted budget.[86] The Minister for External Territories, Bill Morrison, in particular called for the PNGDF to be replaced by a Malaysian-style police field force or paramilitary-style adjunct to the police. However, this suggestion amounted to little, and was rejected by Army and Papua New Guinean authorities.[87] Morrison's idea was more a reflection of his dissatisfaction with the conventional PNGDF rather than a concrete and well-reasoned proposal for the armed forces in PNG. The idea was never seriously examined, despite its being well within the capability of the Department of External Territories under Morrison to do so, and no study of any kind seems to have been conducted. Instead, the suggestion, which in effect called for the Army to become subordinate to the police, should be seen as partly the continuation of the interdepartmental tensions that dominated discussion of PNG Command in the late 1960s.

The suggestion that the plan for the PNGDF be abandoned for something more unorthodox was problematic, but has been tenacious in discussion of the PNGDF since independence.[88] Given the limited time available to make the force then in existence independently viable, it is not surprising that little effort was dedicated to planning a wholesale and radical change of an organisation that had taken ten years to develop and seemed to the Army to have performed capably the tasks asked of it. In addition, even without the time restrictions, proposals such as that for a police field force were rightly considered unworkable in PNG, particularly as they had their basis in political, rather than military, considerations. In an appreciation for the CGS and other senior officers, Eldridge for instance dismissed the proposed police field force as 'obviously cheap, lowly paid, poorly officered with minimum administrative and logistic support'. He criticised it as being 'presumably too anaemic and inert to constitute a threat', pointing to the most likely reason for the support of this option by the Department of External Territories.[89] Moreover, as O'Neill pointed out in 1971, as the police were already armed, downgrading the PIR to a field force 'would simply increase Police numbers rather than add a new capacity'.[90] By contrast, Kiki's acceptance that PNG might face a range of threats beyond those within the purview of the police, but short of invasion, dovetailed with PNG Command's training during the 1960s, which envisaged fighting a conflict that could escalate from small-scale insurgent operations in which patrolling and contact with locals were the focus of the Army, to conventional war. In addition, PNG Command had already been called on to conduct a range of high-intensity activities, including search and rescue, deploying long-range patrols (such as those used to tackle the influenza outbreak in 1969), or protecting fishing grounds. Unlike the police, the PNGDF of the early 1970s had the logistics capability, the training, the equipment and the organisation to undertake these operations, as well as to engage in conventional combat if required.

Drastic reduction in the size of PNG Command was equally problematic, as any smaller force would not retain the capabilities then possessed by PNG Command. Patrolling PNG's long border and rugged terrain dictated a defence force large enough to operate in numerous independent groups around the country. The distances involved and lack of infrastructure also meant that support by air, ocean transport and engineering capabilities were vital aspects of the force. Each of these combat and support elements necessitated a minimum size; there was little point, operationally or financially, in having one patrol boat or a single infantry company. Each ship or subunit required periods of maintenance, training and rest, such that if there were no reserve force, the PNGDF would be subject to periods in which it would lack key capabilities.[91] This could lead to a situation where no patrol was present on the border during periods of tension, or no transport available owing to aircraft maintenance.

As a result, up to 1973, the Army insisted that the PNGDF be based around three battalions of the PIR, with naval, air and logistic support giving it the capability to operate independently and rejected calls to the contrary.[92]

Despite the experience of the Australian Army in PNG and the under-developed nature of alternative suggestions, some commentators have criticised the Army for imposing a 'Western-style' military structure and culture on PNG. In discussing the antecedents to the PNGDF's deterioration after independence, Denoon argues that the Australian Army was too autonomous in its planning, had failed to 'think through [its] strategic perceptions' and was 'determined to be embedded' in PNG rather than accepting independence.[93] Similarly, historian Robert Hall argued that the Army's 'ethnocentrism' retarded the creation of a Papua New Guinean military tradition within the PNGDF, 'despite the possession by the citizens of Papua New Guinea of a military culture at least as long as that of Europe'.[94] Hall's argument is broadly in keeping with the 'fatal impact' view of colonialism in the Pacific, which, although correctly acknowledging the extensive exploitation of indigenous peoples and the imposition of foreign ideas, denies the agency of subject people in negotiating their engagement with colonial powers.[95] The suggestion that the Australian Army imposed its own traditions and structures on those of PNG implies that these were worthless in the PNG context and ignores the imposition of countless other structures, including the Westminster parliamentary system, the economy, the education system and the police force. Hall's idea also presents a grossly simplistic view of PNG as a single cultural monolith, rather than the profoundly diverse country it was and continues to be. At the same time, Denoon's criticisms owe far more to the biases present in the discussions of the 1970s rather than any deep understanding of defence issues, as he was both present at UPNG during the period and relies heavily on Morrison's version of events.[96] Like Morrison, neither Hall nor Denoon suggest how the Army might have better structured the PNGDF, which is symptomatic of the tendency, as Doran points out, to discuss perceived Australian failures rather than the context in which these decisions took place and the options available at the time.[97]

The decision to base the force on infantry battalions was a good example of a Western practice that, although 'imposed' in that it did not originate in PNG, was nonetheless suited to operations there. The decision to structure the PNGDF around a handful of infantry battalions was based on 'experience in the Borneo operations, in Vietnam and in PNG, with contingency planning both during Confrontation and since, and with the terrain, communication and logistic support requirements there', which, according to planners, 'confirmed the requirement to undertake infantry operations with units similar to the present Australian battalions'.[98] Essentially, the Army decided on the battalion structure on the basis of its vast experience in terrain and operations in PNG and in areas that were comparable both in geography and in the types of conflict that might be expected in PNG. Not only did the partition of the infantry force into battalions allow for each to be trained, maintained and rotated as necessary but also it ensured 'the proper coordination, context and support of company operations, [as] a smaller unit would not survive and a larger one is unnecessary'.[99] Companies of around a hundred men were not independent units; only battalion-sized units could provide organic administration and support functions. Moreover, these structures were a firm foundation from which to expand or contract the force, as companies could be added or disbanded without wider upheaval.

FINAL ADJUSTMENTS

The process of moulding the new defence force was gradual and consisted of minor changes: the integration of the services, decoupling from the Australian Army, the provision of independent capabilities, and the paring down of the force to fit with financial constraints. This all occurred at the same time as the role and structure of the force were decided. The first step towards an independent force was the creation of Joint Force Headquarters (JFHQ) in February 1972. This new formation replaced the Army-only PNG Command, combining the three service headquarters in PNG into an integrated entity under a single commander, as the air and naval forces in PNG were considered too small to be viable independent services and operated largely in support of the Army. As it was the largest service in PNG, the Army took the lead in JFHQ, providing the first commander, Brigadier Eldridge, who was replaced shortly after by Brigadier Jim Norrie.[100] JFHQ was always conceived as a halfway point between the colonial organisation of three separate services and a unified, national defence force, and the commander was explicitly instructed 'to promote and gain acceptance of a concept of a PNG Defence Force'.[101] In the Australian context, JFHQ was also innovative. Compared with the integration of the armed forces in Australia, the combination of the three services in this manner, according to Bert Wansley, who served as chief of staff of the HQ, was 'a little bit ahead of things'.[102]

In January 1973, less than a year later, the PNGDF was officially formed. Symbolically it was a substantial change, with new uniforms and flashes introduced to reflect the national identity of the force. Legally, however, the PNGDF remained under Australian control.[103] In terms of the structure of the force, this change was more a redesignation than the creation of a new organisation, based as it was on the JFHQ and PNG Command before it. The operational units that were based in PNG (the PIR, engineers and the patrol boats) changed little in their structure, equipment, training and doctrine. Ironically, while becoming a Papua New Guinean force, the number of Australians, particularly senior officers, was increased to help in its development, and the number of lieutenant colonels in Headquarters PNGDF rose by thirteen.[104] Rounding out the Defence establishment was the creation of a civilian PNG Defence Department in 1974.[105]

With the creation of the PNGDF, the other military force in PNG, the RAN PNG Division, came under the same command structure. The RAN had prepared for independence in a similar manner to the Army, training Papua New Guinean sailors for service on the PNGDF's five patrol boats and landing craft, or as land-based personnel.[106] It did not, however, follow the Army in its extensive education program. The RAAF, by contrast, came to PNG late. Although it had operated in PNG in a transport role, and occasionally on exercises, the RAAF had had little direct relationship with Papua New Guineans, and pilot recruits were called for only in 1972. The first seven cadet pilots were trained in Victoria, eventually forming the PNGDF transport squadron flying Second World War DC3s.[107] After independence, this unit retained one of the highest percentages of Australian personnel, owing to its late formation and the technical skills it required.

In July 1973 Australian and Papua New Guinean planners settled the final size of the PNGDF, allowing for the ultimate form of the force to be decided.[108] One of a handful of proposals for the final size of the PNGDF, a cap at 3500 was chosen as it was deemed the minimum necessary to satisfy the roles then being formulated by the CPC. Moreover, given that the PNGDF then numbered 3200 Papua New Guineans and around 800 Australians, a force any larger would pose significant problems in recruiting and training new recruits before independence. The smaller size also left open the possibility of later expansion, should the new nation desire to do so.[109] In 1973 the Army finally acknowledged that it had neither the time nor the resources to raise the long-planned third battalion of the PIR.[110] Until this time, the Australian Army and the Department of Defence had maintained that a third battalion was desirable, for the same reasons put forward during the last two decades, principally that it provided a balanced force capable of simultaneously engaging in operational, reserve and training activities.[111] Consequently, the already built accommodation for 3PIR in Lae was underutilised.[112] The PNGDF also underwent a process of administrative simplification and reduction in strength to keep within the manpower limit. The complicated accounting and auditing procedures were simplified to suit PNG requirements; for instance, where before rations were accounted down to each individual item (such as one eighth of a pound of pepper), now they were accounted for as whole ration packs.[113] Similarly, subunits such as the ordinance, supply and transport platoons, were combined into single entities to simplify the PNGDF's organisation.[114] Finally, the two infantry battalions were organised on a 'restricted' establishment of three, rather than four, infantry companies, and a combined support and administrative company, for a total of around 550 soldiers per battalion.[115]

In a final cost- and manpower-saving measure, both the PNGVR and PNG's cadet unit, 35th Cadet Battalion, were disbanded. Members of these units lamented the loss of important links to the community, but Diro argued that civilian fear of the Army's connection with the Papua New Guinean public, and the potential that this might be used by the Army to further its political role, were contributing factors.[116] However, the financial burden of maintaining the two widely dispersed units far outweighed their limited utility during conflict and was the more likely reason for their deletion from the order of battle. Moreover, while both the PNGVR and the cadets were impressively multiracial, the senior ranks were still largely made up of Europeans. As a result, the writing had been on the wall for some years. Cutting these two units, like the simplification of others and the abandonment of 3PIR, was a pragmatic and relatively easy solution to manpower and financial constraints in a limited timeframe.

LOCALISATION

Planning the role and structure of the PNGDF was crucial, yet it was the replacement of Australians with Papua New Guineans – a process termed 'localisation' – that made the force an independent one. PNG could not claim that its defence force was completely independent if Australians occupied permanent executive positions within the force, nor could it operate without Papua New Guinean soldiers who knew their trade in theory and practice. The training and mentoring of Papua New Guineans to assume positions of greater responsibility and skill had been going on since 1951, but this process was slow, in keeping with the measured approach of the colonial government, the perceived distance of independence and the initially low education levels of Papua New Guineans. During the 1970s the Australian Army accelerated its localisation program as far as possible, in order to raise the number of Papua New Guineans in the force at independence. Defence authorities hoped that this could be done without prejudicing the standards and efficiency of the PNGDF, particularly given the danger of unrest that a young, inexperienced force posed.[117] Although the force that was created was stable, the speed with which localisation was pursued – a decision largely out of the Army's hands given the pace of the independence process – did result in a lack of experience among Papua New Guinean soldiers.

The Australian Government's self-interested desire to limit its exposure to politically fraught situations applied much of the pressure to the pace of localisation. The dilemma was a delicate one, given that if Australia prematurely removed its soldiers, the PNGDF might deteriorate to such a degree that it would be unable to defend the country from external attack and might also be ineffective in internal security tasks. In the worst case, the training and discipline of the force could deteriorate to such a degree that it represented a danger to others. The removal of Australian defence aid might also cause PNG to turn to a foreign power for material and training support, limiting Australia's influence on the new nation. Conversely, if Australian troops seconded to the force were involved in internal security operations, they might be injured, or the government might attract criticism for involvement in another country's domestic affairs and charges of continuing the colonial relationship in PNG. The image of Australian troops deploying to quell protest in a sovereign country was one that the Australian Government wished to avoid at all costs. A further factor was the expensive nature of long-term and large-scale military aid, particularly in the form of personnel.[118] Ultimately, the Australia Government feared the political repercussions of Australian troops being involved in internal security operations in a former colony far more than the possibility that PNG's military might suffer from the early removal of Australian skills and leadership.

By the 1970s every area of the PNGDF experienced some kind of localisation, and the training and advising of Papua New Guineans became an important role for many Australians, either as their sole task or, more usually, in addition to their primary function. Although different for each position, localisation was a two-stage process. The first was a training stage, in which Papua New Guinean soldiers learnt the basics of their new position at Goldie River, at Army technical schools around Australia and at OCS Portsea. Other ranks in particular were fed into training establishments at a greater rate during the 1970s, in order to provide the PNGDF with specialist personnel. The next stage was the mentoring of Papua New Guinean soldiers to take over from their Australian counterparts. A Papua New Guinean soldier would often act as an understudy or 'shadow', learning from his Australian mentor and eventually assuming his place.[119] Even Diro acted as an understudy to Norrie before taking command of the PNGDF.

Not surprisingly given the short timeframe, localisation was far from complete immediately before independence. In 1973, Australians still made up more than 20 per cent of the force; however, this percentage was far higher among technical personnel and senior officers in the PNGDF. Only 4 to 5 per cent of the infantry battalions were Australians, while this percentage ballooned to 57 per cent in more technically intensive units, such as the PNGDF signal squadron. The Army component of Headquarters PNGDF was at the extreme end of the scale, with 126 Australians to just thirty-four Papua New Guineans.[120]

The commissioning of Papua New Guinean officers to lead the PNGDF after independence, particularly in technical areas, was one of the most pressing aspects of localisation but had been impeded by optimistic assumptions of the timing of independence and a lack of direction from the government. Although the need to create a PNG officer cohort against the possibility of future independence had been recognised by Australian authorities as early as 1960, the assumption that the Army had at least two decades until that date made officer commissioning slow throughout that decade.[121] As a result, the selection of two Papua New Guinean officer candidates each year for the first years of the program created only a tiny foundation of leaders when the PNGDF began to be planned. The Army simply thought it had more time. As late as 1967 the Department of the Army's target was three hundred Papua New Guinean officers by 1984. Even presented with seventeen years to create an officer cohort, the department and PNG Command still felt that the pace of commissioning was slow.[122] In fact, far less time was available. However, it was only after 1970 that the commissioning of Papua New Guineans was drastically increased, as it became clear that independence was a much more likely prospect in the short term.[123] Nonetheless, it is unlikely that an earlier start would have changed the number of Papua New Guinean officers available at independence, given the small pool of suitable candidates during the 1950s and 1960s. In addition, the racial barriers that precluded Papua New Guineans achieving senior NCO rank or a commission before 1960s make any discussion of earlier commissioning moot.

Papua New Guinean officers continued to be commissioned through OCS until 1974, after which they were trained at the newly established Joint Services College in Lae.[124] There, officer cadets from the PNGDF, police and corrective services trained together for one year, after which PNGDF cadets completed an additional year of military-specific training.[125] However, the advanced pace of commissioning took time to come to fruition. In 1971 there were only twenty-six local officers, rising to thirty-eight officers in 1972, fifty-nine in 1973 and seventy-nine the following year.[126] Given that by this time the establishment of officers in the PNGDF was more than 350, this remained far below the required number.[127] Moreover, most of these men were junior officers. Consequently, at independence Australians made up around 14 per cent of the PNGDF but 65 per cent of its officer corps.[128]

The need to localise senior positions in the PNGDF meant that the pace of promotion far outstripped what the Australian Army considered 'normal'. War has long been acknowledged as a boon to soldiers hoping to be promoted; so too was decolonisation, at least for indigenous officers. However, one consequence of the pace of promotion was that Papua New Guinean officers had little time to gain experience in their positions. To reach senior command, an individual officer had to progress through a series of positions, receiving new training and gaining new experience, which took time. During the 1970s, an Australian officer of sufficient capability might command an infantry battalion about eighteen years after having been commissioned.[129] By contrast, after his commission in 1963, Diro commanded a company in 1971 as a major, assumed command of 1PIR as a lieutenant colonel in 1974, and was given command of the PNGDF as a brigadier in 1975, just twelve years after having received his commission. In 1972, as Diro entered his second year as a company commander, only two Papua New Guineans held the rank of major, just two were captains and another thirty-two were subalterns.[130] The speed with which these officers had to be rushed through the system by independence was therefore a significant problem.[131] Bruce Selleck recalled for instance that experience in the quotidian tasks of running a battalion 'became scarce' and that as a major 'I was called on many times by local PNGDF officers to assist with a wide range of tasks for which they were not trained or did not feel confident in undertaking'.[132]

Similarly, Papua New Guinean NCOs, particularly those in technical positions outside the infantry, had little time to gain experience in
their new positions, and 'some floundered' as a result.[133] Sergeant Ken
Swadling, a signals instructor at Goldie River Training Depot during this
period, believed that the speed with which specialist personnel were produced left little time for them to gain the confidence, knowledge and judge-
ment required to excel in a particular position.[134] The lack of experience
at all levels was exacerbated by the departure of Australians after independence. Moreover, a force made up of young officers and NCOs also had
a serious effect on later promotions. Given the small number of positions
and the likelihood that senior men were some distance from retirement,
there was less opportunity for advancement in the late 1970s.[135]

It is difficult to see how the Australian Army could have localised the
PNGDF differently as a result of the unclear timeframe it was given by the
Australian Government. Before the 1970s, commissioning large numbers
of Papua New Guineans was outside its remit, and made difficult by
the slow development of PNG and the racial restrictions of the colonial
context. The Army was also constrained by government policy in the
1960s, when its mandate was only to create a force in accordance with
Australia's defence needs. By the 1970s, the Army had a short timeframe
during which to train most of the officers that would lead the new PNGDF,
while also being influenced by the Australian Government's desire to
remove the hundreds of Australian personnel from PNG as quickly as
feasible. The lack of experience that resulted therefore was to a large
degree not of the Army's making.

INDEPENDENCE AND THE END OF AUSTRALIAN RULE

Independence Day arrived with great fanfare around PNG, with many
celebrations being months in the planning.[136] In Port Moresby, the climax
of a day of activities, speeches and tree-planting came with the ceremony
on Independence Hill, at which George Aibo raised PNG's new flag.
Prince Charles represented the Queen, the RAAF performed flyovers and
HMAS *Stalwart* fired a hundred-gun salute in the harbour. Thousands
of Papua New Guineans braved Port Moresby rain to witness the end
of Australian rule in PNG and listened to speeches by Gough Whitlam,
the new Papua New Guinean Prime Minister, Sir Michael Somare, and
the first Papua New Guinean Governor-General, Sir John Guise. The
PNGDF was prominent on the day, as were the other two security forces

Figure 7.2 Prince Charles inspects a parade, Wewak, 1975 (Sinclair, *To Find a Path*)

in PNG, the RPNGC and the Correctional Service. However, in planning the celebrations, civilian officials in PNG remained as suspicious of the Army as ever, insisting that the Defence Force was 'not to dominate the scene'.[137]

The actual transfer of defence powers to Papua New Guinean control had occurred in March 1975, but independence marked the point from which PNG truly gained complete ownership of its own armed forces and defence policy. Not surprisingly, given the speed of independence and the Australian control of the process, there was a range of reactions within the PNGDF. As the man responsible for commanding the PNGDF in an independent PNG, Diro felt 'relieved' that independence had finally come, as it offered an opportunity to dispel any public misgivings about the PNGDF and the part it would play in PNG's future.[138] Diro was understandably closely invested in independence, but the day also held a degree of importance for other soldiers as well. Some were proud of their country's achievement of nationhood whereas others were glad the Australians were leaving.[139] However, in many respects Independence Day also marked only a short deviation from normal military life, and the following day it was back to 'business as usual'.[140] In the following days, weeks and months, the routine of the PNGDF changed little; patrolling, civic action and training continued as they had done for some years.

In keeping with the hard-won lessons of the previous decades, independence was discussed at length with Papua New Guinean soldiers.[141] Officers and education personnel gave lectures, and platoons held informal discussions.[142] There was also, not surprisingly, a great deal of discussion among the soldiers themselves.[143] The Army also engaged with civilian Papua New Guineans about independence, and a new task for patrols was reassuring the Papua New Guinean public that the government would continue as normal after independence.[144] Some former soldiers recalled a sense of unease about the pace of independence; however, it is difficult to separate these from the knowledge of the PNGDF's later problems.[145] It is telling, though, that when asked about both their best memories of service and the PNGDF's 'finest moment', none of those Papua New Guineans interviewed for this book referred to independence, despite often being closely involved in the ceremony, planning, localisation and structural changes. Instead, patrolling, training, operations and education featured prominently, suggesting that the actual process of independence had less emotional or professional significance for most PNG soldiers when compared with the PNGDF's core activities.

Independence was not the end of the Australian military presence in PNG. More than six hundred Australian servicemen remained in PNG after September 1975. For the most part, day-to-day tasks within the PNGDF for Australians continued as they had before 1975, although they were now under the command of the Australian Defence Assistance Group (ADAG), which had been created following the transfer of defence powers.[146] Australians remained throughout the force, but were concentrated in senior and technical positions. Still more formed part of whole, Australian-based units, such as engineers posted to Mendi in the Highlands working on local infrastructure, particularly roads, and topographical survey teams charged with mapping the new country.[147] It was not until 1979 that the number of Australians fell below two hundred, but Australian troops have remained in PNG almost continuously since 1975 in various capacities.

Figure 7.3 Sir Michael Somare (with sunglasses) and Brigadier Jim Norrie, the
last Australian commander of the PNGDF (second from right) watch the
Independence Day ceremony, 16 September 1975 (Sinclair, *To Find a Path*)

The relationship between troops of the newly separated nations was
codified in a Status of Forces Agreement (SOFA) and a Loan Agreement, developed in the lead-up to independence to provide the legal and
political basis for a continued Australian presence in PNG.[148] Australia's
reluctance to be too closely involved in the PNGDF, and any politically
unsavoury operations it may embark on, also coloured the relationship,
as did an aversion to granting too much power over Australian troops to
the PNGDF and the PNG state. A sticking point in the development of the
SOFA, for instance, was the applicability of Village Courts to Australian
personnel. These informal local courts drew on customary laws, and Australian officials worried that Australian servicemen might be brought in
front of a small court made up of local elders for a minor crime and
be sentenced according to local custom. The two sides eventually solved
the matter by allowing a right of appeal to higher, Western-based, Papua
New Guinean courts.[149] In addition, the Australian Government attached
a great deal of emphasis to the consultative structures between Australia

and PNG with a view to ensuring that Australian troops would not be deployed in politically damaging situations.[150]

Despite the long shared history, the relationship between Australian and Papua New Guinean soldiers gradually changed after 1975. In the first years after independence, Australians based in PNG were mostly those who had served there before, or had arrived before September 1975. This was a body of people to whom PNG culture was well known, which was familiar with the Australian-based structure of the PNGDF, and enjoyed a respected place within that structure. However, this changed when the postings of these men began to end. Diro found that the rapport between Australian and Papua New Guinean soldiers 'deflated' with the high turnover of personnel, the decline in overall numbers and, importantly, the new barrier of different national priorities. Australian soldiers in ADAG were more diplomatic and advisory towards their Papua New Guinean counterparts, and were considered more and more distant from the PNGDF.[151] Tellingly, Patterson Lowa, the most senior PNGDF officer after Diro, argued that Australian officers should be vetted for mentoring skill and tact before posting to the independent PNGDF, suggesting an absence of these qualities among Australians, at least in Lowa's view. However, as men with PNG experience left the Army, Australian selection for posting to PNG was done as 'a "body" became available, regardless of the experience and proficiency of the local replacement', thereby diluting the experience of the Australian cohort with the PNGDF.[152] Equally, Papua New Guineans were increasingly able to ignore Australian advice, should they desire to do so. As Australians departed, Papua New Guineans gained, and took for themselves, more independence and control over their force.[153]

In addition, when Australians left positions of direct responsibility and took on an advisory role, their role became harder and more fraught as they faced the difficult task of developing the PNGDF and maintaining its standards through suggestion, advice and cajoling.[154] They could also be caught between their own government's instructions and the desires of the PNGDF.[155] Some Australians, particularly those in Headquarters PNGDF, had to distance themselves as best they could from PNG politics, while at the same time fending off accusations that they had too large a role in directing the PNGDF. At the same time, the Papua New Guinean Secretary of the Department of Defence, Noel Levi, complained in 1976 that although Australian servicemen brought years of experience to the PNGDF, 'it is difficult for many of them to accept the changes which are necessary to bring about the necessary modification of our force from its previous Australian service orientation. This adds to the conflict of interests within our organisation.' That these comments were made in the context of animosity between the Secretary and the Commander PNGDF only reinforces the difficult and new position in which Australian servicemen found themselves.[156]

Ultimately, the PNGDF was a reflection of both the decisions of the previous decade and the demands of decolonisation. The dramatic shift of Australian policy from gradual development to immediate independence during the early 1970s left little time for further changes to PNG Command, and strained the Australian armed forces' ability to train Papua New Guineans. The Australian Government's desire to limit its involvement in any politically damaging internal security situations further sped up the process of withdrawing Australian soldiers and replacing them with Papua New Guineans. These same issues resulted in the Army becoming involved in internal security for the first time, a role it vehemently opposed. The Army has been accused of having too much control over the final structure of the PNGDF, yet two points are worth emphasising. First, the Army had little time during which to adjust the structure that it had been instructed to create by the Australian Government over the course of a decade. The pace of decolonisation, the lack of direction from the Australian Government and absence of coordination with the Administration until the 1970s meant that the responsibility for the PNGDF of 1975 was shared between civilian and military planners. At the same time, we should not assume that the PNGDF was inherently poorly suited to PNG's needs, simply because of its imposition by Australia or PNG's travails in the decades after independence. The force's structure, although designed to defend Australian interests, was well designed for operations in PNG, as had been proved during the 1960s. It was well educated, well equipped, tested and enthusiastic. Although the PNGDF was perhaps unfinished in 1975, it had strengths as well as its weaknesses.

CONCLUSION

In 1975 the independent PNGDF was an embryonic force that owed as much to its origins in PNG Command as it did to the preparations for independence. Militarily, it was well suited to operations in PNG, having gained extensive experience in the type of patrolling that was to be its chief role and having had its structures tested in the PNG environment for decades. Certainly, the PNGDF's separation from the Australian military diminished its capabilities; far fewer aircraft were available, for instance. Nevertheless, the core capabilities contained within the two infantry battalions, around which the PNGDF was built, remained the same. Moreover, the Army had laid the groundwork for independence relatively early, and the average soldier in 1975 was highly trained and educated compared with the wider Papua New Guinean population.

Like the new nation itself, the PNGDF had a troubled history after 1975, although its decline was not immediate.[1] For the remainder of the 1970s, it continued the process of localisation, following the plan set down before independence. In 1980, the force participated in its 'finest hour', deploying troops to Vanuatu to keep the peace during that country's transition to independence. Although Australian transport planes were needed to ferry troops to Vanuatu, just five years after independence the PNGDF was able to deploy a task force of two companies and support troops on an operation that its government deemed valuable, to help secure the peaceful independence of another Pacific nation, no less.[2]

The performance of the PNGDF in the Vanuatu operation reflected the challenges that faced the force at independence. The PNGDF experienced

trouble with its logistic capability, suggesting that the last-minute simplification of procedures, and the limited experience of Papua New Guinean
soldiers, had restricted its capabilities. There were also discipline problems, and although the origins of these are difficult to determine without
further study, they too point to a lack of experience among officers and
soldiers. Nevertheless, despite these complications, the PNGDF ultimately
succeeded in deploying a force overseas, supporting it and completing its
assigned task. The PNGDF's ability to commit troops to Vanuatu somewhat justified the belief that the best course for the development of a
PNGDF was to provide the PNG government with options, particularly
as this peacekeeping role was not explicitly imagined before independence.[3] Given the need to source soldiers from both battalions, a defence
force of any smaller size would have been hard pressed to provide enough
troops.

However, the PNGDF's later experience was disappointing.[4] The
Bougainville conflict, a continuation of tensions that had begun during the
period of Australian rule and which deteriorated into widespread violence
in 1988, would eventually consume the PNGDF's resources and sap its
morale. The force performed poorly during the conflict, not least because
of inadequate funding for training and operations. It was also involved
in violence and crime on the troubled island, a stark contrast to the discipline during operations that the force had exhibited before 1975.[5] By
the early 2000s, the size of the PNGDF was reduced, in an effort to curb
expenses.[6] The PNGDF's strength today is around two thousand soldiers,
yet it still struggles to be a capable and stable force.[7]

The place of the military in PNG remained controversial after independence. The PNGDF took a greater role in internal security after 1975
as the PNG Government attempted to contain rising levels of crime and
violence, particularly in Port Moresby, where the PNGDF was called out
for the first time in 1984 and periodically thereafter.[8] The threat of a coup
remains a much-discussed possibility in PNG, buoyed by periodic strikes
and riots among soldiers and some more serious incidents, most notably
the 1997 Sandline Crisis, when PNGDF Commander Major General Jerry
Singirok and many of the troops under his command defied orders from
the PNG Government in response to the employment of mercenaries from
the South African company Sandline in Bougainville. Singirok arrested the
company's leader and soldiers, and forced the government to back down.[9]
The PNGDF also experienced a small mutiny during the 2012 political
crisis over the prime ministership of PNG. Nonetheless, in both instances,
the military displayed restraint: in 1997 the PNGDF had clear limits about

how far it would challenge the government, while in 2012 the majority of the force did not join the mutineers.[10]

How much of the blame for the PNGDF's problems after independence can be placed at Australia's feet is difficult to determine without reference to the political and financial context in which the independent PNGDF operated after 1975. As Stewart Firth argues, 'to discuss security in PNG . . . is to be driven back to a consideration of the political systems in that country'.[11] Undoubtedly PNG, like so many other decolonised countries, still feels the effects of its time as a colonial territory, not least because of the almost complete Australian control of the decolonisation process; however, too great a focus on Australia's role risks overlooking Papua New Guinean agency and the context in which Australia granted independence.

It is perhaps, then, the watershed period between 1966 and 1970, after the end of Confrontation but before the rush to independence, that better represents the various forces that acted on the Australian Army in PNG and the strengths and weaknesses of the PIR and PNG Command. It was during this time that Australia's defence needs, the perception of Papua New Guineans and the development of PNG held roughly equal weight in shaping it. PNG Command continued to expand in keeping with its task of guarding an area of strategic importance to Australia, while at the same time it was increasingly focused on preparing for PNG's eventual independence through the creation of a national army. The Papua New Guinean soldiers within the force, newly promoted and increasingly well educated, were conceptualised as soldiers of a nation not yet in existence, while also being servants of Australia's defence needs. The force changed to such a degree before the decision to proceed to full independence that the long-serving Warrant Officer George Aibo believed that PNG Command became a 'different army' during the late 1960s, despite also remaining part of the Australian Army.[12] Finally, during this period the Australian Army engaged with the political context in which it operated, both despite and because of the tenacious suspicions of the military expressed by the Administration and the Department of Territories.

Before 1966, the Army in PNG was different still. Australia's defence needs decided the manner and role in which Papua New Guinean soldiers served. The PIR was initially expected to perform a similar function to the one it had undertaken during the Second World War: as auxiliaries to Australian soldiers. Yet, in spite of its narrow role of patrolling and reconnaissance, the PIR contributed significantly to Australia's defence during the 1950s, being one of only four regular infantry battalions and an inexpensive addition to Australia's defence in a region considered vital and, until 1951, undefended. However, the Army showed itself to be conceptually ill-equipped to manage a force of Papua New Guineans over a long period. The PIR was poorly led, structured and resourced during the 1950s, a fact brought home to the Army by the disturbances of 1957 and 1961. The 1950s marked the only period during which Australia maintained a permanent peacetime force recruited entirely from indigenous peoples and structured along the hierarchical lines of a colonial society. Although there were important differences between the PIR and the forces raised by the British in Africa, such as the fact that the PIR was never used as an instrument of colonial control, the regiment of the 1950s was, in many respects, Australia's colonial army.

The subordinate position of Papua New Guineans under Australian rule shaped the development of the PIR. The perception of Papua New Guineans as simple soldiers influenced the structure and role of the PIR during the 1950s, which in turn contributed to the disturbances. Given the strength of the idea of 'fuzzy wuzzy' soldiers, there was no 'martial race' myth in PNG, nor did Papua New Guineans view themselves as inheritors of a martial tradition. Consequently, while mirroring the subordinate relationship prevalent in other colonial armed forces, the perception of Papua New Guinean soldiers by the Australian Army is an example of how the different historical and cultural contexts have shaped the employment of indigenous soldiers. Despite the dominance of such famous soldiers as the Sikhs and Ghurkhas in the discussion of colonial soldiers, not all colonial armies follow the model set by the Raj.

During Confrontation the PIR expanded in size and took on a position of far greater responsibility in Australia's defence. Essentially, the PIR's auxiliary wartime role was abandoned with the creation of PNG Command and Papua New Guinean troops were expected to shoulder a similar burden to Australian soldiers. The training given to PNG Command and the plans for its use drew on the experience of Australian forces in Borneo, demonstrating that the Australian Army had begun to view the capabilities of Papua New Guinean troops during the 1960s as similar to their Australian counterparts. Although PNG Command was intended to fight only in PNG, given the restrictions on overseas service for New Guineans, the force nonetheless played an important role in a strategically vital area.

Unlike most formations in the Australian Army, PNG Command actively contributed to Australia's security during peacetime through its everyday activities. Its role in patrolling the border can be considered operational, given that the PIR was tasked with identifying Indonesian incursions in addition to training to defeat them, and that the regiment actively laid the groundwork for its wartime role by gathering topographical and human intelligence as well as fostering relationships with local people. In addition, PNG Command's constant patrolling demonstrated its capability to fight a war of small clashes in the jungle. A measure of the significance of PNG Command during this period, particularly in contrast to the 1950s, was the fact that the force received officers of a similar quality to the rest of the Army, even during the Vietnam War.

PNG Command's efforts to construct a national army during the watershed period after Confrontation challenges the idea that the Australian Army was wholly preoccupied with Australia's defence in its dealings with PNG. Remarkably, the Australian Army devoted a great deal of energy to this 'new task' at a time when PNG Command was still, ostensibly, oriented towards Australia's defence and while the Australian Army was fighting the Vietnam War. PNG Command recognised that the creation of a defence force was not only a matter of its structure and size but, as the education program showed, was also a matter of the character of the soldiers who were to man the force.

The Army's acceptance of the shifting position of Papua New Guineans in the Territory, brought about by the dismantling of discriminatory laws during the late 1950s and early 1960s, is further evidence of the degree to which it was influenced by PNG's development. The Australian Army was not a passive actor in this process. Rather it took the initiative by integrating messes, commissioning local officers and removing the barriers to Papua New Guineans commanding Australian soldiers. As a result, by the mid-1960s, all positions within PNG Command were open to Papua New Guineans of appropriate rank and skill. However, there were limits to the integration of Papua New Guinean soldiers into the Australian Army. Papua New Guineans were restricted from joining units other than the PIR, and a distance continued to be maintained between Australians and Papua New Guineans in a social context.

Although Papua New Guineans occupied a subordinate place in the Army, it is worth emphasising that the Australian Army was a profoundly multiracial force for twenty-four years. Although the word 'forgotten' has been overused in Australian military history to the point of absurdity, Papua New Guineans surely qualify. They were a unique group within the Australian Army, and represented the largest non-European group in the Australian military during the Cold War, if not to date. Integrating them into the history of the Australian Army reconceptualises this institution as one that grappled, successfully by the end of the 1960s, with the employment of a considerable number of culturally diverse foreigners. The range of ethnicities, languages and culture in such a small force was almost unmatched in other colonial militaries. Papua New Guineans engaged in a variety of ways with the Australian Army in which they served, as demonstrated by the array of Papua New Guinean motivations for enlistment while also maintaining multilayered allegiances to *wantok*, the Army and the nation.

Most crucially for the development of the Australian Army in PNG, Papua New Guinean soldiers saw themselves as an elite within PNG. This perception fuelled the disturbance in 1957, as Papua New Guinean soldiers defended the regiment from civilian insult, and again in 1961, as they demanded wages that were commensurate with their perceived standing in PNG. However, this elite status, too, was limited to PNG's borders, and the inequalities between Australians and Papua New Guineans, while galling to Papua New Guinean soldiers, did not elicit the same reaction. Nonetheless, despite the limits on the position and treatment of Papua New Guineans, the Australian Army was still one of the few organisations in which Australians and Papua New Guineans worked as professional equals.

From the 1960s, in each of the controversial incidents that dominated discussions of the Army in PNG, including the disturbances, civic action and internal security, and early preparations for independence, the Army displayed an awareness of its role in the future of PNG. That the PIR and PNG Command had been largely ignored by the Administration in planning for the future of PNG made this all the more significant. The tension between the Australian Army and the Administration, and their parent departments, was central to the development of the Australian Army's units in PNG. In particular, the suspicion of the potential for Papua New Guinean soldiers to be a force for disaffection against Australian rule or, as independence came closer, launch a coup, dominated the discussion of the military. These perceptions, although tenacious, were based on faulty assumptions of the inherent threat posed by Papua New Guinean soldiers. Soldiers displayed a propensity towards strikes and at times violence when aggrieved, but these outbursts were not political and had more in common with industrial disputes. In most instances, they represented an appeal to authority, rather than a rejection of it. The civilian anxiety towards the military in PNG, despite ostensibly stemming from a concern for the needs of an independent state, had its origins in a misreading of the disturbances that was based on colonial fears of 'arming the natives'. The continual discussion of the possibility of a coup in PNG owes a great deal to this long-standing fear of Papua New Guinean soldiers; interrogating the origins of this narrative therefore adds to the debate on the stability of the PNGDF today.

Ironically, the rush to independence ensured that the PNGDF that emerged in 1975 was shaped as much by its past as it was by conceptions of the defence needs of the new state. The capabilities of the PNGDF were based around the patrolling and infantry roles of the PIR during Confrontation, and the short time available before independence prevented substantial changes to the force's structure or the creation of a new, experienced and independent officer corps. Equally, the CPC's fear that the military might represent a threat to democratic government mirrored that of the Administration and concerned civilians. In this way, the pace of independence forced a reliance on the structures of the 1960s while simultaneously undermining them.

Ultimately, the success of the Australian Army in PNG during the period of post-war colonial rule should not be judged solely against the PNGDF of 1975, given that the creation of this specific organisation was not the focus of the force until after 1970. Instead, the Australian Army's Papua New Guinean units were a colonial force with significant problems during the 1950s, an active and important part of Australia's defence during Confrontation, and an institution that vigorously sought to create a sense of nationhood among its soldiers during the late 1960s. The force was initially influenced in its structure and treatment of Papua New Guineans by the colonial nature of Australian rule in PNG, but later integrated them into the Army alongside Australian soldiers. All this occurred *before* complete independence from Australia was decided.

The history of the Australian Army in PNG illustrates that the PIR and PNG Command were important parts of both Australia's defence and the preparations for PNG's independence. PNG has been omitted from the Army's history and the Army from PNG's history, yet the two were in fact intertwined during the period of Australian rule. Examining the history of the PIR, PNG Command and PNGDF, and those who served within them, broadens our conception of how Australia was defended and of who defended it. At the same time, the history of these units also demonstrates that the Australian Army during the period between 1951 and 1975 was not a force that existed only on the battlefields of South-East Asia, or that was composed entirely of Australians. Instead it was an institution with far wider and more complex responsibilities, one of which was the establishment and management of a force of Papua New Guineans and the eventual creation of an independent defence force.

APPENDIX
KEY APPOINTMENTS

CO, PIR AND 1PIR

Lieutenant Colonel Herbert Sabin	October 1951 – December 1953
Lieutenant Colonel A. Baldwin	December 1953 – January 1956
Lieutenant Colonel W. Wansley	January 1956 – March 1957
Lieutenant Colonel L. McGuinn	March 1957 – June 1959
Lieutenant Colonel James Norrie	June 1959 – May 1962
Lieutenant Colonel Kenneth McKenzie	June 1962 – May 1965
Lieutenant Colonel Bruce Hearn	May 1965 – May 1968
Lieutenant Colonel Maurie Pears	May 1968 – July 1970
Lieutenant Colonel Ron Lange	July 1970 – April 1973
Lieutenant Colonel J.D.W. Irvine	April 1973 – December 1973
Lieutenant Colonel Ted Diro	January 1974 – November 1974
Lieutenant Colonel Ken Noga	November 1974 –

CO, 2PIR

Lieutenant Colonel Donald Ramsay	March 1965 – November 1967
Lieutenant Colonel E. McCormick	December 1967 – February 1971
Lieutenant Colonel Russell Lloyd	February 1971 – December 1973
Lieutenant Colonel Laurie Lewis	December 1973 – January 1975
Lieutenant Colonel Michael Jeffery	January 1975 – January 1976

COMMANDER, AREA COMMAND PNG

Lieutenant Colonel N. Maddern | June 1952 – April 1953
Lieutenant Colonel T. Young | April 1953 – October 1955
Lieutenant Colonel J. Lynch | November 1955 – March 1957
Lieutenant Colonel W. Wansley | March 1957 – 6 February 1958
Lieutenant Colonel J. Murdoch | February 1958 – January 1960
Colonel Ralph Eldridge | January 1960 – September 1962
Colonel J. Pascoe | September 1962 – August 1963

COMMANDER, PAPUA NEW GUINEA MILITARY DISTRICT

Colonel J. Pascoe | August 1963 – January 1965
(continued)

COMMANDER, PNG COMMAND

Brigadier A.L. McDonald | January 1965 – April 1966
Brigadier Ian Hunter | April 1966 – February 1969
Brigadier Ralph Eldridge | February 1969 – January 1972

COMMANDER, JOINT TASK FORCE, PNG

Brigadier Ralph Eldridge | January 1972 – April 1972
(continued)
Brigadier James Norrie | April 1972 – January 1973

COMMANDER, PNGDF

Brigadier James Norrie | January 1973 – September 1975
(continued)
Brigadier Ted Diro | September 1975 –

ADMINISTRATOR, TERRITORY OF PAPUA AND NEW GUINEA

Jack Keith Murray	1945–52
Brigadier Sir Donald Cleland	1952–66
David Hay	1966–70
Leslie Wilson Johnson	1970–73

AUSTRALIAN HIGH COMMISSIONER, PNG

Leslie Wilson Johnson	1973–74 (continued)
Thomas Kingston Critchley	1974–78

Notes

Introduction

1 George Aibo, interview, 30 July 2013.
2 See Colebatch, 'To find a path'; Mench, *The Role of the Papua New Guinea Defence Force*; Sinclair, *To Find a Path*, vol. I: *Yesterday's Heroes, 1885–1950*, and vol. II: *Keeping the Peace, 1950–1975*.
3 Grey, *The Australian Army*, pp. 192–5, 222–4. See also Palazzo, *The Australian Army*, pp. 302–3.
4 Grey, *A Military History of Australia*, pp. 317, 319, 322.
5 See Sinclair, *Keeping the Peace*, pp. 179–214.
6 Hunt, 'Papua New Guinea in Australia's strategic thinking, 1880–1977', p. 4.
7 Ibid., p. 7.
8 Millar, 'Melanesia's strategic significance', pp. 30–5; Millar, *Australia in Peace and War*, pp. 264–76; Nelson, *Fighting for Her Gates and Waterways*.
9 Grey, 'Cuckoo in the nest?', p. 457.
10 See table 3.11 in Beaumont, *Australian Defence*, p. 128.
11 Riseman, 'War does not discriminate nor should we', *Age* (Melbourne), 18 August 2013.
12 Smith, 'Minorities and the Australian Army', pp. 129–49.
13 See for instance Riseman, 'Racism, indigenous people and the Australian armed forces in the post–Second World War era', pp. 159–79; Riseman, 'Equality in the ranks', pp. 411–26.
14 Nelson, 'The enemy at the door'.
15 Nelson, 'Kokoda: Two national histories', pp. 73, 77.
16 Nelson, 'Hold the good name of the soldier', p. 203.
17 Riseman, 'Australian [mis]treatment of Indigenous labour in World War II Papua New Guinea', p. 163; Reed, '"Part of our own story"', p. 161; Nelson, 'Kokoda', p. 79. See George Silk, untitled photograph, 25 December 1942, AWM 014028.
18 For a discussion of Papua New Guinean loyalty during the war, see Powell, *The Third Force*, pp. 206–23.
19 Laki, 'PNG Defence Force', p. 71. For the use of the term 'native' in recent history, see for instance Bradley, *To Salamaua*, pp. 93, 97, 98, 104.
20 Riseman, *Defending Whose Country?*, p. 153.
21 See for instance the discussion of policy towards indigenous soldiers, without reference to PNG, in Riseman and Trembath, *Defending Country*, p. 21.

22 Doran, 'Wanting and knowing best', p. 311. See also Ritchie, 'Australia, Papua New Guinea, and a communal blindness in our history education'.
23 Doran, 'Wanting and knowing best', p. 321.
24 See for instance East, 'PNGDF', pp. 11–13.
25 Denoon, *A Trial Separation*, p. 191.
26 Nelson, 'Liberation', p. 279.
27 Ibid., pp. 273–4. For alternative views, see Moore, *New Guinea*, p. 185; Waiko, *A Short History of Papua New Guinea*, p. 153.
28 Downs, *The Australian Trusteeship*, pp. 548–52.
29 May, 'The government and the military in Papua New Guinea', p. 1.
30 See Rogers, 'The Papua New Guinea Defence Force'; Mietzner and Farrelly, 'Mutinies, coups and military interventionism', pp. 342–56.
31 See for instance Fraenkel, 'The coming anarchy in Oceania?', pp. 1–34.
32 Mietzner and Farrelly, 'Mutinies, coups and military interventionism', p. 343.
33 Stapleton, '"Bad boys"', p. 1167.
34 Killingray, *Policing and Decolonisation*; Clayton and Killingray, *Khaki and Blue*; Killingray, 'Military and labour recruitment in the Gold Coast during the Second World War', pp. 83–95; Killingray, 'Race and rank in the British army in the twentieth century', pp. 276–90; Parsons, *The African Rank-and-File*.
35 Lovering, 'Authority and identity', p. 301.
36 Roy, 'Military loyalty in the colonial context', p. 528.
37 See Killingray, 'The mutiny of the West African Regiment in the Gold Coast, 1901', pp. 441–54; Rose, 'The anatomy of mutiny', pp. 561–74; Spector, 'The Royal Indian Navy strike of 1946', pp. 271–84; Parsons, *The 1964 Army Mutinies and the Making of Modern East Africa*; Lovering, 'Authority and identity', p. 301.
38 Schaffer, 'Racializing the soldier', p. 213.
39 Walker, '"Descendants of a warrior race"', p. 2.
40 Omissi, '"Martial races"', p. 1.
41 Enloe, 'The military uses of ethnicity', p. 220.
42 Hall, 'Aborigines and Australian defence planning', p. 210.
43 Riseman, *Defending Whose Country?*, p. 28.
44 Rand and Wagner, 'Recruiting the "martial races"', p. 236.
45 Indeed, units such as the Special Air Service (SAS) trained in PNG for a month, entitling their members to the PNG Clasp for the Australian Service Medal (Antony Bowden, Archive No. 2443, AAWFA). However, such units are not integral to the study of the Army in PNG.

1 An 'experimental establishment': The re-raising of the Pacific Islands Regiment, 1951–57

1 Dorney, *Papua New Guinea*, pp. 19–20.
2 Nelson, *Mobs and Masses*, p. 16; Waters and Gardner, 'Decolonisation in Melanesia', p. 118; Dinnen, *Law, Order and the State in Papua New Guinea*, p. 2.
3 See Kerr, *A Federation in these Seas*, pp. 12–41.

4 Fischer, *A History of the Pacific Islands*, p. 161.
5 A discussion of Australia's assumption of a mandate over German New Guinea can be found in Meaney, *Australia and the World Crisis 1914–1923*, vol. 2: *A History of Australian Defence and Foreign Policy 1901–23*, pp. 466–99.
6 Griffin, Nelson and Firth, *Papua New Guinea*, p. 11.
7 Fischer, *A History of the Pacific Islands*, p. 178.
8 Hereniko, 'Representations of cultural identities', p. 410; Denoon, *A Trial Separation*, pp. 13–14.
9 See Riseman, 'Australian [mis]treatment of Indigenous labour in World War II Papua New Guinea'.
10 For a history of the unit, see Powell, *The Third Force*.
11 See Downs, *The Australian Trusteeship*, pp. 3–36.
12 Hudson and Daven, 'Papua and New Guinea since 1945', p. 153.
13 Hasluck, *A Time for Building*, pp. 64, 67; Downs, *The Australian Trusteeship*, p. xviii.
14 Cabinet Submission No. 323, 'Papua and New Guinea development', 13 July 1959, NAA, A5818, vol. 7.
15 Downs, *The Australian Trusteeship*, p. 99. For a description of the Administration's efforts to extend government control during this period, see Hasluck, *A Time for Building*, pp. 77–84.
16 See for instance Hasluck, *A Time for Building*, p. 82.
17 Nelson, 'Papua New Guinea', p. 165.
18 Wolfers, *Race Relations and Colonial Rule in Papua New Guinea*, p. 136.
19 See Sinclair, *Kiap*.
20 For the extensive list of the other departments with a role in PNG, see ibid., pp. xiv–xv.
21 Hasluck, *A Time for Building*, p. 16.
22 Ibid., p. 51.
23 Ibid., p. 13.
24 Ibid., pp. 13–14.
25 Daly to Wade, 20 December 1957, NAA, MP927/1 A5/1/132.
26 Downs, *The Australian Trusteeship*, p. 529.
27 Wolfers, *Race Relations and Colonial Rule in Papua New Guinea*, p. 119. See also Nelson, 'From Kanaka to fuzzy wuzzy angel', p. 172.
28 Wolfers, *Race Relations and Colonial Rule in Papua New Guinea*, pp. 139–40.
29 McCarthy, *South-West Pacific Area First Year*, p. 45; Mench, *The Role of the Papua New Guinea Defence Force*, p. 8.
30 Riseman, *Defending Whose Country?*, p. 150.
31 Sinclair, *Yesterday's Heroes*, pp. 1–4.
32 Ibid., pp. 132, 140.
33 Nelson, 'Hold the good name of the soldier', p. 207.
34 Sinclair, *Yesterday's Heroes*, p. 278.
35 Mench, *The Role of the Papua New Guinea Defence Force*, p. 16.
36 Powell, *The Third Force*, p. 237; Nelson, 'Hold the good name of the soldier', p. 208.

37 Sinclair, *Yesterday's Heroes*, pp. 273–82.

38 Powell, *The Third Force*, pp. 238–9.

39 Cited in Byrnes, *Green Shadows*, p. 198.

40 Hunt, 'Papua New Guinea in Australia's strategic thinking', p. 69; O'Neill, *Australia in the Korean War 1950–53*, vol. 1, *Strategy and Diplomacy*, pp. 21–34. For a detailed discussion of Australian defence policy during the late 1940s, see Horner, *Defence Supremo*, pp. 236–315.

41 See Defence Committee, 'A suitable basis for the distribution of strategic responsibility and war effort', 1950, in Frühling, *A History of Australian Strategic Policy Since 1945*, p. 158.

42 Grey, *The Australian Army*, p. 190.

43 Hunt, 'Papua New Guinea in Australia's strategic thinking', p. 68.

44 Ibid., p. 48; Palazzo, *The Australian Army*, p. 194.

45 O'Neill, *Strategy and Diplomacy*, pp. 31–2.

46 Horner, *Defence Supremo*, p. 299.

47 Horner, 'From Korea to Pentropic', p. 50; O'Neill, *Strategy and Diplomacy*, p. 31.

48 For the an overview of the RAN PNG Division, see Sinclair, *Keeping the Peace*, pp. 179–80.

49 See '"Defence lack in N. Guinea"', *Courier-Mail* (Brisbane), 16 August 1950; 'New Guinea defenceless', *Townsville Daily Bulletin*, 16 August 1950; David Berry, 'They're urging jungle training for Austn troops: New Guinea feels the war menace', *Mail* (Adelaide), 26 August 1950; 'Measures to stop Reds in NG', *Advertiser* (Adelaide), 20 March 1951; 'Close watch on New Guinea', *Queensland Times* (Ipswich) 26 March 1951; 'Cannot hold NG – alone', *Sunday Mail* (Brisbane), 9 December 1951.

50 Taylor to Northern Command, 14 April 1949, NAA, MP729/8 37/431/114; Director Military Operations and Plans, 'New Guinea Volunteer Rifles', 21 June 1949, NAA, MP729/8 37/431/114; J. Hobbs, 'Survey of the Territory of PNG concerning the possible re-formation of a volunteer force', 15 September 1949, NAA, MP729/8 37/431/114.

51 Taylor to Morgan, 30 May 1949, NAA, MP729/8 37/431/114; J. K. Murray to Secretary External Territories, 16 July 1950, NAA, A5954 2331/9.

52 Murray to Secretary External Territories, 16 July 1950, NAA, A5954 2331/9.

53 Secretary RSSAILA to Minister of External Territories, 12 July 1950, PNGNA, 247 1/8/1/44.

54 '"Second Malaya" feared in New Guinea', *Sydney Morning Herald* [hereafter *SMH*], 14 May 1950.

55 McCarthy to Government Secretary, Port Moresby, 22 June 1951, PNGNA, 247 1/8/1/44.

56 'Report by Joint Planning Committee at meeting held on Tuesday 12 September 1950', 12 September 1950, NAA, A5954 2331/9; 'Minute by the Defence Committee at meeting held on Thursday 12 October 1950', 12 October 1950, NAA, A5954 2331/9.

57   J. Hobbs, 'Survey of the Territory of PNG concerning the possible re-formation of a volunteer force conducted', 15 September 1949, NAA, MP729/8 37/431/114.

58   Military Board, 'Raising of a CMF unit in the Territory of Papua and New Guinea', 11 January 1950, NAA, MP729/8 37/431/114.

59   Cited in Sinclair, *Keeping the Peace*, p. 257.

60   G.F. Wootten, 'The Papua and New Guinea Volunteer Rifles', 1 December 1949, NAA, MP729/8 37/431/114; N.P. Maddern, 'Papua New Guinea Volunteer Rifles', AWM113 MH 1/194; Hancock to AHQ, 15 March 1957, NAA, A6059 41/441/34.

61   V. Seacombe, 'Report on Inspection New Guinea 18–30 August 1952', 5 September 1952, NAA, MT1131/1 A259/47/3.

62   Maddern, 'Papua New Guinea Volunteer Rifles'.

63   Secretary External Territories to Secretary Army, 7 July 1950, NAA, A452 1962/8146; Military Board to Northern Command, 6 October 1950, NAA, MP729/8 37/431/114.

64   Spender to Francis, 8 March 1950, NAA, A432 1961/3102.

65   Secretary Territories to Secretary Army, 7 July 1950, NAA, A452 1962/8146; Sinclair, *Keeping the Peace*, pp. 45–6.

66   'PIR – Conditions of Service and Enlistment', n.d. [c. 1951], PNGNA, 16 19/3; Timberley to District Commissioner, Daru, 'Bai-Sigiaba of Isago, Gaima – Certificate of Character', 15 February 1955, PNGNA, 16 19/3; 'The Pacific Islands Regiment (PIR) – Conditions of Enlistment and Conditions of Service', n.d. [c. 1950], NAA, A432 1961/3102.

67   See for instance Sabin to District Commissioner, New Ireland, 4 March 1952, PNGNA, 16 19/3; Sabin to District Commissioner, Madang, 4 March 1952, PNGNA, 16 19/3; Grey, *The Australian Army*, p. 193.

68   H. Sabin, 'Formation of the Pacific Islands Regiment', 12 July 1955, AWM113 11/2/29 [hereafter Sabin, 'Formation of the Pacific Islands Regiment'].

69   Bert Wansley, interview, 27 May 2013.

70   Mench, *The Role of the Papua New Guinea Defence Force*, p. 24.

71   Seacombe to AHQ, 9 March 1951, NAA, MT1131/1 A259/47/3.

72   Sabin, 'Formation of the Pacific Islands Regiment'; Gabi Gewa, interview, 30 July 2013; George Aibo, interview, 30 July 2013.

73   Grey, *The Australian Army*, p. 194. See also Adrian Clunies-Ross, Archive No. 0795, AAWFA.

74   Northern Command, 'Proposal for a New Lower Establishment to Supersede II/23C/2 (LE)', 27 July 1956, NAA, A6059 21/441/15; 'Comparison of organisations', August 1957, NAA, A6059 21/441/15.

75   Seacombe to AHQ, 24 July 1951, NAA, MP729/8 37/431/114; DMO&P to Northern Command, 13 August 1951, NAA, MP729/8 37/431/114; Seacombe to AHQ, 9 November 1951, NAA, MP729/8 37/431/120.

76   '"Watch on Indonesia" post in jungle: Eye on NG border', *Sunday Mail* (Brisbane), 1 February 1953.

77 'NG army camp built', *SMH*, 31 March 1953.
78 Northern Command to AHQ, 2 November 1953, NAA, MP729/8 37/431/114.
79 Sinclair, *Keeping the Peace*, pp. 54–5; Greville, *The Royal Australian Engineers*, pp. 512–13.
80 DMO&P to DCGS, 12 August 1954, NAA, MP729/8 37/431/114.
81 Colin Adamson, Archive No. 1171, AAWFA.
82 William Guest, Archive No. 0588, AAWFA.
83 Bert Wansley, interview, 27 May 2013.
84 Northern Command to AHQ, 11 February 1955, NAA, MT1131/1 A247/1/654.
85 Northern Command to AHQ, 12 March 1956, NAA, MT1131/1 A247/1/654; Assistant Secretary Treasury to Secretary Army, 21 September 1956, NAA, MT1131/1 A247/1/654; Finance Representative Area Command PNG to Northern Command, 27 November 1956, NAA, MT1131/1 A247/1/654.
86 Secretary Army to Secretary Territories, 6 December 1955, NAA, A518 E840/1/4; Nelson, 'Papua New Guinea', p. 164.
87 Bert Wansley, interview, 27 May 2013.
88 'History of the PNG Army (1939–1970)', AWM125 12; Northern Command, 'Establishment – Headquarters Papua New Guinea Area', 9 May 1955, NAA, A10857 III/510B/HE; Sinclair, *Keeping the Peace*, pp. 10, 217.
89 O'Neill, *Strategy and Diplomacy*, p. 97.
90 Secretary Territories to Secretary Army, 7 July 1950, NAA, A452 1962/8146. See for instance the correspondence between Hasluck, McBrie and Francis, 2 May – 16 July 1952, NAA, A663 O214/1/132.
91 Barrett to Daly, 31 December 1957, MP927/1 A5/1/132; Maddern, 'Papua New Guinea Volunteer Rifles'.
92 'PIR treated like pigs: Soldiers complain to Mr Barrett', *South Pacific Post* (Port Moresby), 30 March 1955; Cleland to Barrett, 30 March 1955, PNGNA, 405 47/62.
93 Sinclair, *Keeping the Peace*, p. 57.
94 'Dusky guardians of Australia's back door: Thanks to the Fuzzy-Wuzzies we can sleep easier', *Courier-Mail* (Brisbane), 10 August 1950.
95 'Fuzzy-Wuzzies in the islands: Regiment to form part of our army', *Age* (Melbourne), 3 January 1946. See also 'Papuan army could help defend north', *SMH*, 13 May 1954, 'They're in the army now', *Courier-Mail* (Brisbane), 2 September 1952, 'Mr Francis' fuzzy wuzzy army', *SMH*, 14 May 1954.
96 Sabin, 'Formation of the Pacific Islands Regiment'.
97 Northern Command, 'Proposal for a New Lower Establishment to Supersede II/23C/2 (LE) Pacific Islands Infantry Battalion', 27 July 1956, NAA, A6059 21/441/15; Sabin, 'Formation of the Pacific Islands Regiment'.
98 Sabin, 'Formation of the Pacific Islands Regiment'.
99 M.B.B. Orken, 'Report – Liaison Officer – PIR, 17th – 21st December 1957', 21 December 1957, PNGNA, 82 1/7/1.

100 Enloe, *Ethnic Soldiers*, p. 27.
101 See in particular Rand and Wagner, 'Recruiting the "martial races"';
     Omissi, '"Martial Races"'.
102 Griffin, Nelson and Firth, *Papua New Guinea*, p. 50.
103 For a discussion of the use of the military in maintaining internal security
     in the British context, see Clayton and Killingray, *Khaki and Blue*.
104 See Parsons, '"Wakamba warriors are soldiers of the queen"', p. 672.
105 Sabin to Northern Command, 16 December 1952, NAA, MT1131/1
     A251/6/51.
106 V. Seacombe, 'Role, training and employment of the PIR', 24 July 1951,
     NAA, MP729/8 37/431/114.
107 Sabin, 'Formation of the Pacific Islands Regiment'.
108 Firth, 'Colonial administration and the invention of the native', pp. 261–2.
109 H. Sabin, 'Proposed Reog – PIR', 3 August 1956, NAA, A6059 21/441/15.
110 Sabin, 'Formation of the Pacific Islands Regiment'.
111 Northern Command, 'Proposal for a New Lower Establishment', 27 July
     1956, NAA, A6059 21/441/15.
112 Sabin, 'Formation of the Pacific Islands Regiment'.
113 'Report by E.F. Campbell', 26 July 1957, NAA, MT1131/1 A89/1/161.
114 Seacombe to AHQ, 15 June 1951, NAA, MT1131/1 A89/1/161.
115 'Report on Educational Activities in Papua and New Guinea', 4 August
     1953, NAA, MT1131/1 A89/1/161.
116 Weeden to Director Army Education, 12 April 1954, NAA, MT1131/1
     A89/1/161.
117 Education officer PNG to Education Officer Northern Command, NAA,
     A1361 33/1/15 Part 2 and Ord to D Psych, letter, n.d., NAA, MP927/1
     A5/1/132.
118 Sinclair, *Keeping the Peace*, p. 53.
119 B.J. Hodge, 'PNG Census Jun 69: Frequency distribution and relationships
     between certain variables', Research Report No. 32, April 1972,
     AAPSYCH; Mench, *The Role of the Papua New Guinea Defence Force*,
     p. 113.
120 'An Act to Amend the *Defence Act 1903–1950*, as Amended by the
     Defence Act 1951', ComLaw, <www.comlaw.gov.au>; Secretary of the
     Army to Secretaries of Defence, Air and Navy, 18 September 1950, NAA,
     A432 1961/3102.
121 Department of Defence Minute Paper, 7 July 1965, NAA, A1946
     1968/164.
122 Grey, *The Australian Army*, p. 194; Mench, *The Role of the Papua New
     Guinea Defence Force*, p. 26; Sinclair, *Keeping the Peace*, p. 45.
123 Seacombe, 'Role, training and employment of the PIR', 24 July 1951,
     NAA, MP729/8 37/431/114.
124 Grey, *The Australian Army*, p. 194.
125 Nelson, 'Hold the good name of the soldier', p. 205.
126 Northern Command, 'Proposal for a New Lower Establishment', 27 July
     1956, NAA, A6059 21/441/15.
127 'Report by E.F. Campbell', 26 July 1957, NAA, MT1131/1 A89/1/161.

128 Secretary Territories to Secretary Army, 7 July 1950, NAA, A452 1962/8146.
129 The biographical details of the PIR's officer cohort are taken from Australian Army, *The Army List*, 1953, *passim*.
130 Maddern, 'Papua New Guinea Volunteer Rifles'; Sabin, 'Formation of the Pacific Islands Regiment'; T. Daly, 'Disturbance – Pacific Islands Regiment – 3rd January 1961', 2 February 1961, NAA, MP927/1 A251/1/1133 [hereafter Daly, 'Disturbance'].
131 Sabin, 'Formation of the Pacific Islands Regiment'.
132 Secretary Territories to Secretary Army, 7 July 1950, A452 1962/8146.
133 Bell, 'New Guinea pidgin teaching', p. 672.
134 'No pidgin in army', *Townsville Daily Bulletin*, 28 May 1954; '"Pidgin" is on way out', *Courier-Mail* (Brisbane), 28 May 1954.
135 Sinclair, *Keeping the Peace*, pp. 53–4.
136 Education officer PNG to education officer Northern Command, NAA, A1361 33/1/15 Part 2.
137 Picture caption, *Advocate* (Burnie), 13 February 1954.
138 Wolfers, *Race Relations and Colonial Rule in Papua New Guinea*, pp. 98, 122.
139 George Aibo, interview, 30 July 2013; Sinclair, *Keeping the Peace*, p. 49.
140 HQPIR to Area Command PNG, 19 October 1962, NAA, J2818 R148/1/4.
141 William Guest, quoted in Sinclair, *Keeping the Peace*, p. 49.
142 Ibid.
143 Court Martial of Robert James Dick, 2 December 1953, NAA, A471 83560.
144 Court Martial of Jack Dihm, 21 September 1953, NAA, A471 83561; Sinclair, *Keeping the Peace*, p. 53.
145 Jack Dihm, Archive No. 1698, AAWFA.
146 'Hansard Extract – Pacific Islands Regiment', November 1957, NAA, A6059 21/441/15; Downs, *The Australian Trusteeship*, p. 209.
147 W.F. Cook, 'Investigation into a disturbance at Taurama Barracks 1 December 52', 11 December 1952, NAA, MT1131/1 A251/6/51; Ron Lange, interview, 11 May 2012; Colebatch, 'To find a path', p. 73.
148 Sabin to Northern Command, 3 December 1952, NAA, MT1131/1 A251/6/51.
149 Cook, 'Investigation into a disturbance at Taurama Barracks 1 December 52'.
150 Sabin to Northern Command, 'Disturbance – PIR Taurama', 3 December 1952, NAA, MT1131/1 A251/6/51.
151 Seacombe to AHQ, 24 December 1952, NAA MT1131/1 A251/6/51.
152 Ibid.
153 Ron Lange, telephone interview, 11 May 2012.
154 Cook, 'Investigation into a disturbance at Taurama Barracks 1 December 52'.
155 Sabin to Northern Command, 16 December 1952, MT1131/1 A251/6/51.

156 Sinclair, *Keeping the Peace*, p. 51.
157 AHQ to Northern Command, 12 August 1952, NAA, MT1131/1 A251/6/40.
158 Military Board Submission No. 10/1968, 1968, AAHU.
159 Court Martial of Private Lekira Ajima, PIR, 3 and 12 August 1953, NAA, A471 83388.
160 Court Martial of Private Lawani Mati, PIR, 4 November 1954, NAA, A471 84214.

2 A 'fool's paradise': The disturbances, 1957–61

1 'Native soldiers riot! Army officers lose control', *South Pacific Post* (Port Moresby), 18 December 1957, cited in Sinclair, *Keeping the Peace*, p. 61.
2 Deputy Chief General Staff to Secretary Army, November 1957, NAA, A6059 21/441/15.
3 Sinclair, *Keeping the Peace*, p. 58.
4 Sabin to Brigadier General Staff, 3 August 1956, NAA, A6059 21/441/15; Northern Command, 'Proposal for a New Lower Establishment to Supersede II/23C/2 (LE)', 27 July 1956, NAA, A6059 21/441/15; Director Infantry to Director Staff Duties, 3 September 1957, NAA, A6059 21/441/15.
5 In the PIR, these were Lieutenant Colonels H. Sabin, A. Baldwin, W. Wansley and McGuinn, while the officers commanding Area Command were Lieutenant Colonels N. Maddern, T. Young, J. Lynch and W. Wansley.
6 Daly to Wade, 20 December 1957, NAA, MP927/1 A5/1/132.
7 Rackemann to Police Commissioner, 16 December 1957, PNGNA, 82 1/7/1.
8 Daly to Wade, 20 December 1957, NAA, MP927/1 A5/1/132; Kiki, *Kiki*, pp. 86–7.
9 Kiki, *Kiki*, p. 87.
10 Rackemann to Police Commissioner, 16 December 1957, PNGNA, 82 1/7/1.
11 Gunther to Secretary Territories, 23 December 1957, PNGNA, 82 1/7/1; Kiki, *Kiki*, p. 87.
12 James Cruickshank, Archive No. 0770, AAWFA.
13 Orken, 'Report – Liaison officer – PIR, 17th – 21st December, 1957', 21 December 1957, PNGNA, 82 1/7/1.
14 Daly to Wade, 20 December 1957, NAA, MP927/1 A5/1/132; Gunther to Secretary Territories, 17 December 1957, PNGNA, 82 1/7/1.
15 PNG Command, 'PNG Comd Internal security plan 1/66: Planning for internal unrest involving Pacific Islands (PI) soldiers', 7 May 1966, NAA, A452 1972/4342.
16 McGuinn to Northern Command, 16 December 1957, NAA, MP927/1 A66/1/428.
17 'Troops in NG a disgrace', *Courier-Mail* (Brisbane), 30 January 1958.

18 'Native soldiers riot! Army officers lose control', *South Pacific Post* (Port Moresby), 18 December 1957, cited in Sinclair, *Keeping the Peace*, p. 61; Rackemann to Police Commissioner, 16 December 1957, PNGNA, 82 1/7/1; Assistant Director of Medical Services, 'Taurama Native Hospital – List of Patients at the Hospital in Connection with Riot', 16 December 1957, PNGNA, 82 1/7/1.

19 Normoyle to Gunther, 16 December 1957, PNGNA, 82 1/7/1.

20 Rackemann to Police Commissioner, 16 December 1957, PNGNA, 82 1/7/1.

21 Gunther, radio address, 18 December 1957, PNGNA, 82 1/7/1; Daly to Wade, 20 December 1957, NAA, MP927/1 A5/1/132; George Aibo, interview, 30 July 2013; Gunther to Secretary Territories, 17 December 1957, PNGNA, 82 1/7/1.

22 Rackemann to Police Commissioner, PNGNA, 82 1/7/1.

23 Orken, 'Report', 21 December 1957, PNGNA, 82 1/7/1.

24 Ibid.

25 Fisher to Commissioner of Police, 19 December 1957, PNGNA, 82 1/7/1; Orken, 'Report', 21 December 1957, PNGNA, 82 1/7/1; Daly to Wade, 20 December 1957, NAA, MP927/1 A5/1/132.

26 Fisher to Commissioner of Police, 19 December 1957, PNGNA, 82 1/7/1.

27 Orken, 'Report', 21 December 1957, PNGNA, 82 1/7/1; F.J. Winkle, 'Report on incident at Taurama Barracks on Monday 16th December 1957', 21 December 1957, PNGNA, 82 1/7/1.

28 Rackemann to Police Commissioner, 16 December 1957, PNGNA, 82 1/7/1.

29 Daly to Wade, 20 December 1957, MP927/1 A5/1/132.

30 Winkle, 'Report on incident at Taurama Barracks on Monday 16th December 1957'.

31 'NG magistrate in bid to "avoid loss of prestige"', *SMH*, 22 January 1958.

32 Daly to Wade, 20 December 1957, NAA, MP927/1 A5/1/132; Shanahan to Daly, January 1958, NAA, MP927/1 A66/1/428.

33 'Army sacks 15 men who rioted', *South Pacific Post* (Port Moresby), 5 March 1958; George Aibo, interview, 30 July 2013.

34 Hasluck to Cramer, 7 January 1958, NAA, MP927/1 A66/1/428.

35 Bryant to Gunther, n.d., NAA, MP927/1 A66/1/428; Mench, *The Role of the Papua New Guinea Defence Force*, p. 30.

36 '100 arrests follow brawls at Moresby', *Canberra Times*, 16 December 1957.

37 'New Guinea riots alarm officials', *SMH*, 19 December 1957.

38 Gunther to Hasluck, 17 December 1957, PNGNA, 82 1/7/1.

39 'Regiment officers defended', *Telegraph*, 2 February 1958; 'Claim no officer turned tails', *Courier-Mail* (Brisbane), 2 February 1958. McCarthy, open letter, 31 January 1958; Normoyle, open letter, 31 January 1958 in NAA, MP927/1 A66/1/428.

40 Daly to Wade, 20 December 1957, NAA, MP927/1 A5/1/132.

41 'PIR – Disturbances at Port Moresby, Notes for minister for discussion with minister for Defence and Territories', 10 February 1958, NAA, MP927/1 A66/1/428.

42 Daly to Wade, 20 December 1957, NAA, MP927/1 A5/1/132.

43 Kiki, *Kiki*, p. 87.
44 Normoyle to Gunther, 16 December 1957, PNGNA, 82 1/7/1.
45 McGuinn to Northern Command, 16 December 1957, NAA, MP927/1 A66/1/428.
46 Daly to Wade, 20 December 1957, NAA, MP927/1 A5/1/132.
47 Ibid.
48 Gunther to Daly, 18 December 1957, NAA, MP927/1 A5/1/132; Barrett to Daly, 20 December 1957, NAA, MP927/1 A5/1/132; Daly to Wade, 20 December 1957, NAA, MP927/1 A5/1/132.
49 Grey, *A Soldier's Soldier*, p. 96; Sinclair, *Keeping the Peace*, p. 67.
50 Daly to Wade, 20 December 1957, NAA, MP927/1 A5/1/132.
51 'New Guinea riots alarm officials', *SMH*, 19 December 1957.
52 'Report by E.F. Campbell, D Psych AHQ on visit to Pacific Islands Regiment', 26 July 1957, NAA, MT1131/1 A89/1/161.
53 Nelson, *Mobs and Masses*, p. 16.
54 Cabinet Agendum No. 336, 28 July 1959, NAA, A5818, Vol. 7.
55 Military Board, 'Reorganisation of PIR', 4 February 1958, NAA, A10857 II/23C/LE.
56 Lambert to White, 15 July 1958, NAA, A452 8075.
57 Sinclair, *Keeping the Peace*, p. 67.
58 'Copy of statement made by his honour the Administrator in the Legislative Council – 4 March 1958', NAA, MP927/1 A66/1/428.
59 Mench, *The Role of the Papua New Guinea Defence Force*, p. 31.
60 Nelson, *Papua New Guinea*, p. 204.
61 Treasury to Territories, 27 August 1958, NAA, A452 1962/8146.
62 T. Daly, 'Report on the Pacific Islands Regiment', 2 February 1961, NAA, MP927/1 A251/1/1133.
63 Eldridge to Daly, 6 January 1961, NAA, MP927/1 A251/1/1133.
64 Cabinet Submission No. 1346, 13 September 1961, NAA, A4940 C3436.
65 Sinclair, *Keeping the Peace*, p. 73.
66 Court-Martial of Lance Corporal Ata Lipokia, 24 January 1961, NAA, A471 88590.
67 Stokes, unpublished memoir, p. 189.
68 Norrie to Northern Command, 5 January 1961, NAA, A452 1962/8172.
69 Ibid.
70 Cleland to Lambert, 2 February 1961, NAA, A452 1962/8172.
71 Court-Martial of Lance Corporal Kabeho Kaubabi, 17 January 1961, NAA, A471 88585.
72 Norrie to Northern Command 5 January 1961, NAA, A452 1962/8172.
73 Rose, 'The anatomy of mutiny', p. 569.
74 Stokes, unpublished memoir, p. 189; Cabinet Submission No. 1346, 13 September 1961, NAA, A4940 C3436.
75 Stokes, unpublished memoir, p. 189.
76 Terry Holland, questionnaire, received 26 November 2013.
77 Norrie to Northern Command, 5 January 1961, NAA, A452 1962/8172; Court-Martial of Private Towawaong Dabi, 12 January 1961, NAA, A471 88569.

78 Cabinet Submission No. 1346, 13, September 1961, NAA, A4940 C3436.
79 Court-Martial of Private Kahpou Pahun, 10 January 1961, NAA, A471 88606.
80 Court-Martial of Private Bonyu Titi, 19 January 1961, NAA, A471 88622.
81 Stokes, unpublished memoir, p. 190.
82 Ibid., p. 190.
83 Gabi Gapa, interview, 30 July 2013.
84 Norrie to Northern Command, 5 January 1961, NAA, A452 1962/8172.
85 '74 native troops to be charged over New Guinea riot', SMH, 5 January 1961.
86 Cabinet Submission No. 1346, 13 September 1961, NAA, A4940 C3436.
87 Daly, 'Report on the Pacific Islands Regiment', McCarthy to District Officers, 20 January 1961, NAA, A452 1962/8172.
88 Sinclair, Keeping the Peace, p. 75.
89 See for instance Court-Martial of Private Utera Kipu, 11 January 1961, NAA, A471 88588.
90 Court-Martial of Lance Corporal Kabeho Kaubabi, 17 January 1961, NAA, A471 88585.
91 Stokes, unpublished memoir, p. 190.
92 Court-Martial of Private Takoni Pulei, 17 January 1961, NAA, A471 88611; Court-Martial of Private Kahpou Pahun, 10 January 1961, NAA, A471 88606; Court-Martial of Private Kouna Gari, 24 January 1961, NAA, A471 88575.
93 Court-Martial of Private Takoni Pulei, 17 January 1961, NAA, A471 88611.
94 Court-Martial of Private Utera Kipa, 11 January 1961, NAA, A471 88588.
95 Court-Martial of Private Kouna Gari, 24 January 1961, NAA, A471 88575; Court-Martial of Private Towawaong Dabi, 12 January 1961, NAA, A471 88569; Court-Martial of Private Kalava Amanu, 10 January 1961, NAA, A471 88561; Court-Martial of Private Kahpou Pahun, 10 January 1961, NAA, A471 88606.
96 Daly, 'Disturbance'.
97 Court-Martial of Private Utera Kipa, 11 January 1961, NAA, A471 88588.
98 'Pacific Islands troops discharged', Age (Melbourne), 13 January 1961; Sinclair, Keeping the Peace, p. 75.
99 Stokes, unpublished memoir, p. 190.
100 See for instance 'NG troops and police clash on pay', Canberra Times, 4 January 1961; '74 natives to be charged over New Guinea riot', SMH, 5 January 1961.
101 Secretary Building Workers' Industrial Union of Australia to Menzies, 10 January 1961, NAA, A452 1962/8172. Similar letters were sent by the Queensland Plasterers' Union and the Meat Industry Employees' Union, NAA, A452 1962/8172.
102 Sinclair, Keeping the Peace, p. 74.
103 Ibid., p. 76; Mench, The Role of the Papua New Guinea Defence Force, p. 30.
104 Gunther to Cleland, 4 January 1961, NAA, A452 1962/8172.

105 Cleland to Lambert, 9 January 1961, NAA, A452 1962/8172.

106 Cabinet Submission No. 1346, 'Report on Pacific Islands Regiment', 13
     September 1961, NAA, A4940 C3436.

107 See for instance 'Alleged call to NG rioters', *Canberra Times*, 24 January
     1961; 'NG official gaoled for sedition', *Canberra Times*, 25 January 1961;
     'Native riot pleased man on sedition charge, court told', *Age* (Melbourne),
     24 January 1961.

108 Sinclair, *Keeping the Peace*, p. 77.

109 Roy, 'Military loyalty in the colonial context', p. 507.

110 Correspondence between Cleland and Lambert, 7 April 1961 – 4 January
     1962, NAA, A452 1962/8172.

111 '74 natives to be charged over New Guinea riot', *SMH*, 4 January 1961.

112 'Draft answers to parliamentary question to Minister Cramer – PIR rates of
     pay', n.d., NAA, A452 1962/8146.

113 Cleland to Lambert, 2 February 1961, NAA, A452 1962/8172.

114 McCarthy to all district officers, 20 January 1961, NAA, A452 1962/8172.

115 T. Daly, 'Report', 2 February 1961, NAA, MP927/1 A251/1/1133; Military
     Board Minute No. 10/1961, AAHU; Flint, unpublished memoir, p. 13.

116 Cleland to Lambert, 2 February 1961, NAA, A452 1962/8172.

117 Court-Martial of Private Utera Kipa, 11 January 1961, NAA, A471 88588.

118 'Report by Mr MBB Orken', cited in Mench, *The Role of the Papua New
     Guinea Defence Force*, p. 31.

119 Cramer to Townley, 28 April 1961, in Military Board Minute
     No. 77/1961, 30 March 1961, AAHU; Cramer to Hasluck, 28 April 1961;
     Cleland to Lambert 19 May 1961, NAA, A452 1962/8146; Hasluck to
     Cramer 12 September 1961, NAA, A452 1962/8146; Holt to Cramer, 25
     June 1961, NAA, MP927/1 A251/1/1133.

120 Cabinet Decision No. 1609, 26 September 1961, NAA, A4940 C3436.

121 DMO&P, 'JPC Report 32/1968 Future Size and Role of PIR', 16 May
     1968, AWM121 234/F/2.

122 See for instance, Warwick Smith to Hay, 5 October 1966, NAA, A452
     1966/4989.

3 'Real duty': Confrontation and the creation of PNG Command, 1962–66

1 Edwards and Pemberton, *Crises and Commitments*, pp. 200–7, 230–2.

2 Defence Committee, Minute No. 4/1963, 7 February 1963, NAA, A452
   1972/4342. See also 'Defence Implications of changes in West New
   Guinea', October 1962, NAA, A452 1962/7075.

3 Defence Committee Minute, 4 February 1963, NAA, A1945/40 832/8,
   cited in Horner, *Strategic Command*, p. 203.

4 Ibid.

5 Horner, *Strategic Command*, pp. 203–5; Edwards and Pemberton, *Crises
   and Commitments*, pp. 259–60.

6 Cabinet Decision No. 791, 8 May 1963, NAA, A5619 C174.

7 Defence Committee, Minute No. 5/1963, 7 February 1963, NAA, A452
   1972/4342.

8   Horner, *Strategic Command*, p. 214.
9   Frühling, *A History of Australian Strategic Policy*, pp. 277–336.
10 'Australia's strategic position', February 1963 in ibid., p. 304.
11 'Strategic basis of Australian defence policy', October 1964 in ibid., p. 322.
12 'List of past, current and proposed strengths of PIR c. 1965', n.d., NAA, A452 1966/4989.
13 George Kearney, 'An examination of the 2/68 recruit population', Psychological Report No. 18/68, November 1968, AAPSYCH.
14 Northern Command, 'Role and deployment of the Army in New Guinea', 23 June 1961, NAA, A6059 41/441/124.
15 Defence Committee, Agendum No. 4/1963, 29 January 1963, NAA, A5799 4/1963.
16 Northern Command, 'Organisation of the Army – Papua New Guinea – Subsequent Phase', 13 August 1963, AWM90 WPI.
17 Waters, '"Against the tide"', p. 198.
18 Cabinet Decision No. 791, 8 May 1963, NAA, A5619 C174.
19 Defence Committee, Minute No. 5/1963, 7 February 1963, NAA, A452 1972/4342.
20 Department of Defence, 'Meeting of the Joint Planning Committee', 16 November 1962, NAA, A452 1962/7075.
21 Department of the Army, 'Report on the Pacific Islands Regiment', 15 September 1961, NAA, A4940 C3436.
22 Sinclair, *Keeping the Peace*, p. 86.
23 Northern Command, 'Organisation of the Army – Papua New Guinea – Subsequent Phase', 13 August 1963, AWM90 WPI; Cabinet Submission No. 118, 8 April 1964, NAA, A4940 C3436.
24 Sinclair, *Keeping the Peace*, p. 98.
25 Wade to Taylor, 16 February 1962, NAA, A6059 41/441/124. See Grey, *The Australian Army*, pp. 204–8; Palazzo, *The Australian Army*, pp. 249–52.
26 Cabinet Decision No. 791, 8 May 1963, NAA, A5619 C174.
27 Prime Minister's Department Minute, 20 August 1968, NAA, A5619 C174.
28 Taylor to Wade, 18 April 1962, NAA, A6059 41/441/124; Northern Command, 'Organisation of the Army – Papua New Guinea – Subsequent Phase', 13 August 1963, AWM90 WPI.
29 '1PIR Administrative Instruction 1/65 Raising of 2PIR and handover of 1PIR outstations', 4 February 1965, NAA, J2818 132/3/19A.
30 For a description of the construction process, see Greville, *The Royal Australian Engineers*, pp. 515–24.
31 Grahame Wease, telephone interview, 14 October 2011; Sinclair, *Keeping the Peace*, p. 132.
32 Grahame Wease, telephone interview, 14 October 2011.
33 Sinclair, *Keeping the Peace*, p. 132.
34 Grahame Wease, interview, 14 October 2011.
35 Greville, *The Royal Australian Engineers*, pp. 509–12.
36 Sinclair, *Keeping the Peace*, pp. 27–35.

37 'Administrative appreciation for the expansion of the Army in Papua and New Guinea', 11 January 1965, NAA, J2818, 22/1/7.
38 Abbott to Secretary Department of the Administration, 9 September 1964, NAA, A452 1964/3744.
39 Sinclair, *Keeping the Peace*, p. 96.
40 Ibid., p. 98.
41 Horner, *SAS: Phantoms of War*, p. 61.
42 Sinclair, *Keeping the Peace*, pp. 90–1. See also Quirk to former PIR officers, September 1963, NAA, J2818 R160/1/3.
43 'Recruiting PNGMD', 18 February 1964, NAA, J2818 164/1/4; Pascoe to Bensted, 29 April 1964, NAA, J2818, 164/1/5.
44 George Kearney, 'An examination of the 2/68 recruit population', Psychological Report No. 18/68, November 1968, AAPSYCH.
45 HQPNGMD to Northern Command, 3 January 1964, NAA, J2818, 164/1/3.
46 Sinclair, *Keeping the Peace*, p. 235.
47 Ted Diro, interview, 31 July 2013.
48 Sinclair, *Keeping the Peace*, pp. 233–4.
49 Ibid., p. 238.
50 See for instance the call for 'experienced Territorians' to lead the PIR in 1950, referred to in Grey, *The Australian Army*, p. 194.
51 HQPIR to HQ Area Command PNG, 5 August 1963, NAA, J2818 164/1/1; Geoff Payne, telephone interview, 13 March 2012.
52 George Kearney, telephone interview, 19 September 2011; Sinclair, *Keeping the Peace*, p. 59.
53 Geoff Payne, telephone interview, 13 March 2012.
54 L. Sweeney, 'Annual Report on Education: Papua New Guinea', 27 February 1963, NAA, MT1131/1 A89/1/230; Graeme Manning, questionnaire, received 27 March 2012.
55 Geoff Payne, telephone interview, 13 March 2012; D. Armstrong, 'PNG Army Population Survey', Research Report No. 10/68, November 1968, AAPSYCH.
56 District Commissioner to Director District Services and Native Affairs, 11 July 1952, PNGNA, 16 19/3.
57 John Kelley, telephone interview, 2 August 2012.
58 Geoff Payne, unpublished diary, May–June 1972.
59 Geoff Payne, telephone interview, 13 March 2012.
60 May, *The Changing Role of the Military in Papua New Guinea*, p. 27.
61 Galloway to Recruiting Officer, 13 October 1965, PNGNA, 55 52/2/2; Geoff Payne, telephone interview, 13 March 2012; Administrative Instruction 14/63, 20 September 1963, NAA, J2818 164/1/1; John Kelley, telephone interview, 2 August 2012.
62 Press release for ABC, 1964, NAA, J2818 164/1/5; Major Bower to Director of Posts and Telegraphs, 10 November 1964, NAA, J2818 164/1/6.
63 Manager Kulili Estate to Administrator, 14 August 1961, PNGNA, 82 28/6/4.

64 Recruiting officer, 'Recruiting tour 1/64 13 June – 20 June 1964', NAA, J2818 164/1/5.

65 Military Board Agendum No. 42/1960, 7 August 1960, NAA, A6059 41/441/94. See also Military Board Agendum No. 54/1960, 30 September 1960, NAA, A6059 41/441/94; Submission to Military Board 25/67, 5 April 1967, AAHU.

66 Cabinet Submission No. 1346, 15 September 1961, NAA, A4940 C3436; Military Board Submission 45/1965, 27 July 1965, NAA, A452 1965/5991.

67 'Report of the AHQ Working Committee – Identification of Potential Officers from the Pacific Islands', 21 February 1963, NAA, J2818 160/2/1.

68 Military Board Submission 25/67, 5 April 1967, AAHU.

69 'Report of the AHQ Working Committee – Identification of Potential Officers from the Pacific Islands', 21 February 1963, NAA, J2818 160/2/1.

70 Johnson to Pascoe, 30 May 1963, NAA, J2818 160/2/1; Pascoe to Hosking, n.d., NAA, J2818 160/2/1.

71 JPC Report No 21/64, 'Command and Control in the Territory of Papua and New Guinea', 28 February 1964, NAA, A1946 1968/710.

72 AHQ Operational Instruction 2/63 PIR, 25 February 1963, NAA, A6059 41/441/124. Police and Administration officers also played a role in intelligence-gathering in the border region.

73 Defence Committee Agendum No. 74/1968, 13 December 1963, NAA, A2031 74/1963. See also Edwards and Pemberton, *Crises and Commitments*, p. 279.

74 Defence Committee, Minute No. 5/1963, 7 February 1963, NAA, A452 1972/4342.

75 See for instance Smith, *Gunners in Borneo*, p. 43.

76 Brian McFarlane, interview, 16 February 2013.

77 'Command and control organisation to counter covert Indonesian action in the Territory of Papua New Guinea', 3 June 1967, NAA, A452 1972/4342; JPC Report No. 60/64, 'Extension of the conflict with Indonesia – Plans Spillikin and Hemley', 21 June 1964, NAA, A8738 21; Dennis and Grey, *Emergency and Confrontation*, p. 194.

78 M.F. Brogan, 'Plan Pygmalion: Proposed conference at Port Moresby 19–21 July 65', 28 June 1965, NAA, A1946 1968/710; Department of Defence, 'Plan Pygmalion', 26 May 1966, NAA, A452 1972/4342.

79 Joint Service Plan 'Pygmalion', 9 April 1964, NAA, A452 1972/4342.

80 JPC Report No. 32/1968, 'Future Size and Role of the Pacific Islands Regiment', 10 May 1968, NAA, A8738 39; Cabinet Submission No. 118, 8 April 1964, NAA, A4940 C3436.

81 Wilton to Sherger, 24 October 1963, NAA, A1946 1968/710.

82 'Command and control organisation to counter covert Indonesian action in the Territory of Papua New Guinea', 3 June 1967, NAA, A452 1972/4342.

83 Dennis and Grey, *Emergency and Confrontation*, p. 253.

84 'Badmash' is Nepalese for 'enemy', and was presumably chosen because of the PIR's regimental alliance and officer exchange program with 7th Duke of Edinburgh's Own Ghurkha Rifles Regiment. Sinclair, *Keeping the Peace*, pp. 100–1; 'Soldiers to patrol NG', *Canberra Times*, 21 July 1964.

85 'Patrol Report 63/64 D Coy Ptl', 14 May 1964, NAA, A6847 8.
86 'Suitim Graun' translates roughly as 'suitable ground', or 'ground suiting him'.
87 See Dennis and Grey, *Emergency and Confrontation*, pp. 228–9.
88 K. McKenzie, 'Director's Report for Exercise "Suitim Graun"', 7 February 1965, PNGNA, 55 52/2/2.
89 Ibid.; McKenzie to Galloway, 13 February 1965, PNGNA, 55 52/2/2.
90 Mike Dennis, interview, 15 February 2012.
91 Ted Diro, interview, 31 July 2013.
92 'AHQ Operational Instruction 2/63 PIR', 25 February 1963, NAA, A6059 41/441/124.
93 Sinclair, *Keeping the Peace*, p. 93.
94 Ian Gollings, interview, 3 November 2011; Brian McFarlane, interview, 16 February 2013; Beale, *Operation Orders*, p. 73.
95 Sio Maiasa, interview, 3 August 2013.
96 See for instance 'Patrol Report 63/64 D Coy Ptl', 14 May 1964, NAA, A6847 8; 'Patrol Report 63–63/64', February 1964 NAA, A6847 8; 'Patrol Report 1 PIR 21 65/66', 2 June 66, NAA, A6847 8. Intelligence Officer 1PIR to District Commissioner, 19 May 1967, PNGNA, 55 52/2/2; Maurie Pears, interview, 14 April 2012.
97 '1967/8 PNG Comd Patrol Programme', 18 May 1967, PNGNA, 55 52/2/2; 'Papua and New Guinea Patrol and Exercise Programme 1971/1972', 7 April 1971, PNGNA, 1008 52/2/2; 'PNG Land Forces Patrol and Exercise Programme, July 1973 to June 74', n.d., PNGNA, 1008 52/2/2.
98 Northern Command, 'Administrative Appreciation', 11 January 1965, NAA, J2818, 22/1/7/.
99 Sinclair, *Keeping the Peace*, p. 202.
100 Ronnie Oiwelo, interview, 31 July 2013; Thomas Posi-tute, interview, 30 July 2013; Barney Dinji, interview, 31 July 2013; Moses Kiari, interview, 2 August 2013; Jim Kombukun, interview, 31 July 2013.
101 See for instance PNG Command Serial 3, 'D Company 2PIR operational exercise report, 20 September – 23 October', 14 December 1965, NAA, A6847 8.
102 Harry Bell, '1 PIR Patrol Report 19/65–66', n.d., NAA, A6847 8.
103 Stokes, unpublished memoir, p. 255.
104 Simpson, 'C Coy 2PIR Ptl Report', 14 December 1972, NAA, A6847 5.
105 'Patrol report 9–66/67', n.d., NAA, A6847, 8; Jack Kukuma, interview, 3 August 2013.
106 See for instance any of the PNG Command patrol reports held in NAA series A6847.
107 Bob Sayce, interview, 4 September 2012.
108 E.S. Sharp to District Commissioner, 29 May 1963, PNGNA, 55 52/2/2.
109 'Patrol Briefing Orders – Kiliwas patrol', 15 Dec 1953, NAA, A471 84204; 'Patrol Briefing Orders – Sissano patrol', 12 Jan 1954, NAA, A471 84204.
110 John Suat, interview, 6 August 2013; Moses Kiari, interview, 2 August 2013; Laurie Lewis, interview, 14 July 2012.

111 Bob Sayce, interview, 4 September 2012; Colin Adamson, Archive
     No. 1171, AAWFA; 'Lost New Guinea tribe: Villagers fear dinner date',
     Canberra Times, 15 September 1966; 'Primitive tribe found in NG',
     Courier-Mail (Brisbane), 15 September 1966.
112 See for instance 'Patrol Report 63–63/64', February 1964, NAA, A6847, 8;
     Moses Kiari, interview, 2 August 2013.
113 Stokes, unpublished memoir, p. 259.
114 Ibid., p. 256. See also for instance 'Patrol Report 18–64/65 B Coy Ptl',
     December 1964, NAA, A6847, 8; James Cruickshank, Archive No. 0770,
     AAWFA.
115 Sinclair, *Keeping the Peace*, p. 93.
116 Moses Kiari, interview, 2 August 2013.
117 Defence Committee, Minute No. 74/1963, 13 December 1963, NAA,
     A2031, 74/1963.
118 AHQ Operational Instruction 2/63, 25 February 1963, NAA, A6059
     41/441/124.
119 John Suat, interview, 6 August 2013; Brian McFarlane, interview, 16
     February 2013.
120 Sinclair, *Keeping the Peace*, p. 127.
121 '1PIR patrol report Serial 9, 20 August – 16 September 1969', n.d., NAA,
     A6847 11.
122 Ray Quirk to former officers, September 1963, NAA, J2818 R160/1/3.

4 From 'native' to national: Papua New Guinean soldiers, 1960–75

1 Downs, *The Australian Trusteeship*, p. 240. Griffin, Nelson and Firth,
   Papua New Guinea, pp. 130–1.
2 See chapters 10 and 11, Wolfers, *Race Relations and Colonial Rule in
   Papua New Guinea*, pp. 125–65.
3 Downs, *The Australian Trusteeship*, p. 130.
4 Doran, 'Introduction', in *Australia and Papua New Guinea, 1966–1969*,
   p. xxii; Griffin, Nelson and Firth, *Papua New Guinea*, pp. 133–4.
5 Downs, *The Australian Trusteeship*, p. 385.
6 Wolfers, *Race Relations and Colonial Rule in Papua New Guinea*,
   pp. 136–7.
7 See for instance Native Local Government Council Conference, 12 January
   1962, PNGNA, 82 9/7/2. Downs, *The Australian Trusteeship*, p. 200.
   Wolfers, *Race Relations and Colonial Rule in Papua New Guinea*,
   pp. 136–7.
8 Griffin, Nelson and Firth, *Papua New Guinea*, pp. 129–30.
9 In some cases, Indigenous servicemen and former soldiers led the push for
   greater equality in Australia (Haebich, *Spinning the Dream*, pp. 234–40).
10 Wolfers, *Race Relations and Colonial Rule in Papua New Guinea*,
   pp. 136–7.
11 Griffin, Nelson and Firth, *Papua New Guinea*, pp. 128–9; Wolfers,
   'Trusteeship without the trust', p. 125.
12 Military Board Minute No. 181/1962, October 1962, AAHU.

13   Sinclair, *Keeping the Peace*, p. 247.
14   Quirk to former PIR officers, August 1963, NAA, J2818 R160/1/3. For the RAN perspective, see 'Periodical report for the period 1 October to 31 December 1962', n.d., AWM78, 416/2.
15   Stokes, unpublished memoir, p. 244.
16   Quirk to former PIR officers, August 1963, NAA, J2818 R160/1/3.
17   I.M. Hunter, 'The Army's Tasks in Papua New Guinea', CGS conference, July 1967, NAA, A452 1967/5846.
18   Secretary Defence to Minister for Defence, 7 July 1965, NAA, A1946 1968/164.
19   White to Secretary Defence, 14 November 1962, NAA, A1946 1968/164.
20   For the RAN's discriminatory recruiting policy, see Secretary Navy to Secretary Defence, 'Racial Discrimination', 21 January 1963, NAA, A1946 1968/164.
21   Secretary Department Labour and National Service to Secretary Prime Minister's Department, 31 January 1968, NAA, A1946 1968/164; Secretary Defence to Minister for Defence, 7 July 1965, NAA, A1946 1968/164; Military Board Submission No. 10/1968, 1968, AAHU.
22   See *Defence Act 1903–73*, section 35A, ComLaw, <www.comlaw.gov.au>.
23   'Headquarters, Papua and New Guinea Military District, Tropical Establishment, IV/206/3(TE), 30 October 1964, NAA, A10857 IV/206/TE.
24   Sinclair, *Keeping the Peace*, pp. 28, 30.
25   B.J. Hodge, 'PNG Army Census 1969: Frequency distributions and relationships between certain variables', Research Report No. 32, April 1972, AAPSYCH.
26   Ibid., p. 269; 'Generals want natives in PNGVR but decision up to Canberra', *South Pacific Post* (Port Moresby), 5 November 1963; 'Enlistment of Indigenous – Asiatic & Mixed Race Personnel in PNGVR', 4 October 1963, NAA, J2818 150/3/2.
27   Seacombe to AHQ, 9 Nov 1951, NAA, MP729/8 37/431/120; Military Board, 'Reorganisation of PIR', 4 February 1958, NAA, A10857 II/23C/LE.
28   Military Board Minute 243/1960, 14 October 1960, AAHU.
29   Military Board Instruction 171–1, 1 September 1962, AWM; Military Board Instruction 171–1, Amendment No. 56, 8 March 1968, AWM.
30   Sinclair, *Keeping the Peace*, p. 87.
31   The position of uniforms as a symbol of both status and subordination is discussed in Parsons, *The African Rank-and-File*, p. 118.
32   Sinclair, *Keeping the Peace*, p. 87.
33   Thomas Posi-tute, interview, 30 July 2013.
34   Martin Takoin, interview, 30 July 2013.
35   HQPIR to Area Command PNG, 19 October 1962, NAA, J2818 R148/1/4.
36   'Report on user trial jungle boots', n.d. [c. 1962], NAA, J2818 R148/1/4.
37   Flint, unpublished memoir, p. 13.
38   Ibid.
39   'King size boots', *South Pacific Post* (Port Moresby), 5 November 1963.
40   New Guineans were not Australian citizens but instead 'protected persons'. Cervetto to Boys, 23 March 1965, NAA, J2810 R150/3/2.

41 Israel to Forbes, 9 November 1965, NAA, A452 1966/3828; White to Secretary of Immigration, 28 January 1966, A452 1966/3828; Barnes to Fairhall, 10 May 1966, NAA, A452 1966/3828.

42 Fairhall to Israel, 2 August 1966, NAA, A452 1966/3828.

43 A Papuan applied to join the RAAF the previous year and was also turned down. Warwick Smith to Hay, 19 February 1966, NAA, A452 1966/3828.

44 Lynch to Fox, 25 September 1968, NAA, A452 1966/4989; Ted Diro, 31 July 2013; Jack Kukuma, 3 August 2013.

45 Director-General ASIO to Secretary Prime Minister's Department, 26 October 1964, NAA, A1946 1967/2635 Part 1; Joint Intelligence Committee Report No. 1/1965, 27 October 1965, NAA, A1946 1967/2635 Part 1; Department of Defence, 'Treatment of certain papers', 29 October 1965, NAA, A1946 1967/2635, Part 1.

46 Secretary Navy to Bland, 5 February 1970, NAA, A1946 1967/2635, Part 1.

47 Brian Iselin, interview, 12 December 2011; Department of Defence, 'Procedures for the protective marking of certain papers', 1 June 1971, NAA, A1946 1967/2635, Part 1.

48 See Riseman, 'Racism, indigenous people and the Australian armed forces in the post-Second World War era', p. 162.

49 Roy Beazley, interview, 7 December 2011; Wolfers, *Race Relations and Colonial Rule in Papua New Guinea*, p. 130; Thompson, *Australia and the Pacific Islands in the Twentieth Century*, p. 165.

50 D. Armstrong, 'A Survey of PI Discharge Trends Jan 1964 – Jul 1968', Research Report No. 13, November 1968, AAPSYCH.

51 Quirk to former officers, September 1963, NAA, J2818 R160/1/3.

52 Worland to Assistant Adjutant PIR, 9 August 1962, PNGNA, 1010 52/1/1.

53 Ken Swadling, questionnaire, received 1 August 2011.

54 Worland to Assistant Adjutant PIR, 9 August 1962, PNGNA, 1010 52/1/1.

55 'RSL acts on "racialism"', *Canberra Times*, 29 April 1964; 'Congress to discuss RSL "bias" in Papua', *Canberra Times*, 23 May 1964; Malcolm Macullum, questionnaire, received 28 December 2013.

56 A.F. Dingle, 'Visit to the Territory of Papua and New Guinea, 2nd–5th July 1966', 7 June 1966, NAA, A1838 689/1, Part 2, cited in Doran, *Australia and Papua New Guinea, 1966–1969*, p. 175.

57 Wolfers, *Race Relations and Colonial Rule in Papua New Guinea*, pp. 154–5.

58 Ibid., p. 154.

59 See for instance Ley, 'From colonial backwater to independent state – in a decade', p. 144; Ritchie, 'Australians and Papua New Guinea', p. 299; Wolfers, 'Trusteeship without the trust', p. 127.

60 Wolfers, *Race Relations and Colonial Rule in Papua New Guinea*, p. 154; Kiki, *Kiki*, p. 128.

61 Court martial of Private Punion Takuru, 26 October 1963, NAA, A471 90178.

62 'Patrol Report 63/64 D Coy Ptl', 14 May 1964, NAA, A6847 8.

63 Michael Jeffery, interview, 16 November 2011; Ken Swadling, questionnaire, received 1 August 2011; Norm Hunter, interview, 17 April 2014.
64 Military Board Minute No. 106/1967, 14 April 1967, AAHU.
65 See for instance 'In father's footsteps: New battalion of fuzzy angels', *Canberra Times*, 9 December 1964.
66 Adjutant General, 'Career Structure – Pacific Islands Regiment', July 1965, NAA, A452 1965/5991; Ross Eastgate, interview, 14 April 2012. See also 'Report of the AHQ Working Committee', 21 February 1963, NAA, J2818 160/2/1.
67 Military Board Minute No. 215/1962, 31 October 1962, AAHU.
68 Daly, 'Disturbance'.
69 Daly to Adjutant General, 13 February 1967, NAA, A6059 41/441/94.
70 Almost all those interviewed for this book recalled some degree of close professional relationship with the troops under their command and their colleagues of similar rank.
71 Cliff Brock, interview, 15 March 2013; Jack Kukuma, interview, 3 August 2013.
72 Martin Takoin, interview, 30 July 2013.
73 Don Gillies, telephone interview, 7 December 2012; Ken Swadling, correspondence, 1 August 2011; Mayhew, 'Earthquakes and farewells', p. 117.
74 Grahame Wease, interview 14 October 2011.
75 Ronne Oiwelo, 31 July 2013.
76 Mutuaina Watut, interview, 31 July 2013; Rodney Kanari Daura, interview, 31 July 2013; Thomas Posi-tute, interview, 30 July 2013.
77 Martin Takoin, interview, 30 July 2013; Moses Kiari, interview, 2 August 2013.
78 George Aibo, interview, 30 July 2013; Thomas Posi-tute, interview, 30 July 2013.
79 Wolfers, *Race Relations and Colonial Rule in Papua New Guinea*, p. 154.
80 Phil Adam, interview, 3 May 2011.
81 The study investigated the attitudes of national servicemen teachers, who were chosen as they represented the only group that was not only posted to PNG at the same time but also of similar age, education and rank, making comparison between them possible (Armstrong, 'An examination of the effects of ethnic contact upon the attitudes of some Australians in Papua New Guinea', p. 117).
82 Armstrong, 'An examination of the effects of ethnic contact upon the attitudes of some Australians in Papua New Guinea', p. 120; Azari, Dandeker and Greenberg, 'Cultural stress', p. 594.
83 Ted Diro, interview, 30 July 2013.
84 Colebatch, 'To find a path', p. 127.
85 D. Armstrong and D. Wetherell, 'Attitudes and ideas: A pilot survey of Administration and Mission schools', Research Report No. 25, August 1970, AAPSYCH.
86 John Kelley, interview, 2 August 2012.

87 Recruiting officer, 'Recruiting tour 1/64 13 June – 20 June 1964', NAA, J2818 164/1/5.

88 See 'The Army in Papua/New Guinea', recruiting pamphlet, n.d., UPNG, AP355.109952 P218; 'The Army in Papua New Guinea: Officer careers', recruiting pamphlet, n.d., UPNG, AP355.109952 P218; 'The Pacific Islands Regiment', n.d., PNGNA, 55 52/2/2; 'Your life in the Pacific Islands Regiment', n.d., PNGNA, 55 52/2/2.

89 'Soldier's pay: Army in Papua New Guinea', n.d. [between 1965 and 1972], UPNG, AP355.13509952; Commonwealth of Australia, *Territory of New Guinea Report for 1966–1967*, Commonwealth Govt. Printer, Canberra, 1967, pp. 123, 216.

90 Barney Dinji, interview, 31 July 2013; Anthony Wupu, interview, 6 August 2013.

91 D. Armstrong, 'Service skills used in post service employment', Research Report No. 17 June 1970, AAPSYCH; Colebatch, 'To find a path', p. 314.

92 See Commonwealth of Australia, *Territory of New Guinea Report for 1966–1967*, p. 168.

93 John Kelly, telephone interview, 2 August 2012; Matuaina Watut, interview, 31 July 2013.

94 Martin Takoin, interview, 3 July 2013; Sio Miasa, interview, 3 August 2013; Jack Kukuma, 3 August 2013; Valentine Saese, interview, 6 August 2013; Lincoln Rauletta, interview, 6 August 2013; Patrick Olimomo, interview, 31 July 2013; Tom Levi Chalapan, interview 31 July 2013. See also 'In father's footsteps: New battalion of fuzzy angels', *Canberra Times*, 9 December 1964.

95 Caspar Kakar, interview, 6 August 2013.

96 Anthony Wupu, interview, 6 August 2013; Martin Takoin, interview, 30 July 2013; Sammy Joe Trei, interview, 8 August 2013; Sio Maiasa, interview, 3 August 2013.

97 Jack Kukuma, interview, 3 August 2013.

98 B.J. Hodge, 'Relationship between PNGVR/cadets experience, and rank and employment of Pacific Island soldiers', Research Report No. 36, February 1971, AAPSYCH.

99 Barney Dinji, interview, 31 July 2013; Rodney Daura, interview, 31 July 2013; Ted Diro, interview, 30 July 2013.

100 Raeburn Trindall, 'The Piper', 1973, 16mm film, AWM, F03381.

101 Sio Miasa, interview, 3 August 2013; Ronnie Oiwelo, interview, 31 July 2013; Gapi Gewa, interview, 30 July 2013.

102 Trindall, 'The Piper'.

103 Colebatch, 'To find a path', pp. 36–8.

104 Lovering, 'Authority and identity', p. 302.

105 D. Armstrong, 'An examination of job satisfaction and attitudes to conditions of service of PI soldiers posted to units in the Port Moresby area', Research Report No. 46a, March 1970, AAPSYCH.

106 B.J. Hodge, 'PNG Army Census Jun 1969: Frequency distributions and relationships between certain variables', Research Report No. 32, April 1972, AAPSYCH.

107 B.J. Hodge, 'A demographic study of three rifle companies of 1PIR', Research Report No. 70, July 1973, AAPSYCH.

108 Martin Takoin, interview, 30 July 2013; Anthony Wupu, interview, 6 August 2013; Nadu Gwamse, interview, 6 August 2013; D. Armstrong, 'An examination of job satisfaction and attitudes to conditions of service of PI soldiers', Research Report No. 46b, April 1970, AAPSYCH; D. Armstrong, 'The first four years of service – PI soldiers during initial engagement', Research Report No. 14, April 1969, AAPSYCH; B.J. Hodge, 'PNG Army Census 1969: Marriage and the family', Research Report No. 20, April 1972, AAPSYCH.

109 D. Armstrong, 'A survey of language spoken in the PNG Army', Research Report No. 31, July 1970, AAPSYCH.

110 Bell, 'New Guinea pidgin teaching', p. 674.

111 D. Armstrong, 'PNG Psych Research Unit: Retrospect and prospect', Research Report No. 40, AAPSYCH; B.J. Hodge, 'PNG Army Census Jun 1969: Frequency distributions and relationships between certain variables', Research Report No. 32, April 1972, AAPSYCH.

112 'Report on Recruiting Tour 1/64', 13–30 June 1964, NAA, J2818 164/1/5.

113 B.J. Hodge, 'PNG Army Census Jun 1969: Frequency distributions and relationships between certain variables', Research Report No. 32, April 1972, AAPSYCH.

114 D. Armstrong, 'An examination of job satisfaction and attitudes to conditions of service of PI soldiers posted to units in the Port Moresby area', Research Report No. 46a, March 1970, AAPSYCH.

115 Downs, *The Australian Trusteeship*, p. 208.

116 J.W. Kelly, 'PNG Army Census – 1969: Voting and tax paying behaviour of PI soldiers', Research Report No. 34, May 1971, AAPSYCH.

117 D. Armstrong, 'An examination of job satisfaction and attitudes to conditions of service of PI soldiers posted to units in the Port Moresby area', Research Report No. 46a, March 1970, AAPSYCH.

118 'External disturbances', n.d. [c. 1968], AWM121 234/F/3.

119 DCGS Minute No. 428/1968, 15 November 1968, NAA, A6837 5.

120 See for instance Roy, 'Military loyalty in the colonial context', p. 507; Parsons, *The African Rank-and-File*, pp. 205, 211; Lammers, 'Strikes and mutinies', pp. 559–60.

121 Hearn to soldiers, 11 June 1968, AWM121 234/F/2. For a description of the riot, see Woodford, *Papua New Guinea*, p. 189.

122 A.G. Owens, 'A survey of attitudes of some educated local people of Papua–New Guinea: An interim report', November 1967, Research Report No. 13/1967, AAPSYCH.

123 D. Armstrong, 'PNG Psych Research Unit. Retrospect and prospect', Research Report No. 40, AAPSYCH.

124 D. Armstrong, 'The first four years of service – PI soldiers during initial engagement', Research Report No. 14, April 1969, AAPSYCH.

125 DMO&P, 'Discharge by reason', n.d. [c. 1968] AWM121 234/F/3.

126 D. Armstrong, 'PNG Psych Research Unit. Retrospect and prospect', Research Report No. 40, AAPSYCH.

127 Armstrong, 'The first four years of service – PI soldiers during initial engagement', Research Report No. 14, April 1969, AAPSYCH.
128 D. Armstrong, 'An examination of job satisfaction and attitudes to conditions of service of PI soldiers posted to units in the Port Moresby area', Research Report No. 46a, March 1970, AAPSYCH.
129 D.J. Armstrong, 'Service skills used in post-service employment', Research Report No. 17, June 70, AAPSYCH.
130 D. Armstrong, 'An examination of job satisfaction and attitudes to conditions of service of PI soldiers', Research Report No. 46b, April 1970, AAPSYCH; D. Armstrong, 'Unit differences in PI soldiers' job satisfaction and attitudes to conditions of service', Research Report No. 46c, May 1970, AAPSYCH; D. Armstrong, 'Reintegration of discharged soldiers into community life. Part A – Preliminary study', Research Report No. 15, October 1968, AAPSYCH.
131 Malcolm MacCallum, questionnaire, received 28 December 2013.
132 Ken Swadling, questionnaire, received 1 August 2011.

5 'A new task': Laying the foundations of a national army, 1966–71

1 Department of District Administration to all stations, 5 February 1965, PNGNA, 1017 52/1/1; Prime Minister's Department, 'Notes on Cabinet Submission No. 274', 20 August 1968, NAA, A5619 C174.
2 Sinclair, Keeping the Peace, p. 108.
3 For a detailed discussion of the gradual change in PNG's place in Australia's defence thinking after the end of Confrontation, see Hunt, 'Papua New Guinea in Australia's strategic thinking', pp. 148–76. See also Doran, 'Introduction', p. xliii.
4 Doran, 'Introduction', p. xxv; Doran, 'Wanting and knowing best', p. 314; Hunt, 'Papua New Guinea in Australia's strategic thinking', p. 164; Griffin, Nelson and Firth, Papua New Guinea, p. 139.
5 I.M. Hunter, 'The Army's tasks in Papua New Guinea', CGS conference, July 1967, NAA, A452 1967/5846.
6 'Military thinking reaches its turning point', Age (Melbourne), 11 February 1969.
7 The Department of Territories changed its name to External Territories in 1968.
8 Doran, 'Introduction', pp. xxiii–xxiv.
9 Cabinet Submission No. 71, 10 March 1966, NAA, A1946 68/838.
10 Cabinet Decision No. 138, 24 and 29 March 1966, NAA, A1946 1968/838, in Doran, Australia and Papua New Guinea, 1966–1969, pp. 121–2.
11 Thompson, Australia and the Pacific Islands, p. 173.
12 Doran, 'Introduction', p. xxvii; Waters, 'Against the tide', p. 200; Downs, The Australian Trusteeship, pp. 368–81.
13 Aitkin and Wolfers, 'Australian attitudes towards the Papua New Guinean area since World War II', p. 208.

14 Hunter to Hopton, 30 April 1968, AWM121 234/F/1; Warwick Smith to White, 15 September 1967, NAA, A452 1966/4989.

15 T. Daly, quoted in 'Notes on defence committee discussion by Plimsoll', 30 May 1968, NAA, A1838 689/2, Part 3, in Doran, *Australia and Papua New Guinea, 1966–1969*, pp. 523–7.

16 Doran, 'Introduction', p. xxvi; Grey, *A Soldier's Soldier*, p. 138.

17 David White, 'Police Army conflicts in Port Moresby', *SMH*, 23 August 1966.

18 Department of External Territories, 'Unrest in PIR', 29 September 1969, NAA, A452 1969/4604; Military Area Lae to all units and subunits Lae area, 30 September 1969, NAA, J2810 R271/1/4. Division of District Administration to all District Commissioners, 7 October 1969, PNGNA, 1008 52/2/2; Don Barrett, 'More bungling in Canberra and Kone', *Post-Courier* (Port Moresby), 16 October 1969.

19 M. Fraser, Cabinet Submission No. 419, 25 August 1966, NAA, A5619 C174.

20 Legge to Warwick Smith, 13 September 1966, NAA, A452 1966/4989.

21 Warwick Smith to Hay, 5 October 1966, NAA, A452 1966/4989.

22 'External Disturbances', n.d. [c. 1968], AWM121 234/F/3.

23 Nelson, *Mobs and Masses*, p. 13.

24 DMO&P, 'Disaffection in RP&NGC', 9 July 1968, AWM121 234/F/3.

25 For a detailed list of other contributors to the this discussion, see May, *The Changing Role of the Military in Papua New Guinea*, p. 9.

26 Heatu, 'New Guinea's coming army'.

27 Warubu, 'That army again!', p. 9.

28 David White, 'Who could take over New Guinea', *People*, 1 November 1967.

29 Alan Gilbert, 'The Army in PNG', *Canberra Times*, 4 June 1969.

30 Alan Gilbert, 'A strong army and a weak police force', *Canberra Times*, 4 June 1969.

31 PNG Command, 'PNG Comd Internal security plan 1/66: Planning for internal unrest involving Pacific Islands (PI) soldiers', 7 May 1966, NAA, A452 1972/4342; Albert Jordan, Archive No. 2154, AAWFA.

32 PNG Command, 'Internal security planning contingency plan "Kwik Start" for 1PIR group', 24 May 1966, NAA, A452 1972/4342.

33 Sinclair, *Keeping the Peace*, p. 115.

34 Legge to Warwick Smith, 4 May 1967, NAA, A452 1967/2605.

35 Hunter to Army Canberra, 28 April 1967, NAA, A452 1967/2605.

36 CGS Memorandum No. 168/69, 10 November 1969, NAA, A6837 7; DCGS Memorandum No. 471/69, 7 November 1969, NAA, A6837 7; Stokes, unpublished memoir, pp. 348–51.

37 'RAAF aid to New Guinea famine areas', 19 October 1972, 16mm film, AWM F02822.

38 Hearn to DCGS, 25 June 1968, NAA, AWM121 234/F/2; Michael Jeffery, interview, 16 November 2010; Sinclair, *Keeping the Peace*, p. 154.

39 Warwick Smith to Legge, 13 April 1967, NAA, A452 1967/2605; Warwick Smith to Hay, 17 April 1967, NAA, A452 1967/2605.

40 See Hunter to DMO&P, 20 April 1968, AWM121 234/F/1.

41 Sinclair, *Keeping the Peace*, pp. 134–7. White to Hewitt, 24 February 1969, NAA, A1209 1968/8538, Part 2; Department of Prime Minister, 'Army civic action activities in P.–N. G. Line of Response', n.d., NAA, A1209 1968/8538, part 2.

42 O'Neill, *The Army in Papua-New Guinea*, p. 9.

43 'The Government in Papua New Guinea', March 1967, NAA, A452 1967/5846. The booklet was part of a wider program of 'political education' for Papua New Guineans. See Hay to Department of Territories, 'Report of Significant Events – Papua and New Guinea', 17 November 1967, NAA, A452 1967/7354, in Doran, *Australia and Papua New Guinea, 1966–1969*, p. 410.

44 'The Government in Papua New Guinea', March 1967, NAA, A452 1967/5846.

45 Hunter to Hay, 15 September 1967, NAA, A452 1967/5846.

46 Christopher Forsyth, 'Barnes bows to army storm over booklet', *Australian*, 20 September 1967; David White, 'Who could take over New Guinea', *People*, 1 November 1967; 'Booklet on NG "not anti-Army"', *Canberra Times*, 20 September 1967.

47 'Local Defence Forces Papua and New Guinea: Notes of discussion held in office of Minister for Defence, Parliament House', 18 October 1967, NAA, A452 1966/4989; 'The Army in Papua and New Guinea', January 1969, NAA, A452 1967/5846.

48 'Notes of discussion held in office of Minister for Defence, Parliament House', 18 October 1967, NAA, A452 1966/4989.

49 Ibid.

50 Fraser to Fairhall, 13 March 1967, AWM122 1968/2020; Fairhall to Barnes, 25 May 1967, AWM122 1968/2020; Fraser to Barnes, 21 December 1967, NAA, A452 1966/4989.

51 White to Warwick Smith, 8 April 1968, AWM121 234/F/1.

52 Joint Planning Committee Report No. 32/1968, 10 May 1968, NAA, A8738 39.

53 DMO&P, 'Comments on JPC Report No. 32/1968', 16 May 1968, AWM121 234/F/2.

54 I. Hunter, 'Comments by Commander PNG on JPC Report 32/1968', AWM121 234/F/2.

55 C. Barnes, Cabinet Submission No. 274, 9 August 1968, NAA, A5619 C174.

56 Ibid.

57 Fairhall to Bland, 5 August 1968, NAA, A452 1968/2441, Part 2, in Doran, *Australia and Papua New Guinea, 1966–1969*, pp. 580–1.

58 Bunting to Gorton, 9 September 1968, NAA, A5882 CO320.

59 Cabinet Decision No. 541, 18 September 1968, AWM121 234/F/2. There was again debate on who would lead the review; ultimately Defence retained control. Warwick Smith to Bland, 5 February 1969, NAA, A452 1969/911; 'Notes for File – Discussion with Henry Bland', 10 February 1969, NAA, A452 1969/911.

60   H. Bland, 'Some observations on my visit to PNG, 31 March 1969, NAA, A1838 TS689/2, Part 4.

61   Hunt, 'Papua New Guinea in Australia's strategic thinking', p. 159.

62   Daly to Warwick Smith, 19 September 1969, NAA, A452 1969/4816; Warwick Smith to Daly, 22 December 1969, NAA, A452 1969/4816; DCGS Minute No. 246/1969, 26 May 1969, NAA, A6837 7.

63   HQ PNG Command, 'Future Development of the Army in TPNG – Area of Study I – the Army Structure in Outline', April 1970, NAA, A452 1971/2346.

64   Defence Committee Report No. 17/1970, 31 July 1970, NAA, A1209 1969/9045.

65   Bland, quoted in 'Notes on defence committee discussion by Plimsoll', 30 May 1968, NAA, A1838 689/2, Part 3, in Doran, *Australia and Papua New Guinea, 1966–1969*, p. 526.

66   Kim Beazley, letter to the editor, 'The Army threat: Another view', *Canberra Times*, 26 June 1969.

67   Hunter, 'The Army's tasks in Papua New Guinea'.

68   Ibid.

69   Ibid.

70   See for instance DCGS Minute No. 106/1968, 19 April 1968, AWM121 234/F/1.

71   L. Sweeney, 'Annual Report on Education: Papua New Guinea', 27 February 1963, NAA, MT1131/1 A89/1/230.

72   Dan McDaniel, interview, 13 September 2012; Graeme Manning, questionnaire, received 27 March 2012; Colin Adamson, Archive No. 1171, AAWFA; O'Neill, *The Army in Papua-New Guinea*, p. 13.

73   D.J. Armstrong, 'PNG Army Population Survey', Research Report No. 10, November 1968, AAPSYCH.

74   D.J. Armstrong, 'Relationship between rank and place of origin of Pacific Islands soldiers', Research Report No. 30, July 1970, AAPSYCH; A.J. Affleck, 'Some solicited thoughts on the report by the review committee into future size and role of the Army in PNG', 9 January 1969, AWM121 23/H/I.

75   Bell, 'Goodbye to all that?', p. 49.

76   I. Hunter, 'Brief by Comd PNG Comd', 1 November 1967, NAA, A6059 41/441/94. Colebatch reports on a range of different views among Australian officers towards the *wantok* system: Colebatch, 'To find a path', pp. 120–6. See also O'Neill, *The Army in Papua-New Guinea*, pp. 12–13.

77   A.J. Affleck, 'Some solicited thoughts', 9 January 1969, AWM121 23/H/I; D.J. Armstrong, 'Reintegration of discharged soldiers into community life Part A – A Preliminary Report', Research Report No. 15, 1968. A number of Papua New Guineans interviewed for the book also returned home to marry. Antony Wupu, interview, 6 August 2013; Lincoln Rauleta, interview, 6 August 2013; John Suat, interview, 6 August 2013.

78   Moore, *New Guinea*, p. 183.

79   B.J. Horne, 'Social distance of PNGDF recruits', Research Report No. 68, May 1973, AAPSYCH.

80 Laurie Lewis, interview, 14 July 2012.
81 Interview 3, cited in Colebatch, 'To find a path', p. 32.
82 Ron Lange, interview, 11 May 2012.
83 Michael Jeffery, interview, 16 November 2011.
84 Martin Takoin, interview, 30 July 2013.
85 Moses Kiari, interview, 2 August 2013.
86 May, *The Changing Role of the Military in Papua New Guinea*, p. 29; Nelson, *Mobs and Masses*, p. 13; Rogers, 'The Papua New Guinea Defence Force', p. 278.
87 'Question without notice – House of Representatives Wednesday, 23rd October, 1968 Pacific Islands Regiment', n.d., NAA, A1838 TS689/2, Part 4.
88 O'Neill, *The Army in Papua-New Guinea*, p. 17.
89 Daly to Wade, 20 December 1957, NAA, MP927/1 A5/1/132; Norrie to Northern Command, 5 January 1961, NAA, A452 1962/8172; Cabinet Submission No. 1346, 13 September 1961, NAA, A4940 C3436.
90 White to Treasury Secretary, 4 September 1961, NAA, A452 1962/8146.
91 L. Sweeney, 'Annual Report on Education: Papua New Guinea', 27 February 1963, NAA, MT1131/1 A89/1/230.
92 Ibid.
93 O'Neil to Pascoe, 21 July 1964, NAA, MT1131/1 A89/1/230.
94 'AHQ Education Report No. 2', 14 September 1966, NAA, J2810 R284/1/1. Those who served as teachers were called 'chalkies', a term of affection similar to 'sparky' (electrician) or 'chippy' (builder).
95 Jones, 'The origins of the "chalkies" scheme', <www.nashospng.com>
96 The total number is obscure. See Dymock, *The Chalkies*, p. 73.
97 See for instance Frank Cordingley, 'Frank Cordinley's experience in PNG Jun 67 – Nov 68', <www.nashospng.com>; Phil Adam, interview, 3 May 2011; John Gibson, interview, 3 May 2011; Kevin Horton, interview, 1 May 2011; Greg Ivey, interview, 1 May 2011; George Kearney, telephone interview, 19 September 2011; Ian Ogston, interview, 14 March 2011.
98 Gaynor to many, 8 July 1969, Greg Ivey, private papers.
99 Joint Force HQ Administrative Instruction No. 1/73, 'Reorganisation of Army education in PNG', 9 January 1973, NAA, J2818 R284/1/1; Aston, cited in Ogston, *Chalkies*; Ogston, *Armi Wantoks*, p. iv.
100 R.A.W. Robertson, 'Education Administrative Instruction 1/70', December 1969, NAA, J2818 R284/1/1.
101 J.R. McQuinn, 'Education Administrative Instruction 2/71', 10 June 1971, NAA, J2818 R284/1/1.
102 Ogston, *Armi Wantoks*, p. 20. See also R.A.W. Robertson, 'Education Administrative Instruction 1/70', December 1969, NAA, J2818 R284/1/1.
103 J.R. McQuinn, 'Education Administrative Instruction 2/71', 10 June 1971, NAA, J2818 R284/1/1; Barney Dinji, interview, 31 July 2013.
104 Draft AHQ General Staff Instruction /69, 'Principles and Policies Governing the Army in Papua/New Guinea', 7 March 1969, AWM121 23/H/I; Ed Diery, quoted in Ogston, *Armi Wantoks*, p. 27. See also J.R. McQuinn, 'Education Administrative Instruction 1/71', 15 January 1971, NAA, J2818 R284/1/1.

105 Phil Adam, quoted in Ogston, *Armi Wantoks*, p. 26.
106 Kevin Horton, quoted in Ogston, *Armi Wantoks*, p. 21; Andrew Dalziel, interview, 13 July 2011.
107 Ronnie Oiwelo, interview, 31 July 2013; Mutuaina Watut, interview, 31 July 2013; Barney Dinji, interview, 31 July 2013; Anthony Wupu, interview, 6 August 2013; Greg Ivey, interview, 1 May 2011; Ian Ogston, interview, 14 March 2011; Richard Boddington, interview, 4 May 2011; Terry Edwinsmith, interview, 5 May 2011.
108 Andrew Dalziel, interview, 12 July 2011; Kevin Horton, quoted in Ogston, *Armi Wantoks*, p. 20; Ian Ogston, quoted in Ogston, *Armi Wantoks*, p. 37.
109 Phillip Adam, interview, 3 May 2011.
110 Hunter, 'The Army's tasks in Papua New Guinea'. This was echoed by later commanders. See Norrie to all units, 17 June 1973, NAA, J2818 175/1/1. There is no indication that Brigadier Eldridge, who served in PNG between 1969 and 1972, departed from the views of either Hunter or Norrie, as he cited Hunter's paper, 'The Army's tasks in Papua New Guinea' (1967), as a basis for further planning. Eldridge to Hopton, 4 March 1969, AWM121 234/F/4.
111 Draft AHQ GS Instruction 69, 'Principles and Policies Governing the Army in Papua/New Guinea', 7 March 1969, AWM121 23/H/I; Hunter, 'The Army's tasks in Papua New Guinea'; O'Neill, *The Army in Papua-New Guinea*, p. 17.
112 RAAEC PNG Comd, 'Citizenship Training – Civics Section – Lecture Guides 1968/69', n.d. [c. 1969], NAA, J2818 175/1/1.
113 Hay to Barnes, 24 June 1967, NAA, A452 1966/4989; Hori Howard, interview, 16 May 2013.
114 In addition to Hunter's CGS report, see for instance 'Question without notice – House of Representatives, "Pacific Islands Regiment"', 23 October 1968, NAA, A1838 TS689/2 Part 4; Lynch, 'The coming army'.
115 Megarrity notes for instance that, in some regions, the only source of information about the voting system was through the electoral candidates themselves (Megarrity, 'Indigenous education in colonial Papua New Guinea', p. 55).
116 Terry Edwinsmith, interview, 5 May 2011; Greg Farr, interview, 2 May 2011.
117 Mietzner and Farrelly, 'Mutinies, coups and military interventionism', pp. 343, 352.
118 Eldridge to Hopton, 4 March 1969, AWM121 234/F/4.

6 The 'black handers': Australian soldiers and their families in PNG

1 Northern Command, 'Proposed Amendment to Lower Establishment II/23c/4 – Pacific Islands Regiment', 22 February 1961, NAA, A10857 III/81/PE; 'Pacific Islands Peace Establishment', 18 April 1961, NAA, A10857 III/81/PE.

2 See Aitkin and Wolfers, 'Australian attitudes towards the Papua New Guinean area since World War II', p. 212.
3 Sinclair, *Keeping the Peace*, p. 48.
4 Brian McFarlane, interview, 16 February 2013.
5 Ibid.
6 Graeme Manning, questionnaire, received 27 March 2012; Laurie Lewis, interview, 14 July 2012.
7 Albert Jordon, Archive No. 2154, AAWFA.
8 Ted Diro, interview, 31 July 2013; Colebatch, 'To find a path', p. 277.
9 Hori Howard, questionnaire, received 29 March 2012.
10 Brian McFarlane, interview, 16 February 2013; Ian Gollings, telephone interview, 3 November 2011; Bruce Selleck, questionnaire, received 21 November 2012.
11 Ray McCann, questionnaire, received 2 March 2013. See also John Marsden, telephone interview, 18 November 2011; Peter Warfe, Archive No. 2487, AAWFA; Mike Dennis, interview, 15 February 2012.
12 Bruce Selleck, questionnaire, received 21 November 2012.
13 Adrian Clunies-Ross, Archive No. 0795, AAWFA.
14 Stokes, unpublished memoir, p. 263.
15 Flint, unpublished memoir, p. 15.
16 Bert Wansley, telephone interview, 27 May 2013.
17 Colebatch, 'To find a path', pp. 267, 390.
18 Murray Blake, Archive No. 1850, AAWFA.
19 Ian Gollings, telephone interview, 3 November 2011.
20 Stokes, unpublished memoir, p. 264.
21 Graeme Manning, questionnaire, received 27 March 2012.
22 Cliff Brock, questionnaire, received 3 November 2012. Ray McCann expressed a similar view (McCann, interview, 16 February 2013).
23 Moore and Trout, 'Military advancement', p. 453.
24 Janowitz, *The Professional Soldier*, p. 127.
25 Kim and Crabb, 'Collective identity and promotion prospects in the South Korean Army', pp. 295–309.
26 Peck, 'Assessing the career mobility of US Army officers: 1950–1974', pp. 217–37.
27 See Corona, 'Career patterns in the US Army Officer Corps', pp. 109–34.
28 For instance, the *Army List* shows a preponderance of RMC graduates among those who received brigadier rank or higher during the 1980s.
29 Sinclair, *Keeping the Peace*, pp. 46, 48.
30 'CO for Island Regiment', *Cairns Post*, 8 September 1951.
31 H. Sabin, 'Formation of Pacific Islands Regiment', 12 July 1955, AWM113 11/2/29.
32 N. Maddern, 'Papua New Guinea Volunteer Rifles', AWM113 MH 1/194.
33 Daly, 'Disturbance'.
34 Seacombe to Adjutant General, 16 October 1952, NAA, MP927/1 A240/1/138.
35 Killingray, 'The mutiny of the West African Regiment in the Gold Coast, 1901', p. 442; Omissi, *The Sepoy and the Raj*, p. 104.

36 E. Campbell, 'Report by Colonel EF Campbell, D Psych AHQ on Visit to Pacific Islands Regiment', 26 July 1957, NAA, MT1131/1 A89/1/161.

37 Northern Command, 'Proposal for a new lower establishment to supersede II/23c/2 (LE) Pacific Islands Infantry Battalion', 27 July 1956, NAA, A6059 21/441/15.

38 T. Daly, 'Report on the Pacific Islands Regiment', 2 February 1961, NAA, MP927/1 A251/1/1133.

39 Daly, 'Disturbance'.

40 Daly to Wade, 20 December 1957, NAA, MP927/1 A5/1/132.

41 Bell, 'New Guinea pidgin teaching', p. 672.

42 Stokes, unpublished memoir, p. 263.

43 Ray McCann, interview, 16 February 2013; Mike Dennis, interview, 15 February 2012.

44 Cliff Brock, questionnaire, received 3 December 2012.

45 Peter Murray, interview, 7 October 2011; Ron Lange, telephone interview, 11 April 2012; Mike Dennis, interview, 15 February 2012; Terry Edwinsmith, interview, 5 May 2011; Greg Farr, interview, 2 May 2011.

46 Military Board Instruction 16–1, Amendment No. 12, 'Service in certain overseas areas and remote localities', 23 December 1970, NAA, A6913, 1; Dennis Armstrong, telephone interview, 16 December 2011; George Kearney, telephone interview, 19 September 2011.

47 Dennis Armstrong, telephone interview, 16 December 2011.

48 Ian Gollings, telephone interview, 3 November 2011.

49 Fraser to Fairhall, 13 March 1967, NAA, A452 1966/4989.

50 Eldridge to Graham, 8 May 1969, AWM121 234/F/4.

51 'Copy of statement made by his honour the Administrator in the Legislative Council – 4 March 1958', NAA, MP927/1 A66/1/428.

52 Dennis Armstrong, telephone interview, 16 December 2011; Ross Eastgate, interview, 14 April 2012; Michael Jeffery, interview, 16 November 2010; Brian Iselin, telephone interview, 20 December 2011; Grahame Wease, telephone interview, 14 October 2011.

53 Ross Eastgate, interview, 14 April 2012.

54 AMF Minute, 'Report on officers completing tour of duty with Pacific Islands Regiment', 14 August 1961, NAA, MT1131/1 A251/1/1023.

55 The Army List was first published as the Military List of the Commonwealth of Australia in 1904, and continued to be produced in various iterations until the 1980s when it was discontinued for cost reasons – as well as privacy concerns, presumably (Dennis et al., Oxford Companion to Australian Military History, p. 45). This case study has used all available Army Lists produced between 1960 and 1988.

56 The three Papua New Guinean officers then in commission are not included in this figure, as they were subject to a different promotion track. See White to Warwick Smith, 'Career structure – Pacific Islands Officers of the Australian Regular Army', 2 September 1965, NAA, A452 1965/5991.

57 These men were compared with other officers who did not serve
    in PNG, who were chosen from infantry officers listed directly above
    or below the PIR officers in the *Army Lists*. As the *Army List* is organised
    by seniority, this ensured that the control group was made up of
    individuals at similar points in their careers, but was otherwise
    random.

58 The final ranks achieved by the comparison group were: three captains,
    ten majors, ten lieutenant colonels, one brigadier and one major
    general.

59 Major generals: B. Howard, J. Norrie, M. Jeffery, J. Molan, I. Flawith and
    A. Clunies-Ross; brigadiers: L. Lewis, J.A. Sheldrick, F.K. Cole, I.S. Fisher,
    G.J. Loughton, D.M.M. Francis, J.G. Cosson, W.O. Rogers, J.J. Farry, T.H.
    Holland and R.D.F. Lloyd.

60 Compiled from Appendix C in Horner and Bou, *Duty First*, pp. 439–44.

61 David Butler, Archive No. 1034, AAWFA.

62 Alvah, *Unofficial Ambassadors*, p. 62; Brown, 'Bye, bye Miss American Pie',
    p. 50.

63 See Australian Bureau of Statistics, 'Australian Population Statistics 2006',
    Catalogue No. 3310.0, <www.abs.gov.au>; ABS, 'Australian Social
    Trends, 1997', Catalogue No. 4102.0, <www.abs.gov.au>

64 Wood, *The Forgotten Force*, pp. 115–18.

65 Dennis and Grey, *Emergency and Confrontation*, p. 88.

66 Grey, *A Soldier's Soldier*, p. 132n.

67 Military Board Submission No. 10/1968, 'Discipline in Papua New Guinea',
    1968, AAHU.

68 'Administrative appreciation for the expansion of the Army in Papua and
    New Guinea', 11 January 1965, NAA, J2818, 22/1/7; Cliff Brock,
    interview, 15 March 2013; Quarter Master General to DCGS, 19 June
    1968, AWM121 234/F/2.

69 Grey, *A Soldier's Soldier*, p. 132n.

70 Alvah, *Unofficial Ambassadors*, p. 63.

71 White to Treasury Secretary, 15 December 1961, NAA, A452 1962/8146.

72 David Butler, Archive No. 1034, AAWFA. The *Canberra Times*, for
    instance, advertised lettuce at 1 shilling 10 pence in 1958. 'Cheaper bananas
    available', *Canberra Times*, 18 April 1958.

73 Laurie Lewis, interview, 14 July 2012.

74 Sherie McGuiness, 'Life in a shoe box', p. 123.

75 Stokes, unpublished memoir, p. 180.

76 'PNG Command Accommodation Manual', 1971, NAA, J2810 R6/1/1.

77 Bishop, 'Tarred-paper houses', p. 16.

78 Holding, 'Adding a "guest wing"', p. 13.

79 For a description of how the shortage of married quarters affected even
    senior officers, see Grey, *A Soldier's Soldier*, pp. 119, 132.

80 Department of the Army, 'Report on the Pacific Islands Regiment', 15
    September 1961, NAA, A4940 C3436.

81 Dennis and Grey, *Emergency and Confrontation*, p. 88.

82   I. Hunter, 'CGS Quarterly Briefing – Brief by Comd PNG Command', 1
      November 1967, NAA, A6059 41/441/94; Cabinet Minute 1609, 26
      September 1961, NAA,
      A4940 C3436; Cabinet Submission No. 118, 'Papua New Guinea –
      Military Requirements, 8 April 1964, NAA, A4940 C3436; Cabinet
      Decision No. 173, 23 April 1964, NAA, A4940 C3436.
83   Ray Quirk to many, August 1963, NAA, J2818 R160/1/3.
84   Stokes, unpublished memoir, p. 180.
85   McFarlane, *We Band of Brothers*, p. 144.
86   Ted Clark, telephone interview, 15 May 2011.
87   Department of the Army, 'Report on the Pacific Islands Regiment', 15
      September 1961, NAA, A4940 C3436.
88   Jenny Ducie, 'A heavenly bird of paradise', p. 50.
89   Department of External Affairs Minute, 'P&NG – Comparisons of
      conditions of service Commonwealth Territory public services and ARA
      personnel with the PIR', 8 August 1969, NAA, A452 1969/1803. See also
      Military Board Instruction 90–21, 'Papua New Guinea Education
      Allowance', 6 December 1971, AWM.
90   Rosemary Brock, interview, 15 March 2013; Margaret Purcell, 'Teaching
      in paradise', p. 128.
91   Daly complained: 'The Army in New Guinea is a show piece and is visited
      by almost everyone of any importance who goes to the country' (Daly,
      'Disturbance'). Consequently, the wives of COs might have to provide a
      morning tea befitting a governor-general or government minister (Burns, 'A
      teddy bears' picnic?', p. 25).
92   Daly, 'Disturbance'.
93   Department of the Army, 'Report on the Pacific Islands Regiment', 15
      September 1961, NAA, A4940 C3436; White to Treasury, 15 December
      1961, NAA, A452 1962/8146.
94   Anne Eastgate, interview, 14 March 2012.
95   Lloyd, 'A rushed arrival', p. 69.
96   David Butler, Archive No. 1034, AAWFA; Ducie, 'A heavenly bird of
      paradise', p. 54.
97   The soldier was sentenced to seven years imprisonment. 'A native attacks
      an officer's wife', *Argus* (Melbourne), 13 December 1956.
98   Glendenning, 'Where's the jungle?', p. 44; Burns, 'A teddy bears' picnic?',
      p. 26. Anne Eastgate, interview, 14 March 2012.
99   See for instance Brown, 'Bye, bye Miss American Pie', p. 21.
100 Diane Lewis, interview, 14 July 2012.
101 Lynette Horton, 'Life as an army wife in Papua New Guinea
      1970–71',<www.nashospng.com>; Lynette Horton, interview, 1 May
      2011.
102 Bev Hartwig, interview, 16 February 2012.
103 Tattam, 'Marriage to an officer and a gentleman', p. 68.
104 Diane Lewis, interview, 14 July 2012.
105 Ted Diro, interview, 31 July 2013.
106 Lynette Horton, interview, 1 May 2011.

107 Brian Iselin, telephone interview, 20 December 2011; Dan Winkel, interview, 13 April 2012.
108 Albert Jordon, Archive No. 2154, AAWFA; Stokes, unpublished memoir, 343; Jeffery, 'Yangpela Misis', p. 112.
109 Cliff Brock, interview, 15 March 2013.
110 Sinclair, *Keeping the Peace*, pp. 88–9.
111 Phil Adam, interview, 3 May 2011.
112 Ian Ogston, interview, 3 March 2010; Brian Iselin, telephone interview, 20 December 2011; John Kelly, interview, 2 August 2012.
113 John Kelly, interview, 2 August 2012.
114 Northern Command to AHQ, 6 March 1950, NAA, MP729/8 37/431/114.
115 Mayhew, 'Moem's brown owl', p. 99.
116 Cliff Brock, questionnaire, received 3 December 2012. Richard Knight remembered that social life was 'almost compulsory' (Knight, interview, 23 July 2013).
117 Cliff Brock, interview, 15 March 2013.
118 Ross Eastgate, interview, 14 April 2012. Peter Murray, interview, 15 October 2011.
119 Donald Gillies, 'Nuiguini Armi – today's problems', 1971, article in possession of author.
120 For a discussion of 'stress, morale and alcohol' among Australians in Vietnam, see Ekins and McNeill, *Fighting to the Finish*, pp. 350–6.
121 Ogston, *Armi Wantoks*, p. 45.
122 Dan Winkel, interview, 13 April 2012; 'The story of Dan Winkel's tours', March 2012, <www.nashospng.com>
123 Dan Winkel, 'Dan's TPNG Adventure Tours', <www.nashospng.com>; Norm Hunter, interview, 17 March 2012.
124 Phil Adam, interview, 3 May 2011.
125 HQPNGDF Staff Instruction 19/73, 'Force Sports Policy' 4 July 1973, NAA, J2810 R211/1/8.
126 Robert Coppa, questionnaire, received 15 November 2012; Norm Hunter, interview, 17 March 2012; Jim Kombukun, interview, 31 July 2013.
127 Stokes, unpublished memoir, p. 202; Albert Jordon, Archive No. 2154, AAWFA.
128 Anne Eastgate, interview, 14 April 2012.
129 Lloyd, 'Mrs Osi to the rescue', p. 88.
130 Quirk also remarked: 'I don't know whether I should be writing this – this letter might end up in the hands of the Chaplain General' (Quirk to many, 10 September 1963, NAA, J2818 R160/1/3).
131 See for instance Smith, 'Minorities and the Australian Army', p. 131.
132 Diane Lewis, interview, 14 July 2012.
133 Bert Wansley, telephone interview, 27 May 2013.
134 Peter McDougall, questionnaire, received 19 November 2013.
135 Phil Adam, interview, 3 May 2011. Richard Knight recalled a similar admonition (Knight, interview, 23 July 2013).
136 Stokes, unpublished memoir, p. 244.
137 Diane Lewis, interview, 14 July 2012.

138 Thomas Posi-tute, interview, 30 July 2013.
139 Jeffery, 'Yangpela Misis', p. 111.
140 Lloyd, 'Mrs Osi to the rescue', pp. 84, 90.
141 Dickson-Waiko, 'Women, nation and decolonisation in Papua New Guinea', p. 181.
142 Lloyd, 'Mrs Osi to the rescue', pp. 86–9.
143 Cliff Brock, interview, 15 March 2013; Nadu Gwamse, interview, 6 August 2013.
144 MacDonald to Scragg, 22 February 1965, NAA, A452 1964/3744.
145 Northern Command to AHQ, 2 December 1953, NAA, MT1131/1 A259/47/23.
146 'PNG Command Accommodation Manual', 17 November 1971, NAA, J2810 R6/1/1.
147 Frank Cordingly, 'Frank Cordingley's experience in PNG Jul 67 – Nov 68', <www.nashospng.com>
148 Greg Farr, interview, 2 May 2011; John Marsden, telephone interview, 18 November 2011; Peter Warfe, Archive No. 2487, AAWFA.
149 Ian Gollings, email correspondence, 25 October 2011. Michael Morrison, Archive No. 1928, AAWFA.
150 Brian Iselin, email correspondence, 21 December 2011.
151 Donald Gillies, telephone interview, 7 December 2011; Francis Tilbrook, Archive No. 2354, AAWFA.
152 See Fletcher and Gonara, 'Decriminalisation of prostitution in Papua New Guinea', pp. 145–53.
153 R.T. Sutton, 'Report on activities of Sgt S Warn RAE – Clerk of Works, attached 1PIR Taurama Barracks', September 1970, NAA, J2810 R271/1/4.
154 Dan Winkel, interview, 13 April 2012.
155 'Med Stats and Returns – Causes of Admission to Hosp – PNG Comd', AWM292 4057/51 Part 1 and Part 2.
156 Norm Hunter, interview, 17 April 2012.
157 Downs, The Australian Trusteeship, p. 71.
158 Stewart, 'Not a misis', p. 249.
159 See Radcliffe, 'In defence of White Australia', pp. 184–201. Australians posted as part of the occupation of Japan were similarly discouraged from interracial marriages. See Wood, The Forgotten Force, pp. 118–25.
160 Principal Administrative Officers' Committee (Personnel), 'Marriage between service personnel and aliens', 15 December 1966, NAA, A1946 1967/3762.

7 'A different world': The rush to independence, 1970–75

1 Ted Diro, interview, 31 July 2013.
2 Waters, 'Against the tide', p. 195.
3 Nelson, 'Liberation', pp. 279–80.
4 Doran, 'Introduction', p. lv.

5 Waters, 'Against the tide', p. 204.
6 Nelson, 'Liberation', p. 277; Griffin, Nelson and Firth, p. 162; Downs, *The Australian Trusteeship*, p. 459.
7 Nelson, 'Liberation', pp. 277–8.
8 Wesley-Smith, 'Australia and New Zealand', p. 215. For the election and Somare's government, see Downs, *The Australian Trusteeship*, pp. 486–95.
9 Aitkin and Wolfers, 'Australian attitudes towards the Papua New Guinean area since World War II', p. 208.
10 Griffin, 'Papua New Guinea', p. 357.
11 Denoon, *A Trial Separation*, p. 86; Griffin, 'Papua New Guinea', p. 349.
12 Aitkin and Wolfers, 'Australian attitudes towards Papua New Guinea on the eve of independence', pp. 432–8.
13 Nelson, 'Liberation', pp. 277–8.
14 Denoon, *A Trial Separation*, p. 106.
15 For the involvement of the Papua New Guinean public in the decolonisation process, see Ritchie, 'Defining citizenship for a new nation'. For other discussions of Papua New Guinean involvement, see Millar, *Australia in Peace and War*, p. 275; Doran, 'Wanting and knowing best', p. 316.
16 Nelson, 'Liberation', p. 279.
17 Ibid., p. 277. For a discussion of Australian investigations into British colonial practice, see Goldsworthy, *Losing the Blanket*, pp. 75–6, 85.
18 See the extensive correspondence contained in Foreign and Commonwealth Office (FCO) files 24/1433 and 24/1434. My thanks to Dr Jonathan Ritchie for generously providing these files.
19 Denoon, *A Trial Separation*, p. 86.
20 An RAN study in 1970, for instance, found that 'adequate information on British precedents is lacking' in regard to the process of creating a defence establishment (I.K. Josselyn, 'Measures to foster in PNG an informed understanding of defence matters', 10 June 1970, AWM122 68/2020, Part 4).
21 See Dibb, 'The self-reliant defence of Australia', pp. 13–14.
22 Nelson, *Fighting for Her Gates and Waterways*, p. 19.
23 'Strategic Basis of Australian Defence Policy', June 1973, in Frühling, *A History of Australian Strategic Policy*, pp. 464–75.
24 See Hunt, 'Papua New Guinea in Australia's strategic thinking', pp. 177–208.
25 Denoon, *A Trial Separation*, p. 95; Nelson, *Fighting for Her Gates and Waterways*, p. 20.
26 'Strategic Basis of Australian Defence Policy', June 1973, in Frühling, *A History of Australian Strategic Policy*, pp. 464–75.
27 'Record of Australia/Papua New Guinea Ministerial Defence Meeting – Canberra', 4 April 1974, NAA, A452 1973/2892. See also Barnard to Morrison, 30 March 1974, NAA, A452 1972/3889; Morrison to Barnard, n.d. [April 1974], NAA, A452 1972/3889.
28 Nelson, *Fighting for Her Gates and Waterways*, p. 20.

29 Department of Army, 'Establishment of Defence Branch, Papua New Guinea', 28 September 1972, AWM90 R256/1/1 Part 1; Draft Working Party Report, 'Development of an indigenous defence force in PNG', 24 February 1971, NAA, A452 1972/3573; Sinclair, *Keeping the Peace*, p. 297. For a detailed overview of Papua New Guinean public opinion on defence matters, see the discussion in Mench, *The Role of the Papua New Guinea Defence Force*, pp. 72–84.

30 See for instance PNG Minister for Defence and Foreign Relations to Members of Administrator's Executive Committee, 'Size and Composition of the PNG Defence Force', August 1973, NAA, A4087 D923/26/6; 'PNG Officials Consultation, March 1973 – Report by defence members of the delegation', March 1973, NAA, A1838 689/2/9, Part 2.

31 Defence Committee Minute No. 19/70, 17 September 1970, NAA, A1209 1969/9045; I.K. Josselyn, 'Measures to foster in PNG an informed understanding of defence matters', 10 June 1970, AWM122 68/2020, Part 4.

32 Department of Defence Minute, 'PNGDCC – Papers for Information', 16 February 1973, NAA, A452 1972/3889.

33 Mench, *The Role of the Papua New Guinea Defence Force*, p. 68.

34 Tange to Chief of Air Staff, 13 June 1971, NAA, A703 572/1/110; Fairbairn to McMahon, 29 November 1971, NAA, A1209 1969/9045.

35 For an example of colonial armies' involvement in internal security see Parsons, *The African Rank-and-File*; Killingray, *Policing and Decolonisation*; Omissi, *The Sepoy and the Raj*, pp. 192–231.

36 Doran, 'Introduction', p. xlv.

37 Downs, *The Australian Trusteeship*, pp. 424–37; Griffin, Nelson and Firth, *Papua New Guinea*, pp. 154–9.

38 Doran, 'Introduction', p. xlviii.

39 Defence Committee Minute No. 16/1970, 15 July 1970, NAA, A1838 689/2, Part 7; Defence Committee, 'Papua/New Guinea – Possible Domestic Violence in Rabaul', 2 September 1969, NAA, A1209 1969/9031, Part 1, in Doran, *Australia and Papua New Guinea, 1966–1969*, pp. 902–3.

40 Fraser was also supported by his secretary, Arthur Tange, in opposing the involvement of the Army in internal security. See Tange, *Defence Policy-making*, p. 31.

41 O'Neill, *The Army in Papua-New Guinea*, p. 1.

42 Attachment 7, 'Main steps taken in 1970 call out of PIR' in Department of Defence Discussion Paper, 'Internal security in PNG in the period to independence', September 1973, NAA, A4087 D923/16/1; Ward, 'Call out the troops'; Ron Lange, interview, 29 December 2013.

43 AHQ Operation Instruction No. 3/69, 'Aid to the civil power in New Guinea', 12 July 1973, AWM121 234/F/2; Joint Planning Committee Report No. 32/1968, 'Future Size and Role of the Pacific Islands Regiment', 10 May 1968, NAA, A8738 39.

44 Department of Defence Discussion Paper, 'Internal Security in PNG in the lead up to independence', 6 December 1973, NAA, A4087 D923/16/1.

45 Stokes, unpublished memoir, p. 363; Cliff Brock, interview, 15 February 2013. For a discussion of the three-volume 'Keeping the Peace', see French, *The British Way in Counter-insurgency, 1945–1967*, pp. 204–6.

46 'Draft Outline Report Papua New Guinea Arrangements required at about the time of granting of self-government for the maintenance of internal security as a local responsibility report by the interdepartmental committee set up by cabinet decision 452', 1 December 1971, NAA, A452 1971/3088.

47 Nunn to Secretary Department of Defence, 30 June 1971, AWM122 70/2025, Part 2; Graeme Manning, questionnaire, received 27 March 2012.

48 Department of Defence Discussion Paper, 'Internal Security in PNG in the lead up to independence', 6 December 1973, NAA, A4087 D923/16/1.

49 *Keeping the Peace (Duties in Support of the Civil Power)*, Part 2.

50 Stokes, unpublished memoir, p. 363.

51 'Draft Outline Report Papua New Guinea Arrangements...', 1 December 1971.

52 Department of Defence, 'Internal Security in PNG in the lead up to independence', 6 December 1973, NAA, A4087 D923/16/1.

53 Interdepartmental Study Group, 'Examination of Legal Powers required by the Military Forces if employed in Papua New Guinea in roles short of Direct Intervention in a riot situation', November 1971, NAA, A452 1971/4640.

54 This was done in response to the Sydney Olympics (Smith, 'Aid to the civilian authorities', p. 10).

55 Denoon for instance argues that PNG Command planned to deal with rioters in a 'brusque' fashion, and claims that the Army was overly sanguine about putting down riots, while 'civilian sensibilities were very different' (Denoon, *A Trial Separation*, p. 146). See also O'Neill, *The Army in Papua-New Guinea*, p. 14.

56 Defence Committee Minute No. 5/1970, 'Military Aid to the Civil Power in Papua and New Guinea', 25 March 1970, NAA, A1838 936/3/21, Part 2.

57 Department of Defence Discussion Paper, 'Internal security in PNG in the period to independence', September 1973, NAA, A4087 D923/16/1; George Lambert, 'Functions and Roles of Papua New Guinea Security Forces – Post Independence', December 1972, NAA, A452 1972/3889.

58 Stokes, unpublished memoir, p. 364.

59 Ron Lange, interview, 29 December 2013.

60 Scholars disagree about the attitudes of Papua New Guineans. Mench, as an Australian officer serving in PNG during the 1970s, believed that there was strong support for an internal security role (Mench, *The Role of the Papua New Guinea Defence Force*, pp. 209–10). In contrast, Colebatch found a mix of opinions among soldiers (Colebatch, 'To find a path', pp. 347–8). May argues that after independence PNGDF officers demonstrated a degree of reluctance to undertake this type of operation (May, *The Changing Role of the Military in Papua New Guinea*, p. 40).

61 Colebatch, 'To find a path', 347.

62 Ron Lange, interview, 29 December 2013.
63 Defence Committee Report No. 15/1970, 'Territory of Papua and New Guinea Military Aid to the Civil Power Report by Interdepartmental Committee', 8 September 1970, NAA, A1838 689/2 Part 7; Ron Lange, interview, 29 December 2013, and Colebatch, 'To find a path', pp. 348, 356-8.
64 Stokes, unpublished memoir, p. 361; Ron Lange, interview, 29 December 2013.
65 Department of Territories to Administration, 16 September 1969, NAA, A452 1969/4604; R.P.J. Stevenson, 'Report of Tour of Bougainville, 11–18 September 1969', 20 September 1969, NAA, A452 1969/4604; Hay to Department of Territories, 26 September 1969, NAA, A452 1969/4604.
66 Downs, *The Australian Trusteeship*, p. 491.
67 See for instance 'NG Army could be halved, says speaker', *SMH*, 19 March 1973; Heatu, 'New Guinea's coming army', p. 33; Sundhaussen, 'New Guinea's army', p. 35.
68 Albert Kiki in PNG House of Assembly, *Debates*, 25 April 1974, vol. III, no. 28, p. 3681, cited in Hunt, 'Papua New Guinea in Australia's strategic thinking', p. 224.
69 'Record of meeting between PNG and Australian Officials on Defence Matters, Port Moresby', 6–8 March 1973, NAA, A4087 D923/6/6, Part 1.
70 External Territories, 'Functions and roles of the Papua New Guinea Security Forces – Post Independence', December 1972, NAA, A452 1972/3889.
71 Kiki in PNG House of Assembly, *Debates*, 25 April 1974, vol. III, no. 28, p. 3681, cited in Hunt, 'Papua New Guinea in Australia's strategic thinking', p. 224; Nelson, *Papua New Guinea*, p. 207. See also Millar, 'Melanesia's strategic significance', p. 31.
72 Defence Planning Division, Department of Defence, 'The Defence Relationship with Papua New Guinea', March 1974, NAA, A452 1973/2892.
73 *Report of the Constitutional Planning Committee* (Papua New Guinea House of Assembly, Port Moresby, 1974), chapter 13, 'The disciplined forces', <www.paclii.org>
74 External Territories, 'Functions and roles of the Papua New Guinea Security Forces – Post Independence', December 1972, NAA, A452 1972/3889.
75 See for instance Woolford, *Papua New Guinea*, p. 240; Hastings, 'Thoughts on Taurama'; Hastings, *New Guinea*, p. 277; Sundhaussen, 'New Guinea's army'; Premdas, 'A non-political army'.
76 *Report of the Constitutional Planning Committee*, chapter 13, 'The disciplined forces'.
77 Ibid.
78 May, *The Changing Role of the Military in Papua New Guinea*, p. 12.
79 See Constitution of Papua New Guinea, <http://en.wikisource.org>
80 The necessity of coordinating defence planning with other departments also slowed the process. 'CGS Briefing of GOCs and Commanders', 10 May 1971, AAHU.

81 Working Party draft, 'Development of an indigenous defence force in PNG', 24 February 1971, NAA, A452 1972/3573.

82 George Lambert, 'Functions and Roles of Papua New Guinea Security Forces – Post Independence', December 1972, NAA, A452 1972/3889.

83 Department of Defence, 'Australian services in Papua New Guinea', May 1972, NAA, A703 572/1/110; Fairbairn to Drake-Brockman, 23 July 1972, NAA, A703 572/1/110.

84 These were named after the influential Secretary of Defence from 1970 to 1979, Sir Arthur Tange. See Andrews, *The Department of Defence*, pp. 191–211; Horner, *Making the Australian Defence Force*, pp. 46–9.

85 Defence Committee Minute No. 19/70, 17 September 1970, NAA, A1209 1969/9045.

86 Barry Holloway, interview, 24 August 2011.

87 Bill Morrison, 'Transfer of defence powers', in *Hindsight: A Retrospective Workshop for Participants in the Decolonisation of Papua New Guinea*, 3–4 November 2002, <https://digitalcollections.anu.edu.au>; Jim Nockels, interview, 26 September 2011; Sundhaussen, 'New Guinea's army', p. 33.

88 May, *The Changing Role of the Military in Papua New Guinea*, p. 18; Laki, 'PNG Defence Force', p. 70; East, 'PNGDF', p. 11. There have been similar suggestions more recently; see Anonymous, 'Papua New Guinea proposes to merge defense force, constabulary', *Special Warfare*, vol. 13, no. 2, 2000, p. 42.

89 Eldridge to Graham, 8 May 1969, AWM121 234/F/4.

90 O'Neill, *The Army in Papua-New Guinea*, p. 22.

91 Working Party draft, 'Development of an indigenous defence force in PNG', 24 February 1971, NAA, A452 1972/3573; Robin Morison, Archive No. 1921, AAWFA.

92 Defence Committee Report No. 17/1970, 'Review of the Defence Forces in Papua/New Guinea', 31 July 1970, NAA, A1209 1969/9045; DCGS Memorandum No. 367/71, 'Review of the defence forces in Papua/New Guinea', AWM122 70/2025, Part 1; PNGDCC, 'Interim Report on Size and Shape', December 1972, NAA, A452 1972/3889.

93 Denoon, *A Trial Separation*, p. 194.

94 Hall, 'Aborigines and Australian defence planning', p. 210.

95 For a discussion of 'fatal impact' and the 'islander agency' view of Pacific history, see Fischer, *A History of the Pacific Islands*, pp. xviii–xix.

96 See for instance Denoon, *A Trial Separation*, p. 147.

97 See Doran, 'Wanting and knowing best', p. 321.

98 Annex B to Joint Service Report No. 76/1969, 'Review of Defence Forces in Papua – New Guinea', 8 December 1969, AWM122 68/2020, Part 2.

99 HQ PNG Command, 'Future Development of the Army in TPNG – Area of Study I – The Army Structure in Outline', April 1970, NAA, A452 1971/2346.

100 Hughes to DCNS, DCGS, DCAS, 16 December 1971, AWM122 70/2025, Part 3.

101 Chiefs of Staff Committee, 'Outline plan for the establishment of a Joint Force Headquarters in Papua New Guinea', 10 November 1971, NAA,

A703 635/2/660; JFHQ, 'A plan for the development of HQ Joint Force PNG', 24 July 1972, NAA, A703 635/2/660; Eldridge to COSC, Army, Navy and Air Departments, 31 January 1972, AWM122 72/2003.

102 Bert Wansley, telephone interview, 27 May 2013.

103 Military Board, 'Reorganization/Redesignation Instruction 69/72', 30 November 1972, NAA, A703 635/2/660; Chiefs of Staff Committee Minute No. 88/1972, 'Dress proposals for the PNG Force', 18 December 1972, NAA, A703 635/2/660; Mench, *The Role of the Papua New Guinea Defence Force*, p. 75.

104 Colebatch, 'To find a path', p. 372.

105 Sinclair, *Keeping the Peace*, p. 301.

106 See Mench, *The Role of the Papua New Guinea Defence Force*, pp. 96–103.

107 Frank Cranston, 'PNG defence forces to get an air arm', *Canberra Times*, 4 December 1972. See also PNGDCC, 'PNG Defence Force – Air Element', 7 February 1974, NAA, A452 1972/3573; Sinclair, *Keeping the Peace*, pp. 207–13.

108 'Size and Shape of PNG Defence Force', 10 May 1973, NAA, A4087 D923/26/6; PNGDCC, 'Report by the Department of Defence Delegate to the Joint Steering Committee on PNG Defence Force Development', 27 July 1973, NAA, A4087 D923/26/6.

109 PNGDCC, 'Report by the Department of Defence Delegate to the Joint Steering Committee on PNG Defence Force Development', 27 July 1973, NAA, A4087 D923/26/6.

110 Department of Defence, 'Size and Shape of PNG Defence Force', 10 May 1973, NAA, A4087 D923/26/6.

111 S.C. Graham, 'Development of the PNG Defence Force: Study of the Size and Organization of the Force Post Independence: Detailed Proposal for the Land Element', 15 November 1972, NAA, A452 1972/3574; PNGDCC, 'Interim Report on Size and Shape', December 1972, NAA, A452 1972/3889.

112 Sinclair, *Keeping the Peace*, p. 119.

113 Ron Lange, interview, 29 December 2013; Norman Fearn, Archive No. 1421, AAWFA.

114 'Schedule for reorganisation of the PNG Defence Force', in Wansley to Chairman Chiefs of Staff Committee, 14 August 1973, NAA, A452 1972/3889.

115 Sinclair, *Keeping the Peace*, p. 300; Mench, *The Role of the Papua New Guinea Defence Force*, p. 103.

116 W. Molony, 'The Future of the CMF in PNG after Independence', August 1971, NAA, J2810 R696/1/3; I. Thompson, 'The Future of the CMF in PNG after Independence', NAA, J2810 R696/1/3; Ted Diro, interview, 31 July 2013.

117 See for instance PNGDCC Report, 'Australian personnel serving with the PNG Defence Force after independence', 10 October 1973, NAA, A432 1982/10137; Department of Defence Minute, 'PNG – Transfer of Defence Function', 18 September 1974, NAA, A10756 LC264, Part 1.

118 Defence Planning Division, 'The Defence Relationship with Papua New Guinea', March 1974, NAA, A452 1973/2892.

119 Peter Murray, interview, 14 October 2011; Ronnie Oiwelo, interview, 31 July 2013; Ross Eastgate, interview, 14 April 2012.

120 Department of Defence Discussion Paper No. 6, 'Internal Security in PNG in the period to independence', 6 December 1973, NAA, A4087 D923/16/1; PNGDCC, 'Australia/PNG Transfer of the Defence Function', 11 October 1974, NAA, A4090 723/16/1, Part 3.

121 'Report of the AHQ Working Committee – Identification of Potential Officers from the Pacific Islands', 21 February 1963, NAA, J2818 160/2/1.

122 Department of the Army Cabinet Submission, 'Territory of Papua and New Guinea – Army Expansion', n.d. [1967], NAA, A6059 41/441/94; K.A. Peddle, 'PI officers as a potential source of district commissioners', 24 July 1970, NAA, A6059 41/441/94; I. Hunter, 'Brief by Comd PNG Comd', CGS Quarterly Briefing of GOCs/Comds of Comds, RMC and Comd 1 Division, 1 November 1967, NAA, A6059 41/441/94.

123 'Officers in PIR by Rank', 1971, NAA, A1838 936/4; Mench, *The Role of the Papua New Guinea Defence Force*, p. 79.

124 N. Ross Smith, 'The Joint Services College of Papua New Guinea', 19 May 1976, NAA, A9850 802/7, Part 1.

125 Mench, *The Role of the Papua New Guinea Defence Force*, p. 108.

126 J. Norrie, 'Report by the Commander, Joint Force PNG – Period 18 April to 30 June, 1972', 8 August 1972, NAA, AWM122 72/4014; PNGDCC Report, 'Australian service personnel serving with the PNG Defence Force after independence', 10 October 1973, NAA, A432 1982/10137.

127 PNGDCC Report, 'Australia/PNG Transfer of the Defence Function', 11 October 1974, NAA, A4090 723/16/1, Part 3.

128 May, *The Changing Role of the Military in Papua New Guinea*, p. 15.

129 O'Neill, *The Army in Papua-New Guinea*, p. 5.

130 J. Norrie, 'Report by the Commander, Joint Force PNG, Period 18 April to 30 June, 1972', 8 August 1972, AWM122 72/4014.

131 Mike Dennis, interview, 15 February 2012; Cliff Brock, interview, 15 March 2013; Bruce Selleck, questionnaire, received 21 January 2012.

132 Bruce Selleck, questionnaire, received 12 January 2012.

133 Ibid.; Tom Posi-tute, interview, 30 July 2013.

134 Ken Swadling, questionnaire, received 1 August 2011.

135 Cliff Brock, questionnaire, received 3 December 2012.

136 See for instance files on individual ceremonies approved by the Administration contained in PNGNA 1008 76/6/2.

137 Department of Chief Minister to all District Commissioners, 15 October 1974, PNGNA, 1008 76/6/2; Ted Diro, interview, 31 July 2013.

138 Ted Diro, interview, 31 July 2013.

139 Moses Kiari, interview, 2 August 2013; Bruce Selleck, interview, 21 January 2012; Bev Hartwig, interview, 6 February 2012.

140 Frank Moripi, interview, 3 August 2013.

141 Terry Edwinsmith, interview, 5 May 2011; Don Gillies, telephone interview, 7 December 2011; Dan McDaniel, telephone interview, 13 December 2012.
142 Malcolm Macullum, questionnaire, 28 December 2013.
143 Frank Moripi, interview, 3 August 2013.
144 Cliff Brock, questionnaire, received 3 December 2012.
145 Frank Moripi, interview, 3 August 2013; Hori Howard, questionnaire, received 29 March 2012; William Guest, Archive No. 0588, AAWFA.
146 At the end of 1975, the name of ADAG was changed to the Australian Defence Cooperation Group, reflecting the new relationship. Some in PNG felt that the term 'assistance' sent the wrong message: 'some in PNG saw it as a legacy of Australian defence control over PNG: others saw it, from an Australian point of view, as a type of military intrusion into an independent sovereign nation' (Australian High Commission to Department of Defence, 19 and 28 November 1975, NAA, A4087 D923/19/3).
147 For a discussion of survey teams, see Coulthard-Clark, *Australia's Military Map-makers*, pp. 167-9. For the engineers, see Blaxland, *The Australian Army from Whitlam to Howard*, p. 47.
148 Department of Defence Minute, 'PNG – Transfer of Defence Function', 18 September 1974, NAA, A10756 LC264, Part 1; PNGDCC Minute No. 28/74, 'Draft of Loan Personnel Agreement', 19 September 1973, NAA, A10756 LC264, Part 1; 'Documents relating to interim defence arrangements between Australia and Papua New Guinea', October 1975, NAA, A452 1974/406. Hunt's thesis examines the development of these and other defence agreements at length (Hunt, 'Papua New Guinea in Australia's strategic thinking', pp. 209-56).
149 Department of Foreign Affairs Ministerial Submission, 'Australia/PNG Defence Arrangements', 9 December 1976, NAA, A1838 689/2/18, Part 5.
150 Department of Defence Memorandum No. 369, 'Use of Australian loan servicemen in the PNGDF', 23 April 1975, NAA, A1838 3080/4/5 Part 5; Hunt, 'Papua New Guinea in Australia's Strategic Thinking', p. 232.
151 Ted Diro, interview, 31 July 2013; Mike Dennis, interview, 15 February 2012.
152 Urquhart, 'Australia's military aid programs 1950-1990', p. 205.
153 See for instance R.N. Hamilton, 'Senior PNG Department of Defence official criticizes Australian loan personnel in PNG', 8 November 1976, NAA, A4090 723/16/5, Part 5; Don James, interview, 14 April 2012; Tony Haui, interview, 29 August 2011; Blaxland, *The Australian Army from Whitlam to Howard*, p. 36.
154 Mike Dennis, interview, 15 February 2012; Alan Kilby, interview, 2 May 2011.
155 Ray McCann, questionnaire, received 2 March 2013.
156 Hamilton to Secretary, 'Senior PNG Department of Defence official criticises Australian loan personnel in PNG', November 1976, NAA, A1838 689/2/18, Part 4.

Conclusion

1   The best general overview of PNG's history after independence can be found in Dorney, *Papua New Guinea*.

2   For a description see May, *The Changing Role of the Military in Papua New Guinea*, p. 38; MacQueen, 'Beyond Tok Win', p. 235; Gubb, *Vanuatu's 1980 Santo Rebellion*.

3   For an overview of some of the problems the PNGDF faced, see Rogers, 'The Papua New Guinea Defence Force', pp. 84–5.

4   The clearest account of the PNGDF's recent history can be found in May and Haley, 'The military in Papua New Guinea', pp. 53–70.

5   Nelson, *Fighting for Her Gates and Waterways*, p. 21. For a detailed examination of the conflict, see Claxton, *Bougainville 1988–98*; Downer and Australia, *The Bougainville Crisis*; Polomka, *Bougainville*.

6   Mietzner and Farrelly, 'Mutinies, coups and military interventionism', p. 346.

7   May and Haley, 'The military in Papua New Guinea', p. 63.

8   May, 'Papua New Guinea', p. 53.

9   For a discussion of the Sandline Crisis, see Dinnen, May and Regan, *Challenging the State*; Nelson, *Fighting for Her Gates and Waterways*, p. 22.

10 For the PNGDF's 'grace under pressure' during the 2012 political crisis, see Karl Claxton, 'Defence deal with PNG sharpens our South Pacific focus', *Strategist*, 13 May 2013, <www.aspistrategist.org.au>; Ian Kemish, 'Papua New Guinea: Australia's closet neighbour in transition', Fernberg Lecture, 10 December 2012, <www.png.embassy.gov.au>

11 Firth, 'Security in Papua New Guinea', p. 112.

12 George Aibo, interview, 30 July 2013.

BIBLIOGRAPHY

PUBLISHED RECORDS
Army List of Officers of the Australian Military Forces, 1950–88
Keeping the Peace (Duties in Support of the Civil Power), War Office, London, 1957, Part 2
Commonwealth of Australia, *Territory of New Guinea Report for 1966–1967,* Commonwealth Government Printer, Canberra, 1967

UNPUBLISHED RECORDS
Australian Army History Unit, Canberra
Military Board Minutes, 1950–75
Military Board Secretariat Briefing Notes, 1950–75
Military Board Submissions, 1950–75

Australian Army Psychology Corps, Canberra
1 Psychology Research Unit Reports, 1968–73

Australian War Memorial, Canberra
AWM78   Reports of Proceedings, HMA Ships and Establishments, 1939–
AWM90   Australian Service Canteens Organisation records, 1915–79
AWM113   Records of the Military History Section (Army), 1940–61
AWM121   Records of the Directorate of Military Operations and Plans (DMO&P), 1952–75
AWM122   Department of Defence, Joint Planning Committee records from joint military operations and plans, 1959–75
AWM125   Written records – Miscellaneous – South-East Asian conflicts, 1948–75
AWM292   Records of Assistant Director of Medical Services, Headquarters Australian Force Vietnam, 1962–72

National Archives of Australia, Brisbane
J2810   PNGVR, Correspondence files, multiple number series with 'R' prefix [PNG], 1963–73
J2818   HQ PNG Command, Correspondence files, multiple number series [PNG – Pacific Islands Regiment], 1954–66

National Archives of Australia, Canberra

A432   Attorney-General's Department, Correspondence files, annual single number series, 1929–

A452   Department of (External) Territories, Correspondence files, annual single number series, 1951–75

A471   Department of Defence, Courts-Martial files [including war crimes trials], single number series, 1901–

A518   Department of (External) Territories, Correspondence files, multiple number series with alphabetical prefix, 1928–56

A663   Department of Defence, Correspondence files, multiple number series with 'O' prefix (primary numbers 1–224), 1940–57

A703   Department of Air, Correspondence files, multiple number series with occasional alphabetical prefixes and infixes [Canberra], 1949–75

A1209   Prime Minister's Department, Correspondence files, annual single number series with occasional C [classified] suffix, 1957–

A1361   Commonwealth Office of Education, Correspondence files, multiple number series, 1947–60

A1838   Department of External Affairs/Foreign Affairs, Correspondence files, multiple number series, 1948–89

A1946   Department of Defence, Correspondence files, annual single number series, 1967–73

A2031   Defence Committee minutes, 1926–

A4087   Department of Defence, Correspondence files, multiple number series with 'D' prefix, 1973–74

A4940   Menzies and Holt Ministries – Cabinet files 'C' single number series, 1949–72

A5619   Cabinet files, single number series with 'C' [Cabinet] prefix, 1949–1972

A5799   Defence Committee agenda, annual single number series, 1932–

A5818   Seventh Menzies Ministry – copies of Cabinet submissions and associated decisions (first series), 1958–61

A5882   Gorton and McMahon Ministries – Cabinet files, 'CO' single number series, 1968–72

A5954   'Shedden Collection' [Records collected by Sir Frederick Shedden during his career with the Department of Defence and in researching the history of Australian Defence Policy], two number series, 1931–71

A6059   Department of the Army, Correspondence files, multiple number series [class 441] [classified], 1956–64

A6837   Department of the Army, Outward correspondence files of the Vice or Deputy Chief of the General Staff, 1963–

A6846   Department of the Army, Records of, or concerning, the Army in Papua/New Guinea, 1945–75

A6847   Department of the Army, Patrol reports of the Army in Papua/New Guinea, 1963–75

A6913   Military Board Instructions [functional/amended set], 1962–73

A8738   Reports of meetings of the Joint Planning Committee, 1940–
A10756   Fraser Ministries – Cabinet files, single number series with 'LC'
           prefix, 1975–83
A10857   Department of Defence, Establishment records, two number series
           with roman numeral prefix and occasional alphabetic suffix, 1937–
           71

National Archives of Australia, Melbourne
MP729/8   Department of the Army, Secret correspondence files, multiple
           number series, 1945–55
MP742/1   Department of the Army, General and civil staff correspondence
           files and Army personnel files, multiple number series, 1943–51
MP927/1   Department of the Army, General and civil staff correspondence
           files and Army personnel files, multiple number series, 1952–1962
MT1131/1   Department of the Army, General and civil staff correspondence
           files and Army personnel files, multiple number series, 1952–62

Papua New Guinean National Archives, Port Moresby
16   District Commission, Registry Files
55   District Commissioner's Department, Port Moresby Central Registry
           Files
82   Department of Administrator, Registry Files
245   Department of Administrator, Government House Files
247   Department of Administrator, Government Secretary's Files
405   Department of the Administrator, Registry Files
1008   Department of Central Province, Division of Rural Services and Circu-
           lar Memorandum Instructions
1010   Department of Provincial Affairs (Margarida), Registry Files
1017   Department of Provincial Affairs (Aitape), Registry Files

National Archives, Kew, United Kingdom
FCO 24–1433   Commonwealth Office, Far East and Pacific Department
              and Foreign and Commonwealth Office, South West Pacific
              Department: Registered Files (H and FW Series)

University of Papua New Guinea Archives, Port Moresby
New Guinea Collection

Private papers and other sources in possession of the author
Flint, Dick, unpublished memoir, n.d.
Ivey, Greg, private papers, n.d.
Payne, Geoff, unpublished diary, May–June 1972
Sayce, Bob, private papers, n.d.
Stokes, Peter, unpublished memoir, n.d.

Films and photographs
'RAAF aid to New Guinea famine areas', 19 October 1972, 16mm film, AWM,
    F02822
'RSM Osi in recruitment poster', n.d. [c. 1970], <www.nashospng.com/
    taurama-barracks-soldiers>
Silk, George, untitled photograph, 25 December 1942, AWM, 014028
Trindall, Raeburn, 'The Piper', 1973, 16mm film, AWM, F03381

ORAL HISTORY, QUESTIONNAIRES AND CORRESPONDENCE
Conducted by Tristan Moss
Adam, Sergeant Phil, Brisbane, 3 May 2011
Agwi, Major General Francis, conversation, Murray Barracks, PNG, 25 August
    2011
Aibo, Warrant Officer George, Port Moresby, PNG, 30 July 2013
Ainaka, Sergeant Thomas, Moem Barracks, PNG, 6 August 2013
Armstrong, Major Dennis, telephone interview (Melbourne), 16 December 2011
Beazley, Roy, telephone interview (Sydney), 7 December 2011
Boddington, Sergeant Richard, Brisbane, 4 May 2011
Brock, Major Cliff, Canberra, 15 March 2013; questionnaire received 13 March
    2013
Brock, Rosemary, Canberra, 15 March 2013
Chalapan, Warrant Officer Tom Levi, Taurama Barracks, PNG, 31 July 2013
Clark, Lieutenant Ted, telephone interview (Adelaide), 15 May 2011
Claxton, Dr Karl, conversation, Port Moresby, PNG, 25 August 2011
Coppa, Sergeant Robert, questionnaire received 15 November 2012
Dalziel, Sergeant Andrew, Melbourne, 13 July 2011
Daura, Corporal Rodney, Taurama Barracks, PNG, 31 July 2013
Dennis, Lieutenant Colonel Michael, Adelaide, 15 February 2012
Dinji, Warrant Officer Barney, Taurama Barracks, PNG, 31 July 2013
Diro, Brigadier Ted, Port Moresby, PNG, 31 July 2013
Eastgate, Anne, Gold Coast, 14 April 2012
Eastgate, Major Ross, Gold Coast, 14 April 2012
Edwinsmith, Sergeant Terry, Brisbane, 5 May 2011
Farr, Sergeant Greg, Brisbane, 2 May 2011
Garrett, Richard, correspondence, 10 November 2012
Gewa, Corporal Gapi, Port Moresby 30 July 2013
Gibson, Sergeant John, Brisbane, 3 May 2011
Gillies, Major Don, telephone interview (Sydney), 7 December 2011
Gollings, Lieutenant Ian, telephone interview, 3 November 2011; correspondence,
    received 25 October 2011
Gration, General Peter, Canberra, 15 July 2013
Gwamse, Sergeant Nadu, Moem Barracks, PNG, 6 August 2013
Hartwig, Lieutenant Commander Beverly, Adelaide, 16 February 2012
Haui, Brigadier Tony, Port Moresby, PNG, 29 August 2011
Holland, Brigadier Terry, questionnaire received 26 November 2013
Holloway, Sir Barry, Port Moresby, PNG, 24 August 2011
Horton, Sergeant Kevin, Brisbane, 1 May 2011

Horton, Lynette, Brisbane, 1 May 2011

Howard, Major General Brian (Hori), Canberra, 16 May 2011; questionnaire received 29 March 2012

Hunter, Sergeant Norm, Brisbane, 17 April 2012

Iselin, Sergeant Brian, telephone interview (Sunshine Coast), 12 December 2011; correspondence, 21 December 2011 and 7 January 2012

Ivey, Sergeant Greg, Brisbane, 1 May 2011

James, Major Don, Gold Coast, 14 April 2012; correspondence, 19 December 2011

Jeffery, Major General Michael, Canberra, 16 November 2010

Johnson, Sergeant Graeme, telephone interview (Perth), 27 June 2011

Kairi, Private Moses, Port Moresby, PNG, 2 August 2013

Kakar, Corporal Caspar Nasson, Wewak, PNG, 6 August 2013

Kearney, Colonel George, telephone interview (Brisbane), 19 September 2011

Kelly, Major John, telephone interview (Queensland), 2 August 2012

Kilby, Warrant Officer Alan, Brisbane, 2 May 2011

Knight, Sergeant Richard, Port Moresby, PNG, 23 July 2013

Kombukun, Sergeant Jim, Taurama Barracks, PNG, 31 July 2013

Kukuma, Colonel Jack, Port Moresby, PNG, 3 August 2013

Lange, Colonel Ron, telephone interview (Noosa), 15 May 2012

Lewis, Diane, Adelaide, 14 July 2012

Lewis, Brigadier Laurie, Adelaide, 14 July 2012

McCann, Brigadier Ray, Bowral, NSW, 16 February 2013; questionnaire received 2 March 2013

MacCullum, Major Malcolm, questionnaire received 28 December 2013

McDaniel, Lieutenant Colonel Dan, telephone interview (Perth), 13 August 2012

McDougall, Colonel Peter, questionnaire received 19 November 2013

McFarlane, Major Brian, Bowral, NSW, 16 February 2013

Manning, Lieutenant Colonel Graeme, questionnaire received 27 March 2012

Marsden, Major John, telephone interview (Sydney), 18 November 2011

Miasa, Colonel Sia, Port Moresby, PNG, 3 August 2013

Moripi, Major Frank, Port Moresby, PNG, 3 August 2013

Murray, Lieutenant Colonel Peter, Canberra, 7 and 14 October 2011

Nockels, Jim, Canberra, 26 September 2011

Norrie, Lieutenant Colonel Ben, Canberra, 10 March 2011

Ogston, Sergeant Ian, Canberra, 8 March 2010

Oiwelo, Sergeant Ronnie, Taurama Barracks, PNG, 31 July 2013

Olimomo, Sergeant Patrick, Taurama Barracks, PNG, 31 July 2013

Payne, Lieutenant Colonel Geoff, telephone interview (Sydney), 13 March 2013

Pears, Lieutenant Colonel Maurie, Gold Coast, 14 April 2012

Porteous, Sergeant Peter, questionnaire received 24 November 2013

Posi-tute, Warrant Officer Thomas, Port Moresby, PNG, 30 July 2013

Rauleta, Sergeant Lincoln, Moem Barracks, PNG, 6 August 2013

Renagi, Colonel Reginald, Port Moresby, PNG, 22 and 23 August 2011

Saese, Warrant Officer Valentine, Moem Barracks, PNG, 6 August 2013

Sayce, Colonel Bob, Canberra, 8 November 2012

Singirok, Major General Jerry, Port Moresby, PNG, 29 August 2011 and 25 July 2013
Smith, Sergeant Kevin, Brisbane, 4 May 2011
Suat, Sergeant John, Moem Barracks, PNG, 6 August 2013
Swadling, Captain Ken, questionnaire received 1 August 2011
Takoin, Warrant Officer Martin, Port Moresby, PNG, 30 July 2013
Trei, Private Sammy Joe, Port Moresby, PNG, 8 August 2013
Urr, Captain Tom, conversation, Murray Barracks, PNG, 24 July 2013
Wansley, Colonel Bert, telephone interview (Noosa), 27 May 2013
Watut, Corporal Mutuaina, Taurama Barracks, PNG, 31 July 2013
Wease, Warrant Officer Grahame, telephone interview (Tewantin, Qld), 2 October 2011
Winkel, Warrant Officer Dan, Brisbane, 13 April 2012
Wupu, Warrant Officer Anthony, Moem Barracks, PNG, 6 August 2013

Australians at War Film Archive
Adamson, Colin, Archive No. 1171
Blake, Murray, Archive No. 1850
Bowden, Antony, Archive No. 2443
Butler, David, Archive No. 1034
Clunies-Ross, Adrian, Archive No. 0795
Cruickshank, James, Archive No. 0770
Dihm, Jack, Archive No. 1698
Fearn, Norman, Archive No. 1421
Guest, William, Archive No. 0588
Jordan, Albert, Archive No. 2154
Morison, Robin, Archive No. 1921
Morrison, Michael, Archive No. 1928
Tilbrook, Francis, Archive No. 2354
Warfe, Peter, Archive No. 2487

SECONDARY SOURCES
Official histories
Dennis, Peter, and Jeffrey Grey, *Emergency and Confrontation: Australian Military Operations in Malaya and Borneo 1950–1966*, vol. 5, *Official History of Australia's Involvement in Southeast Asian Conflicts, 1948–1975*, Allen & Unwin in association with Australian War Memorial, Sydney, 1996
Edwards, P.G., and Gregory Pemberton, *Crises and Commitments: The Politics and Diplomacy of Australia's Involvement in Southeast Asian Conflicts 1948–1965*, vol. 1, *Official History of Australia's Involvement in Southeast Asian Conflicts 1948–1975*, Allen & Unwin in association with Australian War Memorial, Sydney, 1992
Ekins, Ashley, and Ian McNeill, *Fighting to the Finish: The Australian Army and the Vietnam War, 1968–1975*, vol. 9, *Official History of Australia's Involvement in Southeast Asian Conflicts 1948–1975*, Allen & Unwin in association with Australian War Memorial, Sydney, 2012

McCarthy, Dudley, *South-West Pacific Area First Year*, vol. V, *Australia in the War of 1939–1945*, Australian War Memorial, Canberra, 1959
O'Neill, Robert John, *Australia in the Korean War 1950–53, vol. 1, Strategy and Diplomacy*, Australian War Memorial and AGPS, Canberra, 1981

Books

Alvah, Donna, *Unofficial Ambassadors: American Military Families Overseas and the Cold War, 1946–1965*, New York University Press, New York, 2007
Andrews, Eric, *The Department of Defence*, vol. 5, *The Australian Centenary History of Defence*, OUP, Melbourne, 2001
Ball, Desmond (ed.), *Aborigines in the Defence of Australia*, Australian National University Press, Canberra, 1991
Beale, Pat, *Operation Orders: The Experiences of an Infantry Officer*, Australian Military History Publications, Loftus, NSW, 2003
Beaumont, Joan, *Australian Defence: Sources and Statistics*, vol. 6, *The Australian Centenary History of Defence*, OUP, Melbourne, 2001
Blaxland, J.C., *The Australian Army from Whitlam to Howard*, CUP, Melbourne, 2013
Bradley, Phillip, *To Salamaua*, CUP, Melbourne, 2010
Byrnes, G.M., *Green Shadows: A War History of the Papuan Infantry Battalion, 1 New Guinea Infantry Battalion, 2 New Guinea Infantry Battalion, 3 New Guinea Infantry Battalion*, G.M. Byrnes, New Market, Qld, 1989
Claxton, Karl, *Bougainville 1988–98: Five Searches for Security in the North Solomons Province of Papua New Guinea*, Strategic and Defence Studies Centre, Australian National University, Canberra, 1998
Clayton, Anthony, and David Killingray, *Khaki and Blue: Military and Police in British Colonial Africa*, Research in International Studies, Africa Series, Ohio University Press, Athens, 1989
Coulthard-Clark, C.D. *Australia's Military Map-makers: The Royal Australian Survey Corps 1915–96*, OUP, Melbourne, 2000
Dennis, Peter, Jeffrey Grey, Ewan Morris and Robin Prior (eds), *The Oxford Companion to Australian Military History*, 2nd edn, OUP, Melbourne, 2008
Denoon, Donald, *A Trial Separation: Australia and the Decolonisation of Papua New Guinea*, Pandanus Books, Canberra, 2005
Dinnen, Sinclair, *Law, Order and the State in Papua New Guinea*, State Society and Governance in Melanesia Discussion Paper 97/1, Research School of Pacific and Asian Studies, Canberra, 1997
Dinnen, Sinclair, R.J. May and A.J. Regan, *Challenging the State: The Sandline Affair in Papua New Guinea*, Pacific Policy Papers no. 30, Australian National University, Canberra, 1997
Doran, Stuart, (ed.), *Australia and Papua New Guinea, 1966–1969*, vol. 26, *Documents on Australian Foreign Policy*, Department of Foreign Affairs and Trade, Barton, ACT, 2006
Dorney, Sean, *Papua New Guinea: People, Politics and History Since 1975*, rev. edn, ABC Books, Sydney, 2000

Downer, Alexander, *The Bougainville Crisis: An Australian Perspective*, Department of Foreign Affairs and Trade, Canberra, 2001

Downs, Ian, *The Australian Trusteeship, Papua New Guinea, 1945–75*, AGPS, Canberra, 1980

Dymock, Darryl R., *The Chalkies: Educating an Army for Independence*, Australian Scholarly Publishing, North Melbourne, 2016

Enloe, Cynthia H., *Ethnic Soldiers: State Security in a Divided Society*, Penguin, Harmondsworth, 1980

Fischer, Steven R., *A History of the Pacific Islands*, Palgrave, New York, 2002

French, David, *The British Way in Counter-Insurgency, 1945–1967*, OUP, Oxford/New York, 2011

Frühling, Stephan, *A History of Australian Strategic Policy Since 1945*, Australian Department of Defence, Canberra, 2009

Goldsworthy, David, *Losing the Blanket: Australia and the End of Britain's Empire*, MUP, Melbourne, 2002

Granter, N.E.W., *Yesterday and Today: An Illustrated History of the Pacific Islands Regiment from Its Formation on 19th June 1940 until the Present Day*, [Pacific Islands Regiment], Port Moresby, 1970

Greville, P.J., *The Royal Australian Engineers, 1945 to 1972: Paving the Way*, Australian Military History Publications, [Sydney], 2002

Grey, Jeffrey, *The Australian Army*, Oxford University Press, Melbourne, 2001

——*A Military History of Australia*, 3rd edn, CUP, Melbourne, 2008

——*A Soldier's Soldier: A Biography of Lieutenant General Sir Thomas Daly*, CUP, Melbourne, 2012

Griffin, James, Hank Nelson and Stewart Firth, *Papua New Guinea: A Political History*, Heinemann Educational, Richmond, Vic., 1979

Gubb, Matthew, *Vanuatu's 1980 Santo Rebellion: International Responses to a Microstate Security Crisis*, Canberra Papers on Strategy and Defence, no. 107, Strategic and Defence Studies Centre, Australian National University, Canberra, 1994

Haebich, Anna, *Spinning the Dream: Assimilation in Australia 1950–1970*, Fremantle Press, Fremantle, 2008

Hasluck, Paul, *A Time for Building: Australian Administration in Papua and New Guinea, 1951–1963*, MUP, Melbourne, 1976

Hastings, Peter, *New Guinea: Problems and Prospects*, Australian Institute of International Affairs, Melbourne, 1969

Horner, D.M., *Defence Supremo: Sir Frederick Shedden and the Making of Australian Defence Policy*, Allen & Unwin, Sydney, 2000

——*Making the Australian Defence Force*, vol. 4, *The Australian Centenary History of Defence*, OUP, Melbourne, 2001

——*SAS: Phantoms of War*, 2nd edn, Allen & Unwin, Sydney, 2002

——*Strategic Command: General Sir John Wilton and Australia's Asian Wars*, OUP, Melbourne, 2005

Horner, D.M., and Jean Bou (eds), *Duty First: The Royal Australian Regiment in War and Peace*, Allen & Unwin, Sydney, 1990

Janowitz, Morris, *The Professional Soldier: A Social and Political Portrait*, Free Press, Glencoe, Ill., 1960

Kerr, Alan, *A Federation in These Seas: An Account of the Acquisition by Australia of Its External Territories, with Selected Documents*, Attorney-General's Department, Canberra, 2009

Kiki, Albert Maori, *Kiki: Ten Thousand Years in a Lifetime, a New Guinea Autobiography*, Cheshire, Melbourne, 1968

Killingray, David, *Policing and Decolonisation: Politics, Nationalism, and the Police, 1917–65*, Manchester University Press, Manchester/New York, 1992

Lloyd, Stephanie, Marlena Jeffery and Jenny Hearn, *Taim Bilong Misis Bilong Armi: Memories of Wives of Australian Servicemen in Papua New Guinea 1951–1975*, Pandanus Books, Canberra, 2001

McFarlane, Brian W., *We Band of Brothers: A True Australian Adventure Story*, B.W. McFarlane, Bowral, 2000

May, R.J., *The Changing Role of the Military in Papua New Guinea*, Canberra Papers on Strategy and Defence, no. 101, Strategic and Defence Studies Centre, Canberra, 1993

Meaney, Neville, *Australia and the World Crisis 1914–1923, vol. 2, A History of Australian Defence and Foreign Policy, 1901–23*, Sydney University Press, Sydney, 2009

Mench, Paul, *The Role of the Papua New Guinea Defence Force*, Australian National University, Canberra, 1975

Millar, T.B., *Australia in Peace and War: External Relations Since 1788*, 2nd edn, Australian National University Press, Sydney, 1991

Moore, Clive, *New Guinea: Crossing Boundaries and History*, University of Hawai'i Press, Honolulu, 2003

Nelson, Hank, *Fighting for Her Gates and Waterways: Changing Perceptions of New Guinea in Australian Defence*. State Society and Governance in Melanesia Discussion Paper, Australian National University, Canberra, 2005

Ogston, Ian, *Chalkies: Conscript Teachers in Papua New Guinea: 1970–1971*, Ian Ogston, West Chermside, Qld, 2003

——*Armi Wantoks: Conscript Teachers in Papua New Guinea: 1966–1973*, Ian Ogston, West Chermside, Qld, 2004

Omissi, David, *The Sepoy and the Raj: The Indian Army, 1860–1940*, Macmillan Press, London, 1994

O'Neill, Robert John, *The Army in Papua-New Guinea: Current Role and Implications for Independence*. Canberra Papers on Strategy and Defence, no. 10. Australian National University Press, Canberra, 1971

Palazzo, Albert, *The Australian Army: A History of Its Organisation 1901–2001*, OUP, Melbourne, 2001

Parsons, Timothy, *The African Rank-and-File: Social Implications of Colonial Military Service in the King's African Rifles, 1902–1964*, Heinemann, Portsmouth, 1999

——*The 1964 Army Mutinies and the Making of Modern East Africa*, Praeger, Westport, Conn., 2003

Polomka, Peter, *Bougainville: Perspectives on a Crisis*, Canberra Papers on Strategy and Defence, no. 66, Strategic and Defence Studies Centre, Australian National University, Canberra, 1990

Powell, Alan, *The Third Force: ANGAU's New Guinea War, 1942–46*, OUP, Melbourne, 2003

Riseman, Noah, *Defending Whose Country? Indigenous Soldiers in the Pacific War*, University of Nebraska Press, Lincoln/London, 2012

Riseman, Noah, and Richard Trembath, *Defending Country: Aboriginal and Torres Strait Islander Military Service since 1945*, University of Queensland Press, Brisbane, 2016

Sinclair, James, *Kiap: Australia's Patrol Officers in Papua New Guinea*, 2nd edn, Robert Brown & Associates, Bathurst, 1984

——*To Find a Path: The Life and Times of the Pacific Islands Regiment, vol. I, Yesterday's Heroes, 1885–1950*, Boolarong Publications, Brisbane, 1990

——*To Find a Path: The Papua New Guinea Defence Force and the Australians to Independence, vol. II, Keeping the Peace, 1950–1975*, Crawford House Press, Gold Coast, 1990

Smith, Alan H., *Gunners in Borneo: Artillery during Confrontation, 1962–66*, Royal Australian Artillery Historical Company, Manly, NSW, 2008

Spark, Ceridwen, Seumas Spark and Christina Twomey (eds), *Australians in Papua New Guinea, 1960–1975*, University of Queensland Press, Brisbane, 2014

Tange, Arthur, *Defence Policy-making: A Close-up View, 1950–1980*, ed. Peter Edwards, Canberra Papers on Strategy and Defence 169, ANU E Press, Canberra, 2008

Thompson, Roger C., *Australia and the Pacific Islands in the Twentieth Century*, Australian Scholarly Publishing, Melbourne, 1998

Waiko, John, *A Short History of Papua New Guinea*, OUP, Melbourne, 1993

Ward, Elizabeth, 'Call out the troops: An examination of the legal basis for Australian Defence Force involvement in "non-defence" matters', Australian Parliamentary Research Paper 8, 1997–98

Whitlam, Gough, *The Whitlam Government, 1972–1975*, Viking, Melbourne, 1985

Wolfers, Edward P., *Race Relations and Colonial Rule in Papua New Guinea*, Australia and New Zealand Book Co., Sydney, 1975

Wood, James, *The Forgotten Force: The Australian Military Contribution to the Occupation of Japan 1945–1952*, Allen & Unwin, Sydney, 1998

Woolford, Don, *Papua New Guinea: Initiation and Independence*, University of Queensland Press, Brisbane, 1976

Articles and book chapters

Aitkin, Don, and Edward P. Wolfers, 'Australian attitudes towards the Papua New Guinean area since World War II', *Australian Outlook*, vol. 27, no. 2, 1973, pp. 202–14

——'Australian attitudes towards Papua New Guinea on the eve of Independence', *Australian Outlook*, vol. 30, no. 3, 1976, pp. 432–8

Azari, Jaz, Christopher Dandeker and Neil Greenberg, 'Cultural stress: How interactions with and among foreign populations affect military personnel', *Armed Forces and Society*, vol. 36, no. 4, 2010, pp. 585–603

Bell, Harry, 'Goodbye to all that? Integration in the PIR', *New Guinea and Australia, the Pacific and South-East Asia*, vol. 2, no. 2, 1967, pp. 49–58

Bell, Henry L., 'New Guinea pidgin teaching: Pidgin and the army – an example of Pidgin in a technically orientated environment', in *New Guinea Area Languages and Language Study, vol. 3, Language, Culture, Society and the Modern World*, ed. S.A. Wurm, pp. 671–90, Australian National University, Canberra, 1977

Bishop, Mickie, 'Tarred-paper houses', in *Taim Bilong Misis Bilong Armi*, ed. Lloyd, Jeffery and Hearn, pp. 16–20

Burns, Heather, 'A teddy bears' picnic?', in *Taim Bilong Misis Bilong Armi*, ed. Lloyd, Jeffery and Hearn, pp. 21–7

Corona, Victor P., 'Career patterns in the US Army Officer Corps', *Public Organization Review*, vol. 11, no. 2, 2011, pp. 109–34

Dibb, Paul, 'The self-reliant defence of Australia: The history of an idea', in *History as Policy: Framing the Debate on the Future of Australia's Defence Policy*, ed. Ronald Herman Huisken, pp. 11–26, ANU E Press, Canberra, 2007

Dickson-Waiko, Anne, 'Women, nation and decolonisation in Papua New Guinea', *Journal of Pacific History*, vol. 48, no. 2, 2013, pp. 177–93

Doran, Stuart, 'Wanting and knowing best: Motive and method in Australia's governance of PNG, 1966–69', *Journal of Pacific History*, vol. 40, no. 3, 2005, pp. 311–21

——'Introduction', in *Australia and Papua New Guinea, 1966–1969*, vol. 26, Documents on Australian Foreign Policy, ed. Stuart Doran, pp. xvii–lvii, Department of Foreign Affairs and Trade, Barton, ACT, 2006

Ducie, Jenny, 'A heavenly bird of paradise', in *Taim Bilong Misis Bilong Armi*, ed. Lloyd, Jeffery and Hearn, pp. 49–56

East, Colin, 'PNGDF: Colonial legacy or independent force?', *Pacific Defence Reporter*, vol. 12, no. 5, 1985, pp. 11–13, 60

Enloe, Cynthia, 'The military uses of ethnicity', *Millennium – Journal of International Studies*, vol. 4, 1975, pp. 220–34

Firth, Stewart, 'Colonial administration and the invention of the native', in *Cambridge History of the Pacific Islanders*, ed. Donald Denoon, Stewart Firth, Jocelyn Linnekin, Malama Meleisea and Karen Nero, pp. 253–87, CUP, Cambridge/New York, 1997

——'Security in Papua New Guinea: The military and diplomatic dimensions', *Security Challenges*, vol. 10, no. 2, 2014, pp. 97–113

Fletcher, Karen, and Bomal Gonara, 'Decriminalisation of prostitution in Papua New Guinea', in *Civic Insecurity: Law, Order and HIV in Papua New Guinea*, ed. Vicki Luker and Sinclair Dinnen, pp. 145–53, ANU E Press, Canberra, 2011

Fraenkel, Jon, 'The coming anarchy in Oceania? A critique of the "Africanisation" of the South Pacific thesis', *Commonwealth and Comparative Politics*, vol. 42, no. 1, 2004, pp. 1–34

Glendenning, Maureen, 'Where's the jungle?', in *Taim Bilong Misis Bilong Armi*, ed. Lloyd, Jeffery and Hearn, pp. 39–48

Grey, Jeffrey, 'Cuckoo in the nest? Australian military historiography: The state of the field', *Military Compass*, vol. 6, no. 2, 2008, pp. 455–68

Griffin, James, 'Papua New Guinea', in *Australia in World Affairs, 1971–1975*, ed. W.J. Hudson, pp. 347–83, George Allen & Unwin, Sydney, 1980

Hall, Robert, 'Aborigines and Australian defence planning', in *Aborigines in the Defence of Australia*, ed. Desmond Ball, pp. 205–22, Australian National University Press, Canberra, 1991

Hastings, Peter, 'Thoughts on Taurama: The myth of the "non-political" army', *New Guinea*, vol. 6, no. 1, 1971, pp. 28–34

Heatu, Basita, 'New Guinea's coming army: To prevent a coup or lead one?', *New Guinea*, vol. 2, no. 3, 1967, pp. 32–3

Hereniko, Vilsoni, 'Representations of cultural identities', in *Tides of History: The Pacific Islands in the Twentieth Century*, ed. K.R. Howe, Robert C. Kiste and Brij V. Lal, pp. 406–34, Allen & Unwin, Sydney, 1994

Holding, Kathleen, 'Adding a "guest wing"', in *Taim Bilong Misis Bilong Armi*, ed. Lloyd, Jeffery and Hearn, pp. 12–15

Horner, David, 'The Australian Army and Indonesia's Confrontation with Malaysia', *Australian Outlook*, vol. 43, no. 1, 1989, pp. 61–76

——'From Korea to Pentropic: The Army in the 1950s and early 1960s', in *The Second Fifty Years: The Australian Army 1947–1997*, Proceedings of the Chief of Army's History Conference, 23 September 1997, ed. Peter Dennis and Jeffrey Grey, pp. 48–71, Australian Defence Force Academy, Canberra, 1997

Hudson, W.J., and Jill Daven, 'Papua and New Guinea since 1945', in *Australia and Papua New Guinea*, ed. W.J. Hudson, pp. 151–79, Sydney University Press, Sydney, 1974

Jeffery, Marlena, 'Yangpela Misis', in *Taim Bilong Misis Bilong Armi*, ed. Lloyd, Jeffery and Hearn, pp. 111–14

Killingray, David, 'Military and labour recruitment in the Gold Coast during the Second World War', *Journal of African History*, vol. 23, no. 1, 1982, pp. 83–95

——'The mutiny of the West African Regiment in the Gold Coast, 1901', *International Journal of African Historical Studies*, vol. 16, no. 3, 1983, pp. 441–54

——'Race and rank in the British Army in the twentieth century', *Ethnic and Racial Studies*, vol. 10, no. 3, 1987, pp. 276–90

Kim, Insoo, and Tyler Crabb, 'Collective identity and promotion prospects in the South Korean Army', *Armed Forces and Society*, vol. 40, no. 2, 2014, pp. 295–309

Laki, James, 'PNG Defence Force: An analysis of its past, present and future roles', in *Building a Nation in Papua New Guinea: Views of the Post-Independence Generation*, ed. David T. Kavanamur, Charles Yala and Quinton Clements, pp. 69–91, Pandanus Books, Canberra, 2003

Lammers, Cornelis J., 'Strikes and mutinies: A comparative study of organizational conflicts between rulers and ruled', *Administrative Science Quarterly*, vol. 14, no. 4, 1969, pp. 558–72

Ley, John, 'From colonial backwater to independent state – in a decade', in *Australians in Papua New Guinea, 1960–1975*, ed. Spark, Spark and Twomey, pp. 141–63

Lloyd, Stephanie, 'A rushed arrival', in *Taim Bilong Misis Bilong Armi*, ed. Lloyd, Jeffery and Hearn, pp. 68–73

——'Mrs Osi to the rescue', in *Taim Bilong Misis Bilong Armi*, ed. Lloyd, Jeffery and Hearn, pp. 84–91

Lynch, P.R., 'The coming army', *New Guinea*, vol. 4, no. 1, 1969, pp. 21–3

McGuiness, Sherie, 'Life in a shoe box', in *Taim Bilong Misis Bilong Armi*, ed. Lloyd, Jeffery and Hearn, pp. 120–4

MacQueen, Norman, 'Beyond Tok Win: The Papua New Guinea intervention in Vanuatu, 1980', *Pacific Affairs*, vol. 61, no. 2, 1988, pp. 235–52

May, R.J., 'The government and the military in Papua New Guinea', in *The Military and Democracy in Asia and the Pacific*, ed. R.J. May and Viberto Selochan, ANU E Press, Canberra, 2004

——'Papua New Guinea: Issues of external and internal security', *Security Challenges*, vol. 8, no. 4, 2012, pp. 47–60

May, R.J., and Nicole Haley, 'The military in Papua New Guinea: A "culture of instability" but no coup', *Security Challenges*, vol. 10, no. 2, 2014, pp. 53–70

Mayhew, Norma, 'Earthquakes and farewells', in *Taim Bilong Misis Bilong Armi*, ed. Lloyd, Jeffery and Hearn, pp. 115–19

——'Moem's brown owl', in *Taim Bilong Misis Bilong Armi*, ed. Lloyd, Jeffery and Hearn, pp. 95–102

Mediansky, F.A. 'New Guinea's coming army: Acquiring politically useful skills', *New Guinea*, vol. 5, no. 2, 1970, pp. 37–42

Megarrity, Lyndon, 'Indigenous education in colonial Papua New Guinea: Australian government policy, 1945–1975', *History of Education Review*, vol. 34, no. 2, 2005, pp. 41–58

Mietzner, Marcus, and Nicholas Farrelly, 'Mutinies, coups and military interventionism: Papua New Guinea and South-East Asia in comparison', *Australian Journal of International Affairs*, vol. 67, no. 3, 2013, pp. 342–56

Millar, T.B. 'Melanesia's strategic significance: An uncertain future', *New Guinea*, vol. 5, no. 2, 1970, pp. 30–5

Moore, David W., and B. Thomas Trout, 'Military advancement: The visibility theory of promotion', *American Political Science Review*, vol. 72, no. 2, 1978, pp. 452–68

Nelson, Hank, 'From Kanaka to Fuzzy Wuzzy Angel', *Labour History*, no. 35, 1978, pp. 172–88

——'Hold the good name of the soldier: Discipline of Papuan and New Guinea infantry battalions, 1940–1946', *Journal of Pacific History*, vol. 15, no. 4, 1980, pp. 202–16

——'The enemy at the door: Australia and New Guinea in World War II', Seminar Paper, Tsukuba University, Japan, 21 July 1998

——'Liberation: The end of Australian rule in Papua New Guinea', *Journal of Pacific History*, vol. 35, no. 3, 2000, pp. 269–80

——'Kokoda: Two national histories', *Journal of Pacific History*, vol. 42, no. 1, 2007, pp. 73–88

——*Mobs and Masses: Defining the Dynamic Groups in Papua New Guinea*, State Society and Governance in Melanesia Discussion Paper, Canberra, 2009

Omissi, David, '"Martial races": Ethnicity and security in colonial India 1858–1939', *War and Society*, vol. 9, no. 1, 1991, pp. 1–27

Parsons, Timothy, '"Wakamba warriors are soldiers of the queen": The evolution of the Kamba as a martial race, 1890–1970', *Ethnohistory*, vol. 46, no. 4, 1999, pp. 671–701

Peck, B. Mitchell, 'Assessing the career mobility of US Army officers: 1950–1974', *Armed Forces and Society*, vol. 20, no. 2, 1994, pp. 217–37

Premdas, R., 'A non-political army', *New Guinea*, vol. 9, no. 1, 1974, pp. 29–37

Purcell, Margaret, 'Teaching in paradise', in *Taim Bilong Misis Bilong Armi*, ed. Lloyd, Jeffery and Hearn, pp. 128–31

Radcliffe, Matthew, 'In defence of White Australia: Discouraging "Asian marriage" in post-war South-East Asia', *Australian Historical Studies*, vol. 45, no. 2, 2014, pp. 184–201

Rand, Gavin, and Kim A. Wagner, 'Recruiting the "martial races": Identities and military service in colonial India', *Patterns of Prejudice*, vol. 46, no. 3–4, 2012, pp. 232–54

Reed, Liz, '"Part of our own story": Representations of indigenous Australians and Papua New Guineans within Australia Remembers 1945–1995 – The continuing desire for homogeneous national identity', *Oceania*, vol. 69, March 1999, pp. 157–70

Riseman, Noah, 'Australian [mis]treatment of indigenous labour in World War II Papua New Guinea', *Labour History*, no. 98, May 2010, pp. 163–82

——'Equality in the ranks: The lives of Aboriginal Vietnam veterans', *Journal of Australian Studies*, vol. 36, no. 4, 2012, pp. 411–26

——'Racism, indigenous people and the Australian armed forces in the post-Second World War era', *History Australia*, vol. 10, no. 2, 2013, pp. 159–79

Ritchie, Jonathan, 'Australia, Papua New Guinea, and a communal blindness in our history education', *Australian Policy and History*, March 2010, <http://aph.org.au/papua-new-guinea>

——'Defining citizenship for a new nation', *Journal of Pacific History*, vol. 48, no. 2, 2013, pp. 144–61

——'Australians and Papua New Guinea: A reflection', in *Australians in Papua New Guinea, 1960–1975*, ed. Spark, Spark and Twomey, pp. 297–315

Rose, Elihu, 'The anatomy of mutiny', *Armed Forces and Society*, vol. 8, no. 4, 1982, pp. 561–74

Roy, Kaushik, 'Military loyalty in the colonial context: A case study of the Indian Army during World War II', *Journal of Military History*, vol. 73, no. 2, 2009, pp. 497–529

Schaffer, Gavin, 'Racializing the soldier: An introduction', *Patterns of Prejudice*, vol. 46, no. 3–4, 2012, pp. 209–13

Smith, Hugh, 'Minorities and the Australian Army: Overlooked and underrepresented?' In *A Century of Service: 100 Years of the Australian Army. The 2001 Chief of Army's Military History Conference*, ed. P. Dennis and J. Grey, pp. 129–49, Australian Army History Unit, Department of Defence, Canberra, 2001

——'Aid to the civilian authorities', in *Oxford Companion to Australian Military History*, 2nd edn, pp. 9–10, OUP, Melbourne, 2008

Spector, Ronald, 'The Royal Indian Navy strike of 1946: A study of cohesion and disintegration in colonial armed forces', *Armed Forces and Society*, vol. 7, no. 2, 1981, pp. 271–84

Stapleton, Timothy Joseph, '"Bad boys": Infiltration and sedition in the African military units of the Central African Federation (Malawi, Zambia and Zimbabwe), 1953–1963', *Journal of Military History*, vol. 73, no. 4, 2009, pp. 1167–93

Stewart, Christine, 'Not a misis', in *Australians in Papua New Guinea, 1960–1975*, ed. Spark, Spark and Twomey, pp. 248–62

Sundhaussen, Ulf, 'New Guinea's army: A political role?', *New Guinea*, vol. 8, no. 2, 1973, pp. 29–39

Tattam, Danae, 'Marriage to an officer and a gentleman', in *Taim Bilong Misis Bilong Armi*, ed. Lloyd, Jeffery and Hearn, pp. 60–3

Walker, Franchesca, '"Descendants of a warrior race": The Maori Contingent, New Zealand Pioneer Battalion, and martial race myth, 1914–19', *War and Society*, vol. 31, no. 1, 2012, pp. 1–21

Warubu, Kokou, 'That army again! Fences, boots and all that', *New Guinea*, vol. 3, no. 2, 1968, pp. 8–10

Waters, Christopher, '"Against the tide": Australian government attitudes to decolonisation in the South Pacific, 1962–1972', *Journal of Pacific History*, vol. 48, no. 2, pp. 194–208

Waters, Christopher, and Helen Gardner, 'Decolonisation in Melanesia', *Journal of Pacific History*, vol. 48, no. 2, 2013, pp. 113–21

Wesley-Smith, Terence, 'Australia and New Zealand', in *Tides of History: The Pacific Islands in the Twentieth Century*, ed. K.R. Howe, Robert C. Kiste and Brij V. Lal, Allen & Unwin, Sydney, 1994, pp. 195–226

Wolfers, Edward P., 'Trusteeship without the trust', in *Racism: The Australian Experience*, ed. Edward P. Wolfers and F.S. Stevens, vol. 3, pp. 61–148, Australia and New Zealand Book Co., Sydney, 1972

Theses

Armstrong, Dennis James, 'An examination of the effects of ethnic contact upon the attitudes of some Australians in Papua New Guinea', MA, University of Queensland, 1972

Brown, Elizabeth I, 'Bye, bye Miss American Pie: Wives of American servicemen in Southeast Asia, 1961–1975', PhD, University of Colorado, 2005

Colebatch, Peta, 'To find a path: The army in Papua New Guinea', PhD, Sussex University, 1974

Hunt, Bruce Geoffrey, 'Papua New Guinea in Australia's strategic thinking, 1880–1977: The path to the 1977 Statement on the Defence Relationship', PhD, University of New England, 2003

Lovering, Timothy John, 'Authority and identity: Malawian soldiers in Britain's colonial army, 1891–1964', PhD, University of Stirling, 2002

Rogers, Trevor A., 'The Papua New Guinea Defence Force: Vanuatu (1980) to Bougainville (1990)', PhD, Australian National University, 2002

Urquhart, D.A.K., 'Australia's military aid programs 1950–1990', MA, Australian
    Defence Force Academy, 1991

Newspapers and periodicals
Advertiser (Adelaide)
Advocate (Burnie)
Age (Melbourne)
Argus (Melbourne)
Australian
Australian Financial Review
Cairns Post
Canberra Times
Courier-Mail (Brisbane)
Mail (Adelaide)
People
Post-Courier (Port Moresby)
Queensland Times (Ipswich)
South Pacific Post (Port Moresby)
Sunday Mail (Brisbane)
Sydney Morning Herald
Telegraph
Townsville Daily Bulletin

Index

Note: page numbers in bold type indicate illustrations.